SAPscript®
Made Easy

A Step-by-Step Guide to Form Design and Printout in R/3

SAP Labs, Inc.

Palo Alto, California

Simplification Group
SAP Labs, Inc.
3475 Deer Creek Road
Palo Alto, CA 94304

www.saplabs.com/simple
simplify-r3@sap.com

Printed in the United States of America.
ISBN 1-893570-14-2

C O N T E N T S

Part 1: Learning SAPscript Basics

Chapter 1: SAPscript Forms: The Big Picture

19

Chapter 2: SAPscript Forms: The Basics 27

Part 2: Modifying SAPscript Forms

Chapter 3: Getting Started with Forms 47

Chapter 4: Modifying SAPscript Forms: The Basics   **63**

Chapter 5: Modifying SAPscript Forms: Advanced Topics   **113**

Part 3: Customizing Applications for SAPscript Forms

Chapter 6: Customizing Sales and Distribution for Print Forms   161

Chapter 7: Customizing Materials Management for Print Forms   181

Chapter 8: Customizing Financial Accounting for Print Forms 207

Part 4: Appendixes

Appendix A: SAPscript Control Commands 221

Appendix B: Sample Forms   263

Appendix C: Third-Party Solutions   273

Introduction

Overview

Forms streamline the process of conducting business. Invoices, credit memos, and delivery notes are just a few examples of the types of forms companies routinely use.

With SAPscript, SAP's programming tool, you can easily design, build, and print a wide variety of business forms. R/3 comes with a library of predesigned forms that can be quickly customized to fit the needs of every business.

Filled with step-by-step instructions and screenshots, this guidebook helps you understand how to use SAPscript to design and print business forms.

What Is this Guide About?

This guidebook is all about SAPscript forms. Using this guidebook, you will be able to:

- Use graphical tools (Form Painter and PC Editor) to quickly adapt SAPscript forms for your needs

- Reduce the consulting time and effort required to develop or modify SAPscript forms

The topics covered in this guidebook will help you:

- Modify the layout of SAPscript forms

- Modify the content of SAPscript forms

- Customize R/3 application for SAPscript forms

Who Should Read this Guide?

This guidebook is written for:

- R/3 application consultants

- R/3 implementation team members

- Individuals with little or no knowledge of SAPscript

Assumptions

To help you get the most out of this guidebook, the following assumptions are being made:

- Forms are intended for the U.S., Canadian, and Australian markets.

- Except checks, U.S. and Australian companies do not routinely use preprinted forms. A company logo is usually the only preprinted item on a form.

- Implementation teams are using the latest version of the predeveloped forms.

  To download preconfigured forms, go to http://www.saplabs.com/forms

This guide does not cover the following topics. Consult your system administrator for more information.

- Using the Change and Transport System (CTS)

- Uploading predeveloped forms into your system

- Using the Online Support Service to get an access key to modify R/3 objects

How to Use this Guide?

If you are a new SAPscript user, you should read parts 1 and 2 to familiarize yourself with SAPscript.

If you are a more experienced SAPscript user, you should read part 2. You may choose to skim part 1.

All examples and step-by-step intructions covered in part 2 are based on the SAPscript standard form for sales order confirmation (technical name *RVORDER01*).

Note

Although you can use parts of this guide as a tutorial, it is not intended to be a substitute for the SAP training course *BC 460 SAPscript: Forms Design and Text Management in R/3*.

How Is the Guide Organized?

Part 1: Learning SAPscript Basics

- **Chapter 1: SAPscript Forms: The Big Picture**
  Understanding concepts, architecture, and runtime environment of SAPscript forms

- **Chapter 2: SAPscript Forms: The Basics**
  Form management tools and types of form components

Part 2: Modifying SAPscript Forms

- **Chapter 3: Getting Started with Forms**
  Importing predeveloped forms into your system landscape

- **Chapter 4: Modifying SAPscript Forms: The Basics**
  Modifying windows and content

What's New in this Guide?

Since the publication of the *SAPscript Made Easy* guidebook for Release 4.0B, the following new topics have been added:

Using the graphic management tool to include graphic files in a form

You learn how to import a graphic file (in Windows BMP format) into the document server, preview the graphic, and include the graphic in a form using the new graphic management tool. Additionally, you learn how to organize your own folder structure within the document server.

For more information, see Chapter 5, "Modifying SAPscript Forms: Advanced Topics" on page 113.

Printing text vertically

You learn how to print text vertically using print controls.

For more information, see Chapter 5, "Modifying SAPscript Forms: Advanced Topics" on page 113.

Using the PERFORM command instead of changing the print program

You learn how to use the SAPscript PERFORM command to receive additional data during the printing process. Often it is easier to use the PERFORM command than changing the print program.

For more information, see Chapter 5, "Modifying SAPscript Forms: Advanced Topics" on page 113.

Preparing forms for modification

Language and page format differences exist for SAP standard forms and preconfigured forms used in the U.S. and Canadian markets. If you use the standard or preconfigured forms, you learn how to change the original language and page format for certain forms.

For more information, see Chapter 3, "Getting Started with Forms" on page 47.

Conventions

Throughout this guide, you will find the symbols shown below. These mark special information that supplements the main discussion or theme.

TechTalk: This symbol flags information that is highly technical. It is included for those who want to dig deeper into particular concepts or explore background theory.

Tips & Tricks: This symbol flags suggestions, hints, and practical techniques to help you become more efficient in the way you use the R/3 System.

Caution: This symbol flags information that can help you steer clear of common pitfalls. It demands careful reading.

In the table below, you will find some of the text conventions used throughout this guide.

Text convention	What it means
sans-serif	Command syntax.
sans-serif italic	Screen names or on-screen objects (buttons, fields, etc.).
monospace	User input (text the user types verbatim).
name1 → name2	Menu selection. *name1* is the menu name, and *name2* is the item on the menu.

Figure 1–1 Sample *Enjoy R/3* (Release 4.6) screen

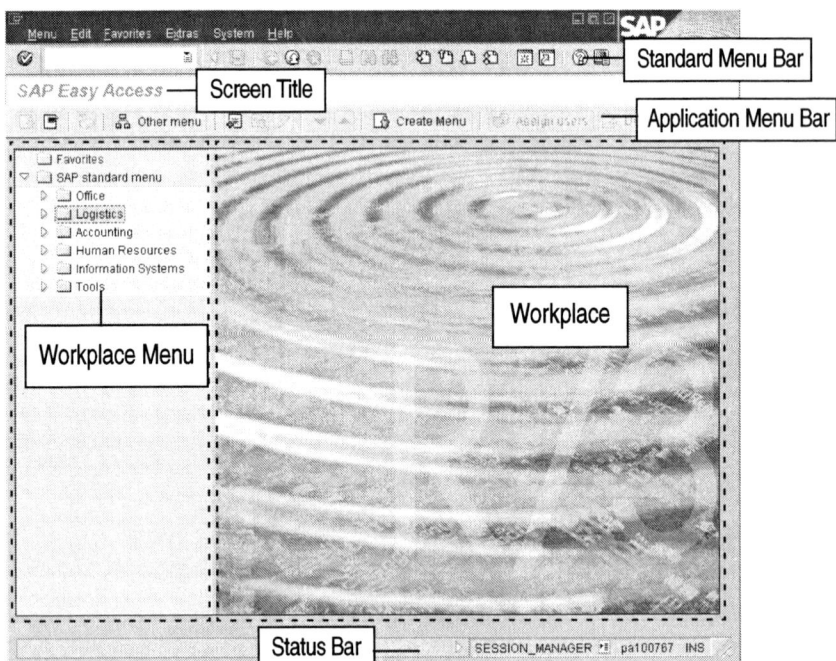

Figure 1–2 Detailed screen elements

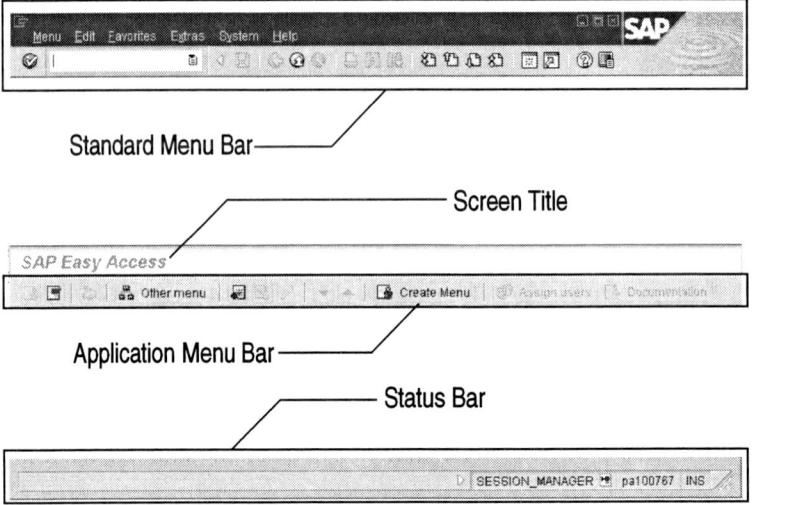

PART ONE

Learning SAPscript Basics

SAPscript Forms: The Big Picture

Overview

This chapter provides an overview of SAPscript forms. After reading this chapter, you will be able to answer the following questions:

- What are SAPscript forms?
- What is the architecture of SAPscript forms?
- How are SAPscript forms processed?
- What are the different sources of SAPscript Forms?
- Where can you find the SAPscript forms you need?

What Are SAPscript Forms?

To help you build the business forms (for example, invoices, purchase orders, etc.) you need, the R/3 System provides you form management tools and SAPscript forms.

A SAPscript form is a *template* that simplifies the process of designing business forms. It supplies the layout (for example, page size) and content (for example, sales data for an invoice) for your business forms. You need SAPscript forms to print, distribute, or display the business forms.

Examples of SAPscript Forms

Some examples of SAPscript forms are shown in Figure 1–1:

- Sales order confirmations
- Invoices
- Purchase orders
- Prenumbered and unnumbered checks
- Accounting statements
- Packing and picking lists

Figure 1–1 Sample SAPscript forms

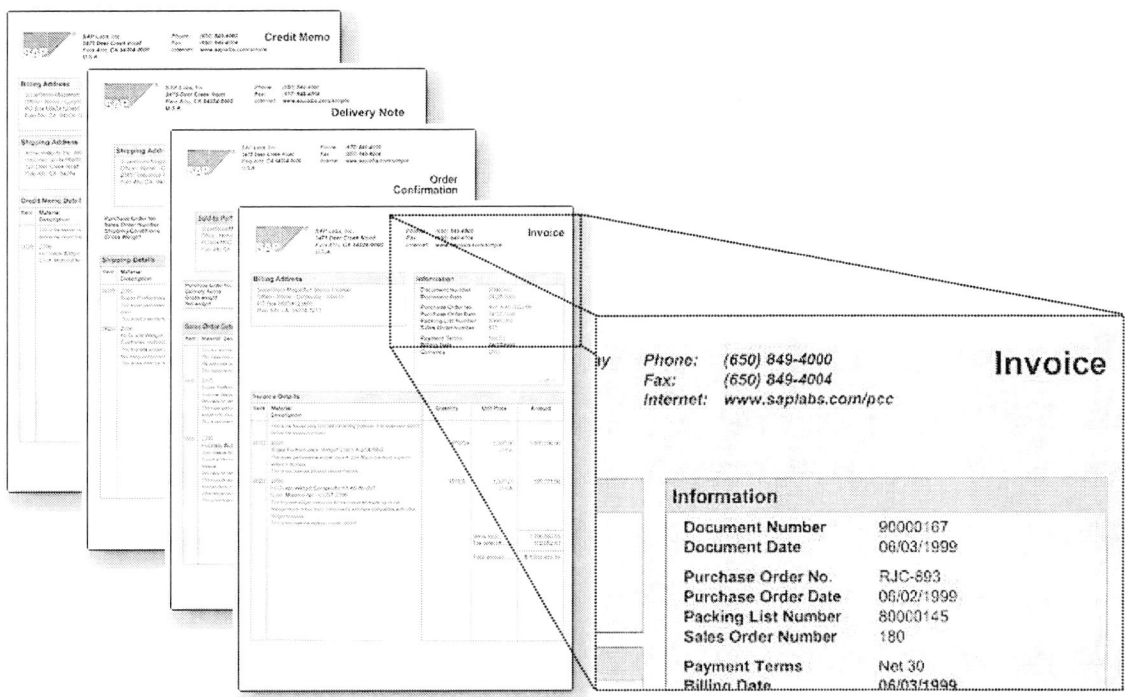

What Is the Architecture of SAPscript Forms?

Each SAPscript form consists of two main components:

- **Layout:** The layout is defined by a set of *windows* in which the content appears.

- **Content:** The content is either text (for example, business data for an invoice) or graphics (for example, a company logo).

Figure 1–2 shows an invoice created with a standard SAPscript form. There are seven separate windows which define the overall layout of the invoice. Windows house the form content. To help you understand the architecture of a SAPscript form, the contents of the *Payment Information* window have been highlighted.

Figure 1–2 Understanding the architecture of a SAPscript form

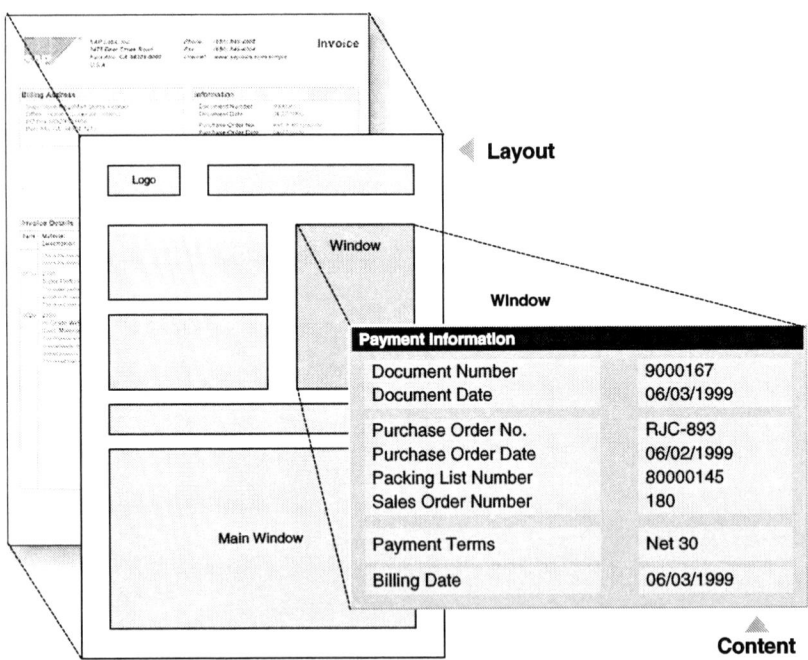

The central object in a SAPscript form is the **window**. You can define the size, position, and content of each window in a form. As shown in Figure 1–3, a SAPscript form derives its structure from a set of windows (for example, logo, billing address, and information windows), each with its own content. For more information, see "What Are the Form Components?" on page 35.

Figure 1–3 The role of windows in SAPscript forms

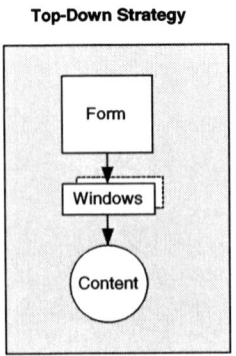

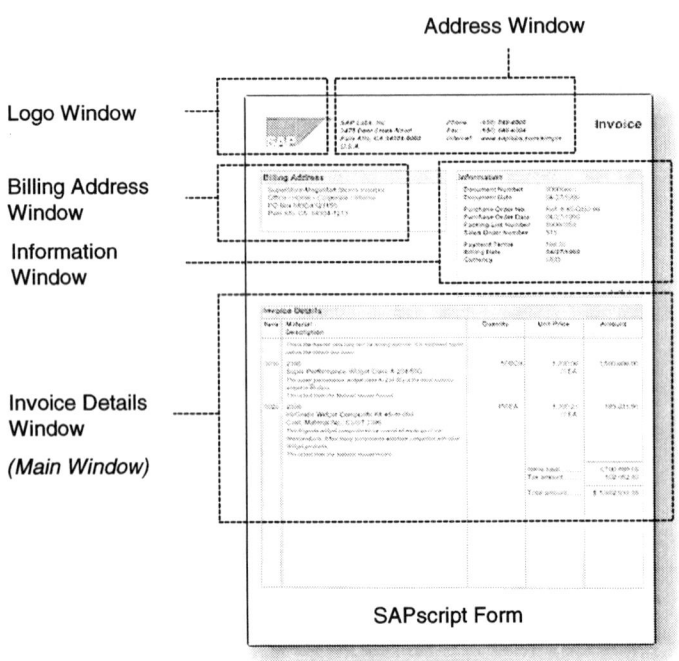

How Are SAPscript Forms Processed?

1

The SAPscript runtime environment coordinates the processing of SAPscript forms.

As shown in Figure 1–4, the SAPscript runtime environment:

- Retrieves layout and content data from the SAPscript form

- Collects the necessary business data from the R/3 database

- Generates the final SAPscript form

The resulting business form can be printed, e-mailed, faxed, or displayed.

Figure 1–4 How SAPscript forms are processed in the R/3 System

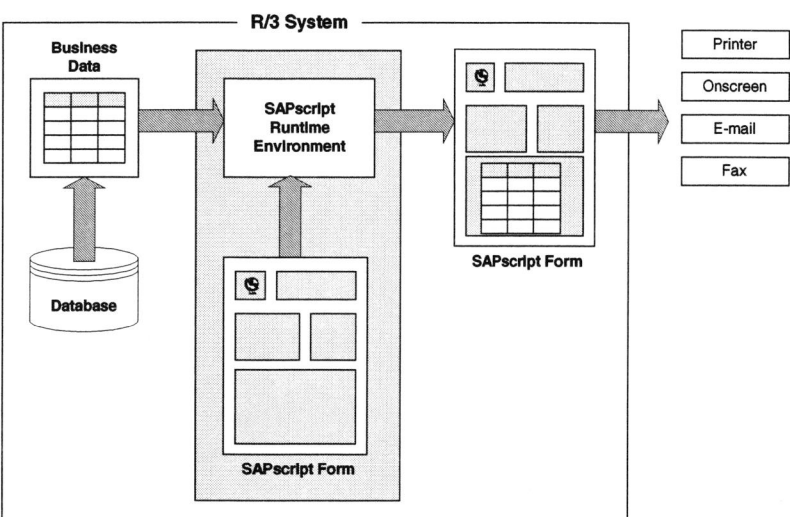

What Are the Different Sources of SAPscript Forms?

SAP provides you with two different sources for SAPscript forms:

- **Standard SAPscript forms:** Standard SAPscript forms are delivered with the SAP standard client (usually referred to as client 000).

- **Preconfigured SAPscript forms** (also called preconfigured forms): Developed for the U.S. and Canadian markets, the preconfigured SAPscript forms are delivered with the Preconfigured Client (PCC).

- **Current Preconfigured SAPscript forms:** You can download current versions of the preconfigured forms from the Internet at: http://www.saplabs.com/forms.

- **SAPscript forms for R/3 Release 3.x:** SAPscript forms are also available as separate files. For R/3 releases 3.0E, 3.0F, and 3.1H, SAP provides sets of SAPscript forms you can download from the Internet at: http://www.saplabs.com/forms.

Standard SAPscript Forms: Some Examples

Here are some examples of standard SAPscript forms that are delivered with client 000:

Table 1–1 Examples of standard SAPscript forms

Form Description	Standard Form Name
Sales Order Confirmation	RVORDER01
Packing List	RVDELNOTE
Invoice	RVINVOICE01
Purchase Order	MEDRUCK
Prenumbered Check	F110_PRENUM_CHCK

Preconfigured SAPscript Forms: Some Examples

Here are some examples of preconfigured forms delivered with the Preconfigured Client:

Table 1–2 Preconfigured SAPscript forms

Form Description	Preconfigured Form Name
Sales Order Confirmation	YPCC_ORDCONF_STD
Packing List	YPCC_PACKLIST
Purchase Order	YPCC_CHECK_NUM
Invoice	YPCC_INVOICE_STD
Remittance Advice	YPCC_REMITT_STD
Account Statement / Open Item List	YPCC_STATEMT_STD
Balance Carried Forward Statement / Open Item List	YPCC_STMBCF_STD
Unnumbered Check	YPCC_CHECK_UNN
Prenumbered Check	YPCC_CHECK_NUM

Where to Find the SAPscript Forms you Need

Use Table 1–3 to help you find the SAPscript form you need.

Table 1–3 Where to find the SAPscript forms you need

For...	Go to...
Standard SAPscript forms (complete list, organized along the application component hierarchy)	From the SAP standard menu, choose *Tools →* *SAPscript → SE71 - Form*. From the *Form Painter: Request* screen choose 🗗 at right of the *Form name* field. The *SAPscript Form Tree (Display Mode)* screen shows the complete list.
Preconfigured forms (updates and current development)	`http://www.saplabs.com/forms`
SAPscript forms (for R/3 releases 3.0E, 3.0F, and 3.1H)	`http://www.saplabs.com/forms`

SAPscript Forms: The Basics

Overview

This chapter introduces you to the basics of SAPscript forms. To understand the "how-to's" described in later chapters, you first need to become familiar with the following:

- What are the form management tools in R/3?

- What are the main components of SAPscript forms?

For more information about SAPscript, see the R/3 online documentation (*Basis* → *Basis Services/Communication Interfaces* → *SAPscript*).

What Are Form Management Tools?

The task of managing forms typically involves layout and content considerations. To manage SAPscript forms, the R/3 System provides the following tools:

- **Form Painter** – a graphical tool to manage form design and layout

- **PC Editor** – a text-based tool to manage business content

Form Painter

You use the Form Painter to manage the page layout of SAPscript forms.

Accessing the Form Painter

Task

Start working with Form Painter.

1. From the *SAP standard menu*, choose *Tools → SAPscript → SE71 - Form*.

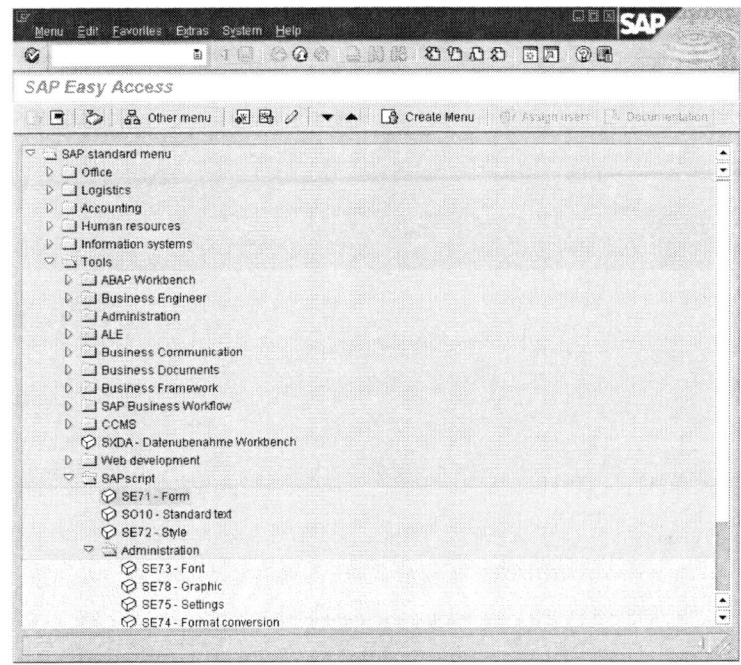

2

Tips & Tricks

Depending on your display settings, the *SAP Easy Access* screen on your system may look different from the one shown above. To specify display settings, choose *Extras → Settings*. Then, select the desired options (for example, *Show technical name*).

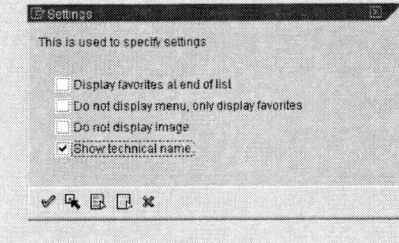

2. On the *Form Painter: Request* screen:

   a. Enter a form name and language (for example, **ZVORDER01** as the form and **EN** (English) as the language).

   b. Choose a form component option (for example, *Header*) in the *Subobjects* section.

   c. Choose 🔍 *Display* or ✏ *Change*.

In the *Subobjects* section, select the form component you want to process as well as the processing mode (displaying or changing mode).

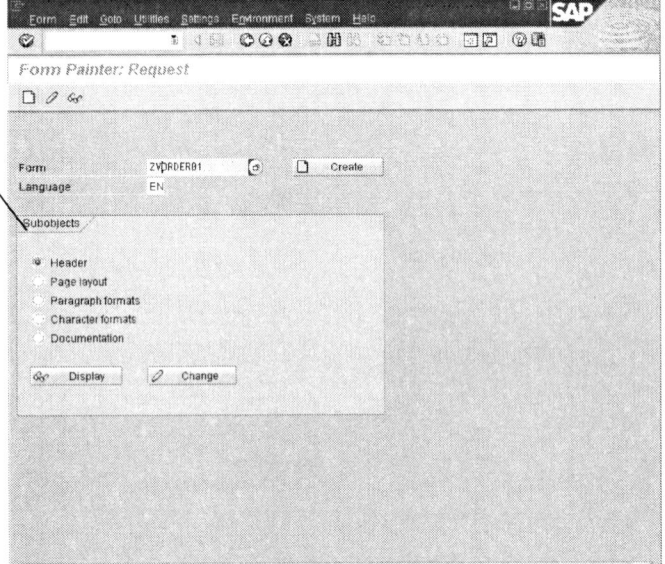

The Form Painter consists of two screens:

- *Administrative Screen*

- *Design Window*

You can modify each form component using the *Administrative Screen*. The *Design Window* (synchronized with the *Administrative Screen*) only appears, if you choose the form component Page Layout.

For more information, see "What Are the Form Components?" on page 35.

Tips & Tricks

> The default setting under *Subobjects* is *Header*. To modify a form layout immediately, choose *Page layout*. Both synchronized screens of the graphical Form Painter appear. For more information, see "Page Layout" on page 40.

PC Editor

You use the PC Editor to modify the content of SAPscript forms. With the PC Editor you can modify text elements or SAPscript command controls, and standard text.

You can access the PC Editor in one of two ways:

- Using the Form Painter

- Using Standard Text

To simultaneously modify form layout and content (for example, text elements or control commands), SAP recommends option 1 (see "Accessing the PC Editor via Form Painter" on page 31).

To modify standard text only, use option 2 (see "Accessing the PC Editor via Standard Text" on page 32).

Accessing the PC Editor via Form Painter

Task

Accessing the PC Editor from Form Painter.

1. From the *SAP standard menu*, choose *Tools → SAPscript → SE71 - Form*.

2. On the *Form Painter: Request* screen:

   a. Enter a form name and language (for example, **ZVORDER01** as the form and **EN** (English) as the language).

   b. Select *Page Layout* in the *Subobjects* section.

   c. Choose 👓 *Display* or 🖉 *Change*.

3. To start the PC Editor directly from the *Administrative Screen* in Form Painter, choose 🖉 .

The name of the currently selected window is displayed in the *Name* field.

To access the PC Editor for the currently selected window, choose 🖉 .

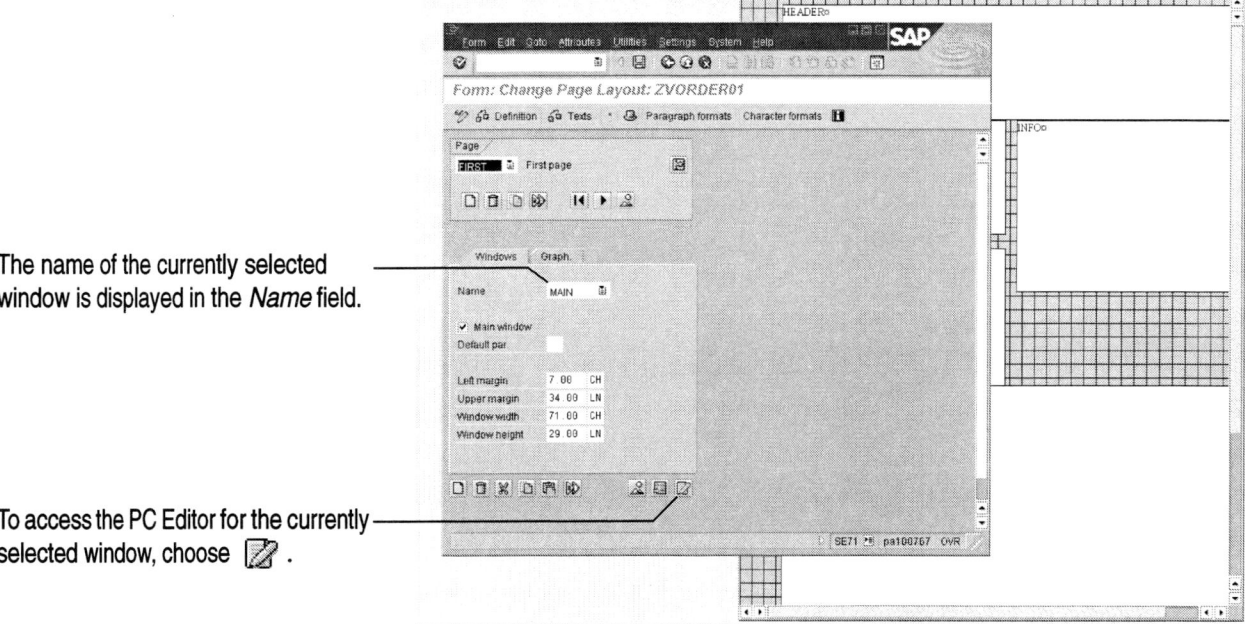

On the *Administrative Screen*, the PC Editor shows the content of the currently selected window.

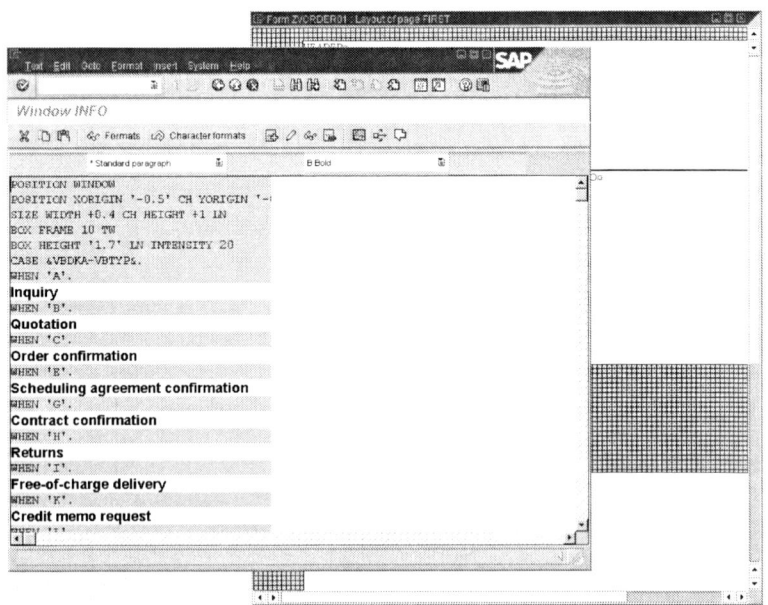

Accessing the PC Editor via Standard Text

If you only want to change standard text, start the PC Editor without using Form Painter. Using Standard text is quicker than accessing through Form Painter, but you need the technical name of the text object you want to edit.

Task

Open the PC Editor using Standard text.

1. From the *SAP standard menu*, choose *Tools → SAPscript → SO10 - Standard Text*.

2. On the *Standard Text: Request* screen:

   a. Choose the standard text by specifying *Text name*, *Text ID* and *Language*.

   b. Choose 🖉 *Change*.

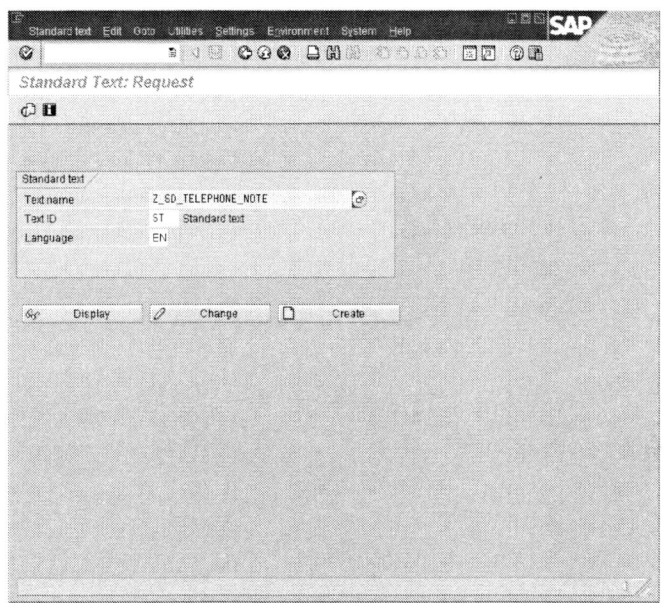

The PC Editor appears for the chosen standard text.

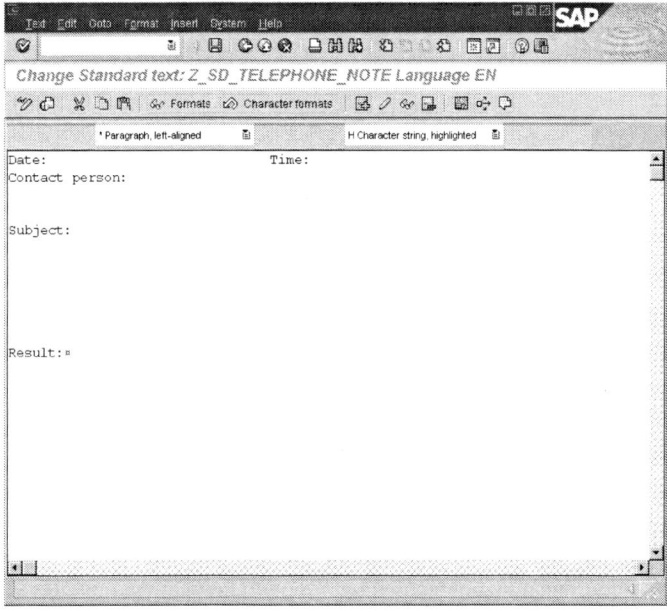

Activating the Graphical Form Painter and PC Editor

The Form Painter provides graphical functionality for manipulating forms (see "Manipulating the Layout of a Form" on page 69). Before using the graphical Form Painter and the graphical PC Editor, you have to activate them.

Task

Activate the graphical Form Painter and PC Editor.

1. From the *SAP standard menu*, choose *Tools → SAPscript → SE71 - Form.*

2. On the *Form Painter: Request* screen, choose *Settings → Form Painter.*

This screen already shows the Form Painter. If the Form Painter is not activated yet, the screen may differ from the one shown.

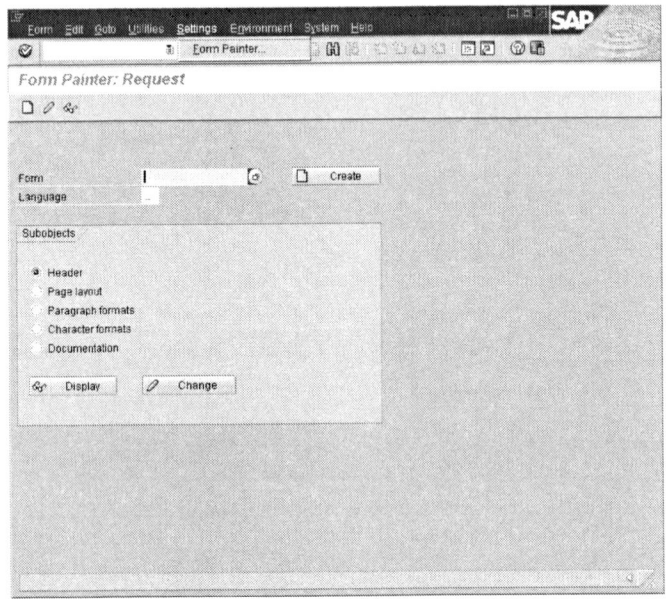

3. On the *User-Specific Settings* screen:

    a. Make sure the *Graphical Form Painter* checkbox is selected.

    b. Make sure the *Graphical PC Editor* checkbox is selected.

    c. To activate user specific settings, choose ✅ .

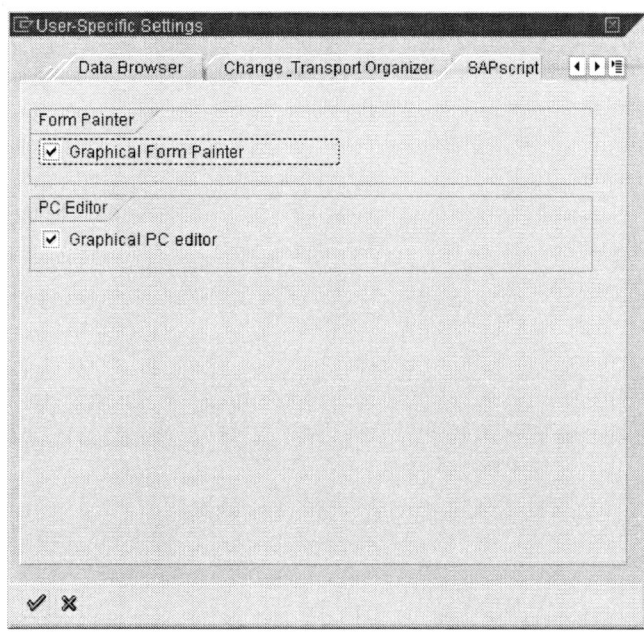

2

What Are the Form Components?

SAPscript provides functions for form manipulation in the following areas:

Table 2–1　SAPscript form components

Form Component	Description	See Page
Header	General information and default settings	36
Paragraph formats	Font and tab information for paragraphs	37
Character formats	Font information within a paragraph	38
Page layout	Page names with page flow information, position, and size of windows on the pages	40
Documentation	Technical documentation about the form components	43

Header

The header consists of either administrative data for the form or basic settings that can be overridden in other parts of the form.

The two elements most important to your customization are font and page format within the basic settings.

Except for checks, the page format for the U.S. and Canada is *LETTER* and *DIN A4* for Australia.

The only purpose for the values "Lines per inch" and "Characters/inch" is to convert the measures specified in lines and characters to absolute values.

Caution

Do **not** change the values for "Lines per inch" and "Characters/inch" because you will readjust all tabs and window coordinates. We will discuss fonts later in this section.

The *Lang. attributes* section gives you important information about the called form. The *Language* field shows the language version you specified when you called the form.

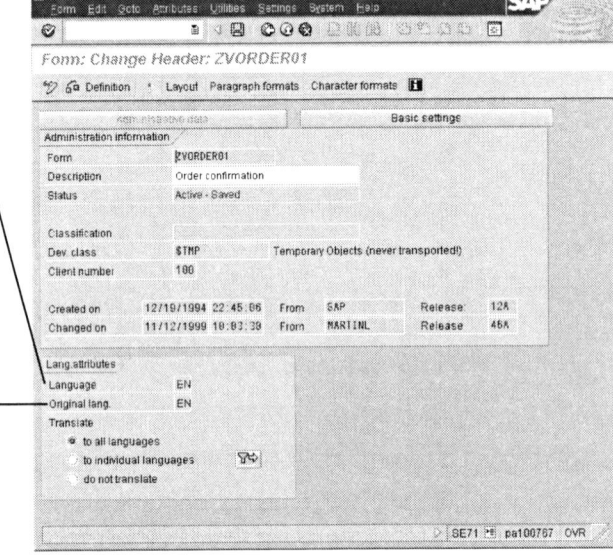

The *Original lang.* field shows the language to which you can change the form. It is usually the language in which the form was originally created.

Tips & Tricks

You can easily move to other components without leaving the above screen by choosing the related button of a component in the menu bar. For example, to move from the header to the page layout, choose *Layout* in the menu bar.

Paragraph Formats

A paragraph contains all the information needed to format text. In forms, not all of the formatting possibilities are used because most form paragraphs consist of only a line or a word.

Font and tabs are the important paragraph formats. If you do not specify a font, the form uses the default font from the form header. If you want to create columns for outputting line items of a document, specify a list of tabs.

2

Tips & Tricks

If a paragraph uses a small font, set the line spacing to less than one line. Ensure that the printer can print more than six lines per inch.

The following screenshot illustrates the font attributes of a paragraph definition.

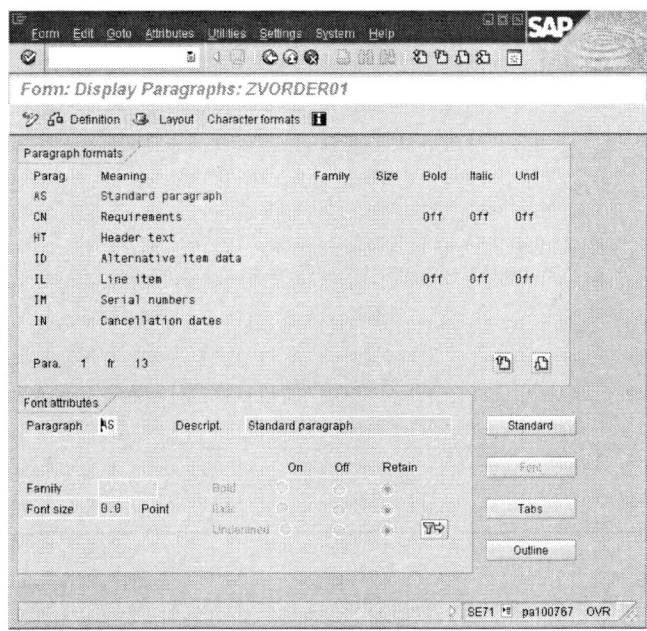

The following screenshot illustrates the tab attributes of a paragraph definition. Tab positions are specified as the number of characters from the left. The system uses the characters per inch value in the header basic settings to convert the number of characters into an absolute value. For this conversion, font size does not matter.

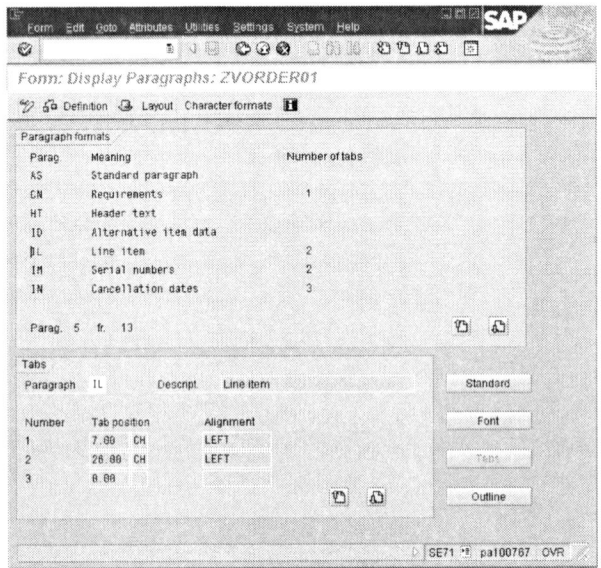

Character Formats

Character format overrides paragraph settings for specific words in a paragraph. For example, you might want to italicize a single word and not the entire paragraph.

TechTalk

To apply character strings within a paragraph using the PC Editor, mark the specific text and select the desired character format from the character string box.

To apply character strings using the text editor, turn on the settings for the character string by enclosing the character string name in angle brackets < > before the specific text. To return to the standard paragraphs settings, insert a slash within angle brackets </> at the end of the specific text. For example: `<B>These words will be bold</>.`

You can assign character formats to bar code printing. The standard attributes show:

- Whether a character format is used for bar code printing

- Which bar code format is used (you can choose predefined bar code formats form a list)

For more information about bar code printing, see Chapter 5, "Modifying SAPscript Forms: Advanced Topics" on page 113.

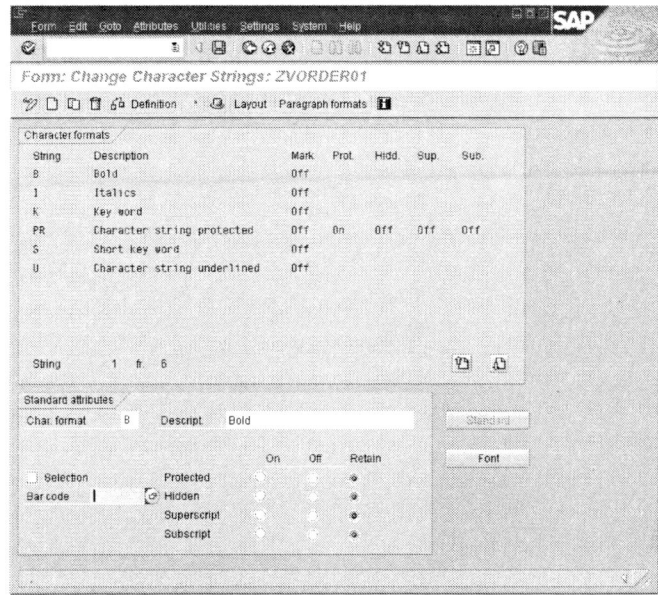

2

To access the font attributes of a character string, choose *Font*.

For *Font attributes,* radio buttons can be used to underline, italicize, or bold the typeface.

Retain means that underline, italic, or bold settings are retained from the paragraph. If a character string has no specified font, the paragraph font is used.

The following screenshot displays the character string *B*, which changes the format to *Bold*, while the settings for *Italics* and *Underline* are retained from the paragraph.

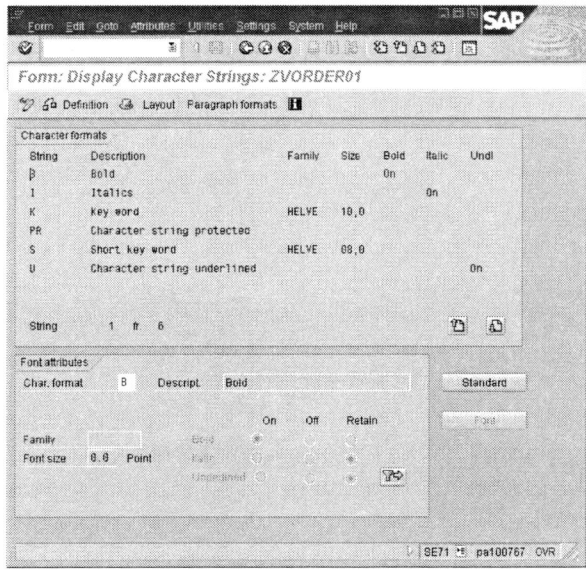

Page Layout

In page layout you can define or change windows.

A window contains SAPscript text, which consists of text elements and the to-be-printed variables.

There is one special window, *MAIN*, that contains the output of the document line items.

Except for *MAIN*, the window type can be either variable (VAR) or constant (CONST). SAPscript does not distinguish between the two window types, although both types are mentioned in the SAPscript documentation.

TechTalk

SAP online documentation on window types:

Variable window content is regenerated on every new page. The content of a constant window is generated once and printed on every page.

This means that, for better performance, windows that contain different information on different pages must be VAR; all others are CONST. The content of the window is defined in the SAPscript editor.

If you activate the Form Painter and choose *Page layout* from the *Form Painter: Request* screen, the following two screens appear:

- *Form: Change Page Layout* screen (also referred to as the *Administrative Screen*)

- Graphical Form Painter (also referred to as the *Design Window*)

Figure 2–1 shows the synchronized screens you work with to modify page layout. You can easily move between screens by clicking on the desired screen.

Figure 2–1 Form Painter screens

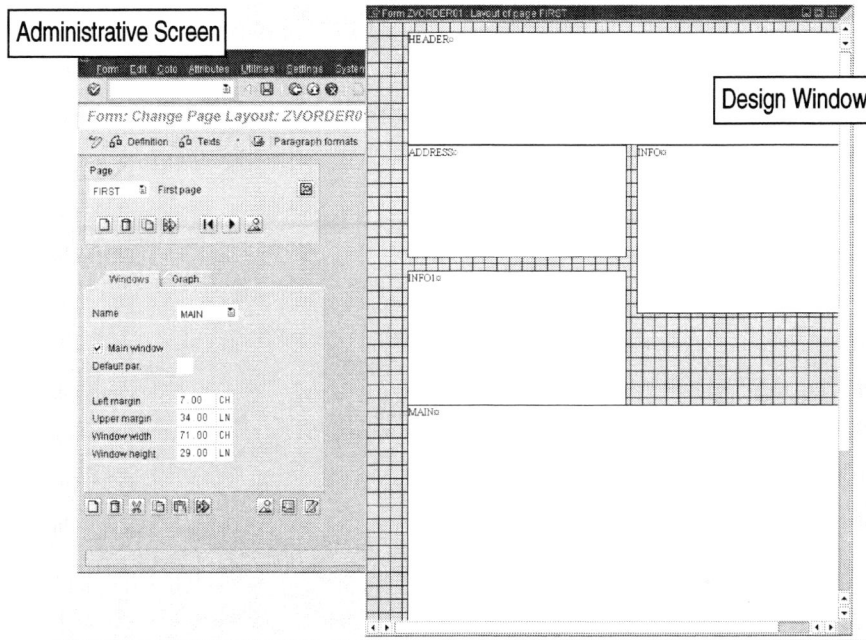

On the *Administrative Screen*, choose ✎ to move to the window text.

In this example the *Window: INFO* screen appears.

- A gray shaded section represents SAPscript commands (including variables).

- A white section shows you the content and layout.

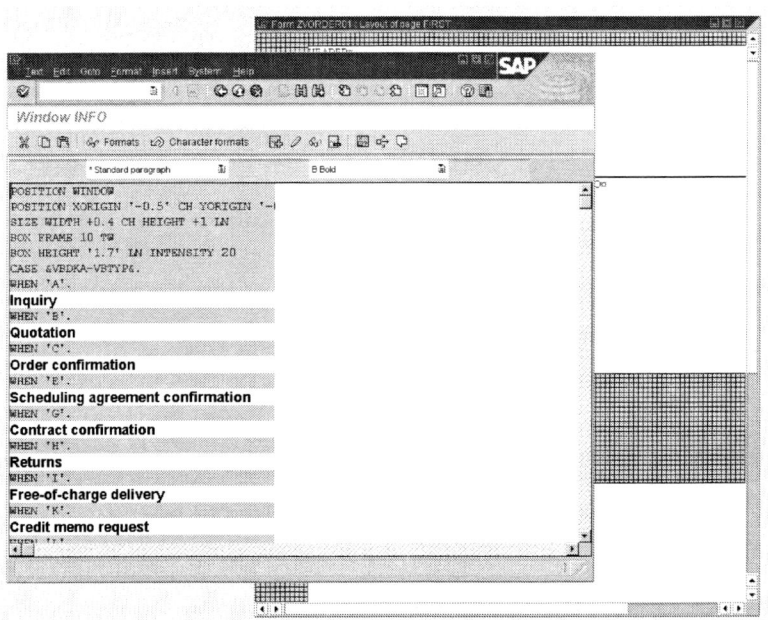

Variables

A variable name consists of the name of a DDIC structure, a hyphen, and a field name. All variable names must also be enclosed in ampersands (&). If you want to output variables, you may format them. This step is necessary if you do not want the standard formatting of the variables coming from the data dictionary.

Table 2–2 Common formatting options

Common formatting options	Syntax
Truncating the variable length	`&table-field(n)&` prints the first *n* characters of the variable
Specifying the number of decimals	`&table-field(.1)&` prints the variable with *l* decimals
Outputting the variable with an offset	`&table-field+m&` prints the rest of the variable after the first *m* characters
Omitting leading zeros	`&table-field(Z)&` omits the leading zeros

Tips & Tricks

Only the combinations of the first three formatting options are allowed. The syntax used to combine all three formatting options is: `&table-field+m(n.1)&`

For a detailed list of formatting options, see Appendix A, "SAPscript Control Commands" on page 221.

Documentation

Storing technical documentation for forms is a useful feature of
SAPscript. Here, you can look for information about form variables,
know when the print program fills the variables, and easily describe
all your changes. We highly recommend using this feature, especially
if you want to modify a form.

In this example, we chose the display mode for the documentation. In
the *Display Documentation* screen, you will find useful information
about the form. The form, usage of windows, and text elements are
described.

2

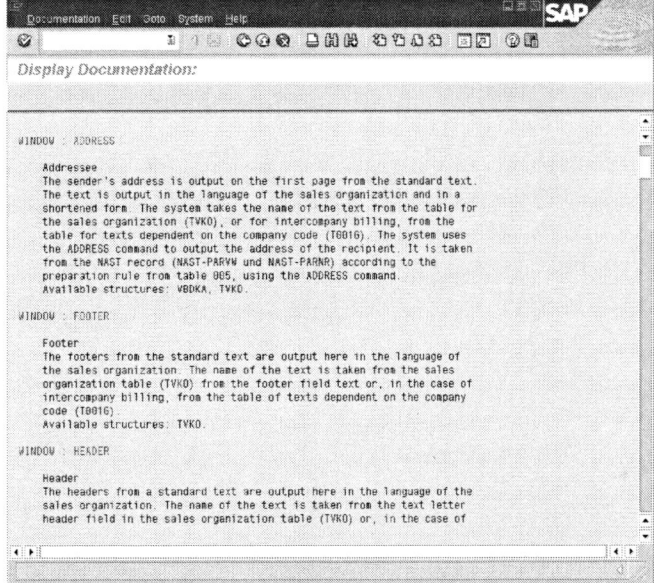

Modifying SAPscript Forms

Getting Started with Forms

Overview

In the previous chapters you learned how SAPscript forms supply the basic layout and structure for your business forms. You are now ready to take the first step toward customizing SAPscript forms.

To help you get started with SAPscript forms, this chapter covers the following:

- What are the methods for importing (or copying) forms?

- How to choose the best method for importing (or copying) forms?

- How to import or copy forms?

Working with SAPscript Forms: First Steps

SAPscript forms are client-dependent. Before you can customize a SAPscript form, you must import (or copy) the form into the appropriate R/3 client.

What Are the Methods for Importing Forms?

Depending on how the forms are available, there are two different methods for importing forms into your appropriate client.

Forms Available on an R/3 Client

If the forms are already available on an R/3 client (for example, on the SAP standard client 000, a preconfigured client, or another client), you must execute a client copy to import the forms into the appropriate client. For more information, see "Copying Forms between Clients" on page 49.

Forms Available as Separate Files

If the forms are available at a file location (for example, on the D drive), you must first import the forms into your client. For more information, see "Importing Forms from a File" on page 58.

How to Choose the Best Method?

Use the table below to determine which import method applies to your situation. Each number represents a different procedure. If more than one procedure is applicable, try to use the one with the lower number.

Table 3–1 Choosing the best method to import forms

Type of Forms Needed	Using Preconfigured Client		Using SAP Client	
U.S. or Canadian	0	Copy preconfigured form from PCC client to yours	1	Copy standard form from client 000 to yours
	1	Copy standard form from client 000 to yours	2	Import forms from file
	2	Import from file		
All other countries	1	Copy standard form from client 000 to yours	1	Copy standard form from client 000 to yours
	2	Import forms from file	2	Import forms from file

If you are using the Preconfigured Client, simply copy the forms from the PCC client to your client. For more information, see "Copying Forms between Clients" on page 49.

U.S. and Canadian customers not using the Preconfigured Client may want to begin by importing the forms from a file. For more information, see "Importing Forms from a File" on page 58.

Caution

Before modifying forms, make sure that you only modify copies.

Copying Forms between Clients

If you want to use preconfigured forms or standard forms that are available in another client than your specific development client, you have to copy the forms between clients. Since we assume you will not perform any development directly in the preconfigured client or standard client, you have to copy the forms—either from the standard client 000 or the preconfigured client—to your specific development client.

The task in this section describes how to copy forms from one client to another. You will learn to execute a client copy for standard forms between the standard client 000 and the client you are currently logged on to.

3

If you are using the Preconfigured Client, you may have to copy preconfigured forms from the PCC to another client. Copying forms from the PCC is analog to copying forms from standard client 000; you only have to replace the client number 000 with the client number of your preconfigured client.

Make sure you are working in the client that is going to receive the forms.

Task

Copy forms between clients.

The following procedure describes how to copy the form *RVORDER01* for sales order confirmation.

1. From the *SAP standard menu*, choose *Tools → SAPscript → SE71 - Form*.

2. On the *Form Painter: Request* screen, choose *Utilities → Copy from client*.

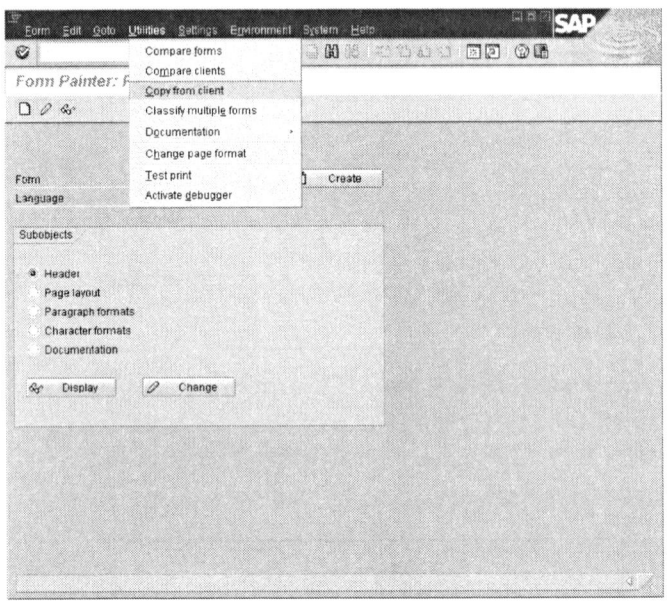

3. On the *Copy Forms Between Clients* screen:

   a. Enter the form name (for example, **RVORDER01**) in the *Form name* field.

   b. Enter the target form name, replacing the first letter of the form name with Z (for example, **ZVORDER01**), in the *Target form* field.

   c. Choose ⊕ .

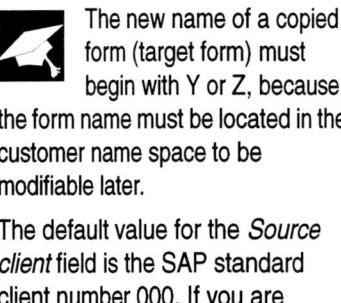

The new name of a copied form (target form) must begin with Y or Z, because the form name must be located in the customer name space to be modifiable later.

The default value for the *Source client* field is the SAP standard client number 000. If you are copying the forms from the preconfigured client (for example, the preconfigured client number is 010), you have to overwrite the source client number 000 (for example, with 010).

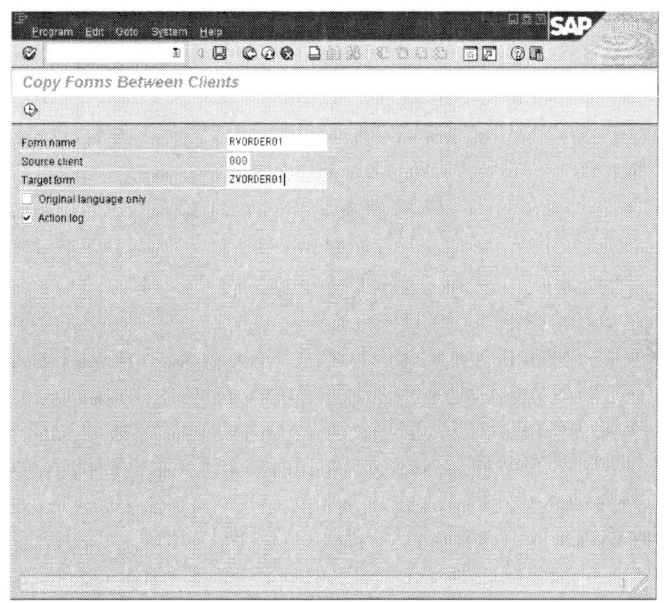

3

4. On the *Create Object Directory Entry* screen:

   a. Enter a development class.

   b. Choose 💾 .

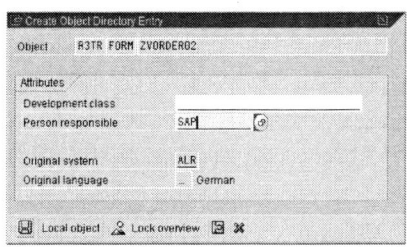

You have now copied the form from one client to another. The system displays an action log.

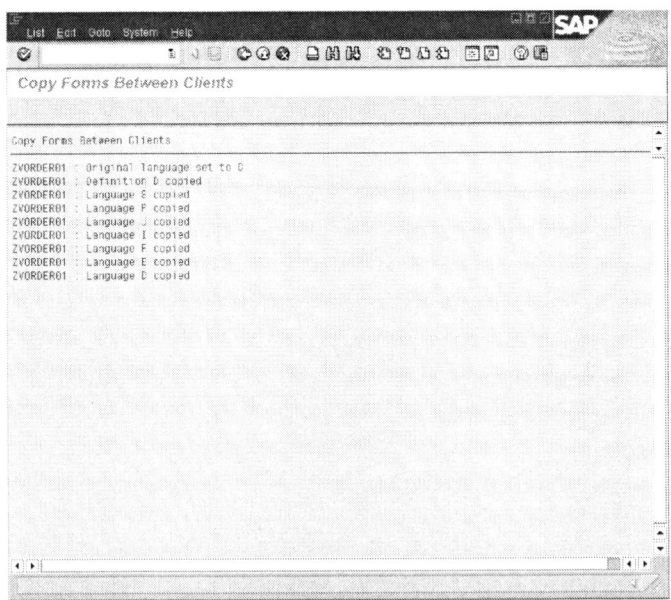

5. Go *Back* three times to return to the SAP standard menu.

Preparing Copied Forms: Additional Tasks

Every time you copy forms between clients, you have to consider two important attributes of the form: The original language and the assigned paper size.

- Standard SAPscript forms are delivered with original language *DE* (German) and paper size *DIN A4* (210 x 297 mm.).

- Preconfigured SAPscript forms are delivered with original language *EN* (English) and paper size *LETTER* (215 x 279 mm.).

Note

Since the forms delivered with the Preconfigured Client use English, you do not have to change the original language for forms copied from the PCC.

Original Language

You can modify forms only in the original language. Before you change a copied form, make sure you choose the correct language version of the form. Since the SAP standard forms currently use *DE*

(German) as the original language, you may want to change the original language to *EN* (English). The following task shows how to change the original language for a form.

Task

Change the original language German (DE) of the copied standard form ZVORDER01 to original language English (EN).

1. From the *SAP standard menu*, choose *Tools → SAPscript → SE71 - Form*.

2. On the *Form Painter: Request* screen:

  a. Enter **ZVORDER01** in the *Form* field.

  b. Enter **DE** in the *Language* field.

  c. Choose ⌀ *Change*.

If you activate the Change and Transport System (CTS), put your new form *ZVORDER01* on a correction request.

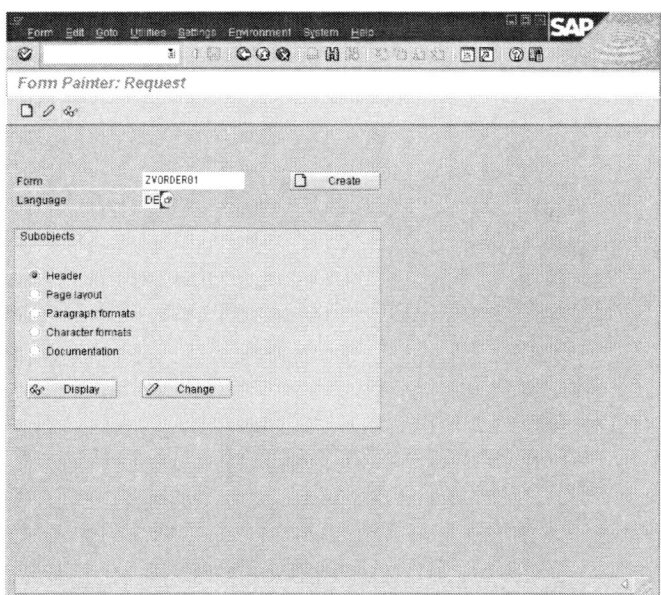

3

3. Choose *Utilities → Convert orig. lang.* to change the original language of the copied form.

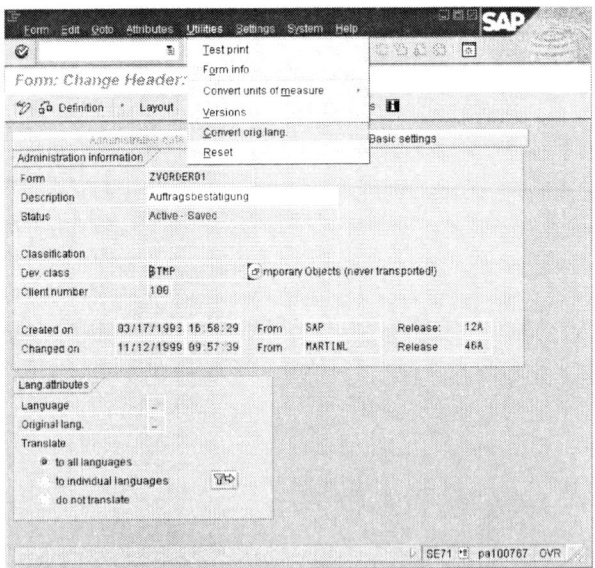

4. In the *Convert Original Language* window:

   a. Enter **EN** in the *To original language* field.

   b. Choose ✔ .

The system converts the original language from *DE* to *EN*, as shown in the message displayed in the status bar.

If a message is not displayed in a separate information window, the message will be displayed in the window's status bar.

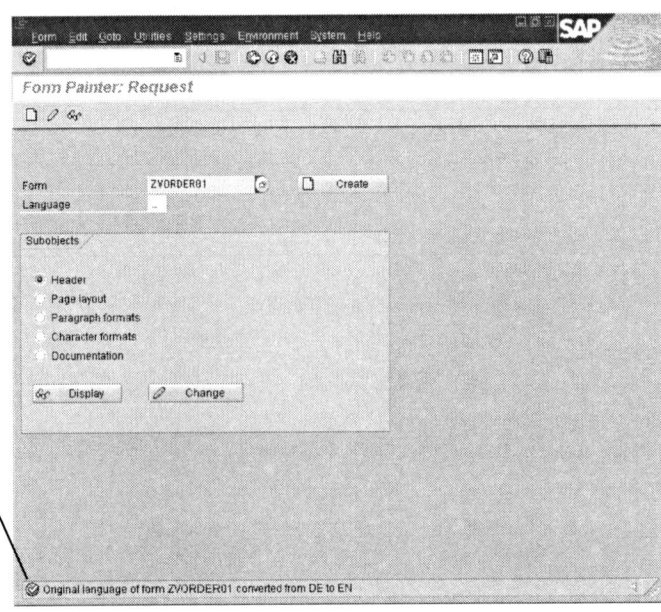

Changing Page Format of a Form

Since the preconfigured forms are developed with page format *LETTER* and the standard forms with page format *DIN A4*, you may want to change the page format for a form. You can easily convert the page format *DIN A4* to *LETTER* and vice versa by executing the program *RSTXFCON*.

The program *RSTXFCON* converts the current form page format to the specified page format checking the position and size of each window on each page. In general, the program tries to hold the position and size of a window. The program first moves the window, and only if necessary, reduces the window size. It is important to understand the program will never enlarge a window. In general, you should execute the conversion program only for page formats that are very similar. The more different the page format, the more additional manual changes are necessary after executing the program.

3

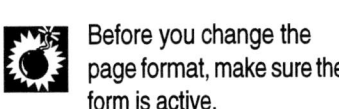 Before you change the page format, make sure the form is active.

Task

Change the page format DIN A4 to LETTER for form ZVORDER01.

1. From the SAP standard menu, choose *Tools → ABAP Workbench → Development → SE38 – ABAP Editor.*

2. On the *ABAP Editor: Initial Screen:*

a. In the *Program* field, enter **RSTXFCON**.

b. Choose ⊕ .

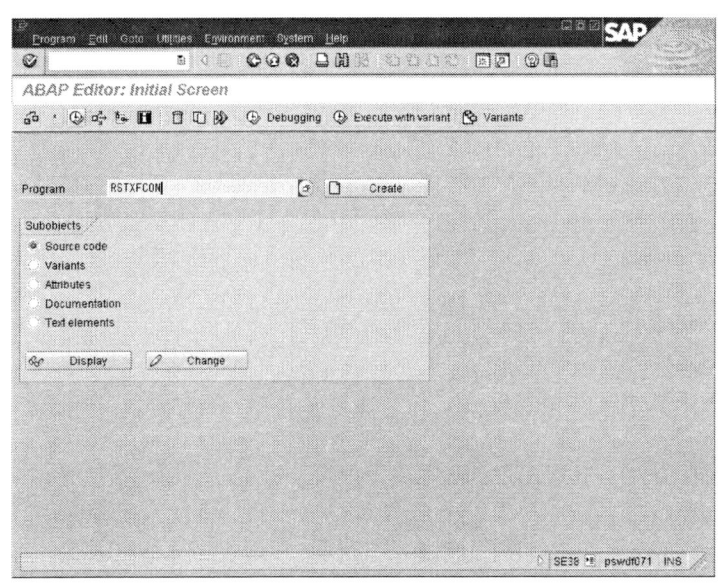

3. On the *SAPscript: Conversion of Page Format for Forms* screen:

    a. In the *Form name* field, enter the desired form name (for example, *ZVORDER01*).

    b. In the *New page format* field, enter the desired page format (for example, *LETTER*).

    c. Make sure that the check box *Test run, do not save* is selected.

    d. Choose ⊕ .

Click ⊡ at the right of the New page format field and then choose the desired page format from the list of available standard page formats.

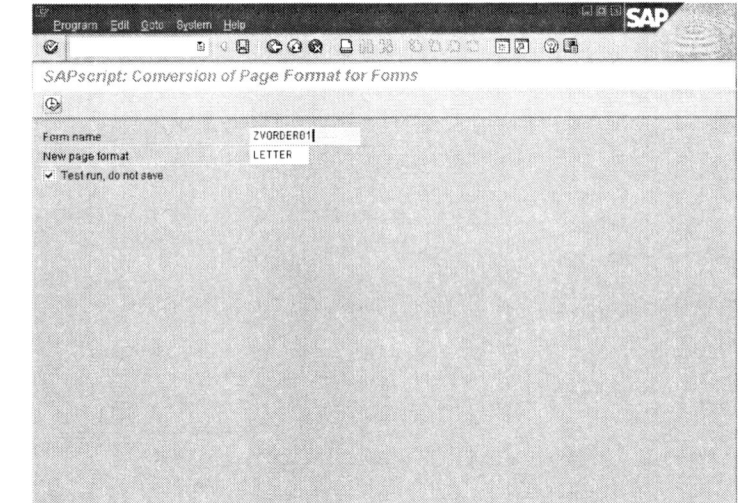

    e. Review the action protocol for the test run.

Tips & Tricks

> Print the protocol to have a copy of the parameters that will be changed by the conversion program.

    f. Go *Back*.

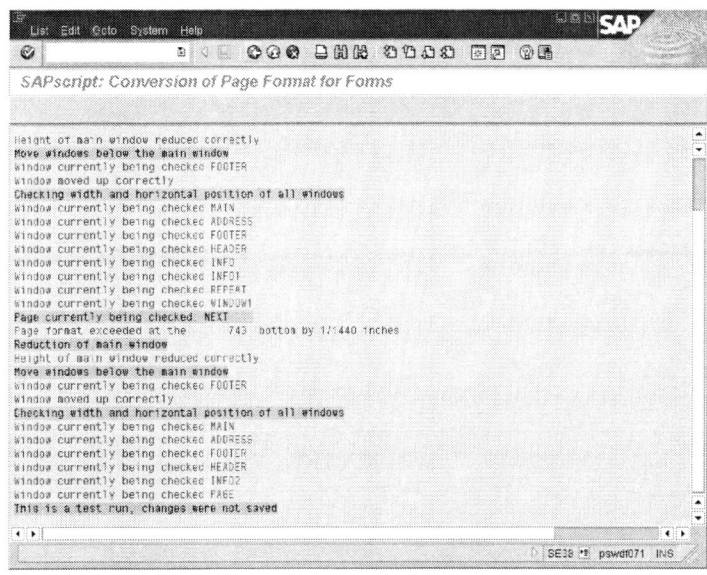

4. If you want to change the paper format, execute the conversion program again, by deselecting the check box *Test run, do not save* and choose ⏼ .

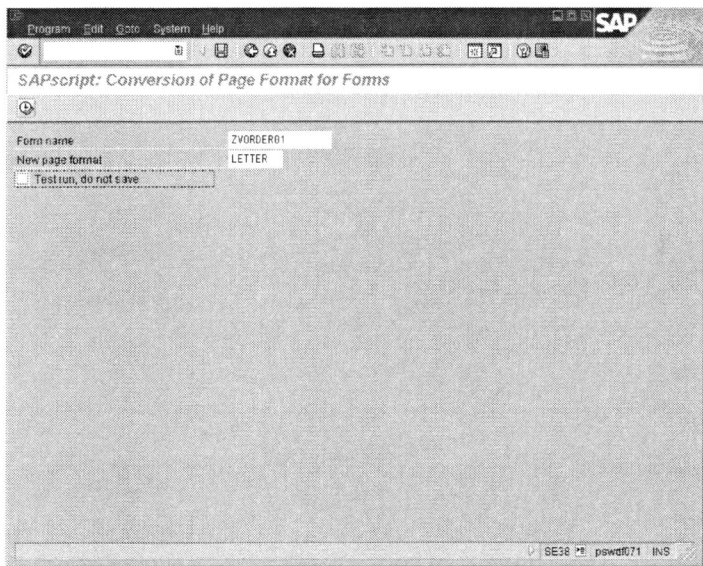

5. If you do not want to change the paper format, go *Back* twice to return to the *SAP standard menu*.

3

Importing Forms from a File

The following section describes how to import forms from a file. Importing from a file is a very practical way to start your form development process in order to save time and money.

Importable files with SAPscript forms can be found on the Internet at: http://www.saplabs.com/forms.

The easiest way to import forms into your R/3 System is to make the files available on the presentation server (that is, the computer where the SAPGUI is running).

Note

You may also place the files on the application server. However, this process is somewhat complicated, particularly if the R/3 System is running on a multi-server machine.

Task

Import a form from a file into your client.

1. Log on to the presentation server where you want to make the forms available.

2. Copy the to-be-imported forms to the desired drive of your presentation server.

3. Log on to the client that is going to receive the imported forms.

TechTalk

Forms are client dependent. Therefore, the upload program only creates forms in the client where the program has been executed.

4. From the *SAP standard menu,* choose *Tools → ABAP Workbench → Development → SE38 - ABAP Editor.*

5. On the *ABAP Editor: Initial Screen*:

   a. Enter **RSTXSCRP** in the *Program* field. *RSTXSCRP* is the name of the upload program in the R/3 System.

   b. Choose ⊕ .

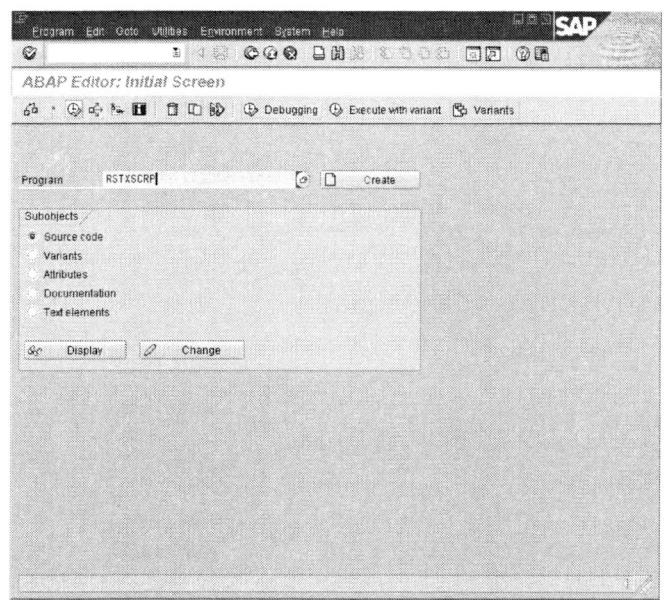

3

TechTalk

Although the *RSTXSCRP* report is an easy and quick way to get a form into the R/3 System, there are some restrictions. Make sure that you also read SAPNet - R/3 frontend note 3355 to learn more about this and similar import functions for forms.

6. On the *SAPscript Export to Dataset / SAPscript Import from Dataset* screen:

   a. Enter the object name of the form (for example, **ZVORDER01**) in the *Object name* field.

   b. Enter **IMPORT** in the *Mode* field.

   c. If you use the presentation server, select *From/on frontend*, otherwise select *From/on application server*.

   d. Enter the name of the dataset and the path (for example, **C:\order01.scr**) in the *Dataset name* field.

   e. Choose 🕀 .

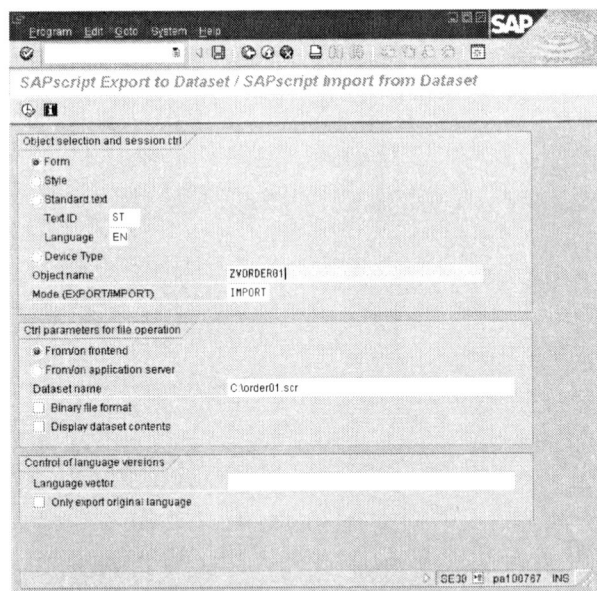

7. In the *Import from a Local File* window:

   a. Enter the full path to the file containing the desired dataset in the *File name* field.

   b. Choose *Transfer*.

The file transfer is now complete. To import other forms, repeat the steps shown in this task.

The result of the file transfer is the protocol displayed below.

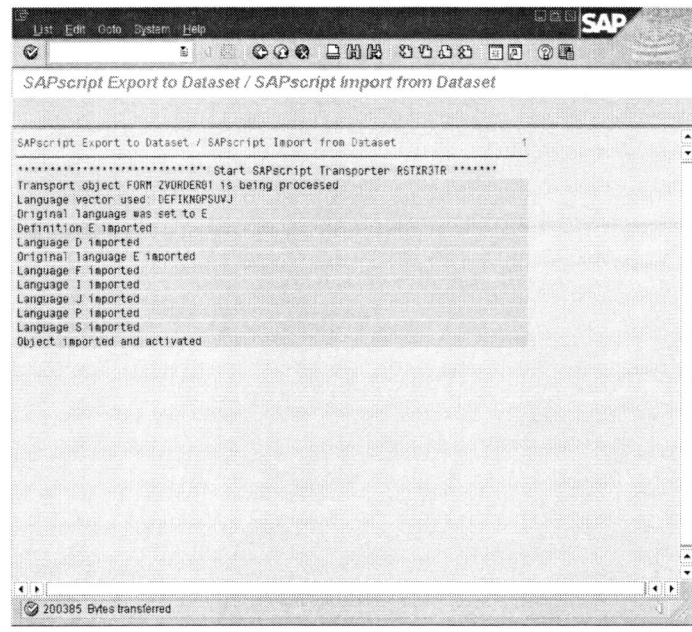

8. Go *Back* three times to return to the *SAP standard menu*.

Modifying SAPscript Forms: The Basics

Overview

In the previous chapter you learned how to import SAPscript forms in your development client. You already know the form management tools Form Painter and PC Editor and how to access them. You are now ready to start modifying forms.

This chapter focuses on basic form modifications as:

- Copying a form

- Test printing a form

- Modifying the layout of a form (creating, renaming, moving, resizing, or deleting a window)

- Modifying the content of a form (moving fields or tabs, looking up a field in the data dictionary, adding fields to your form, or adding fields to a print structure)

Caution

To make your next system upgrade easier and smoother, do not modify the standard forms or the forms from the disk. Copy these forms and modify the copies, not the standard forms.

Copying a Form

Forms must be copied before changes are made. The following example shows how to copy a form.

Task

Copy a form for a sales order confirmation.

1. From the SAP standard menu, choose *Tools → SAPscript → SE71 - Form*.

2. On the *Form Painter: Request* screen:

   a. Enter the name of the new form in the *Form* field. This name should be as similar as possible to the old name and has to begin with Z or Y, since the new form name has to be in the name range for customer objects (for example, the new name for the *Sales Order Confirmation* is **ZVORDER02**).

   b. Enter **EN** in the *Language* field.

   c. Choose ⬜ *Create*.

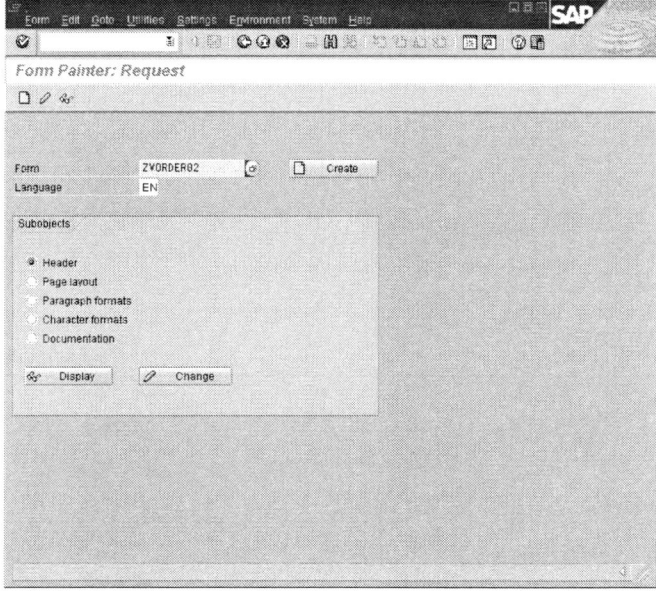

4

3. Choose 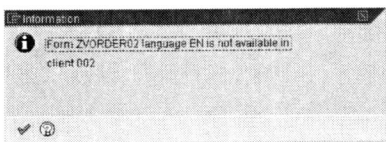 to accept the message displayed in the popup window.

4. On the *Administrative Screen*:

   a. Enter `Sales Order Confirmation` in the *Description* field.

   b. From the menu bar, choose *Form → Copy from*.

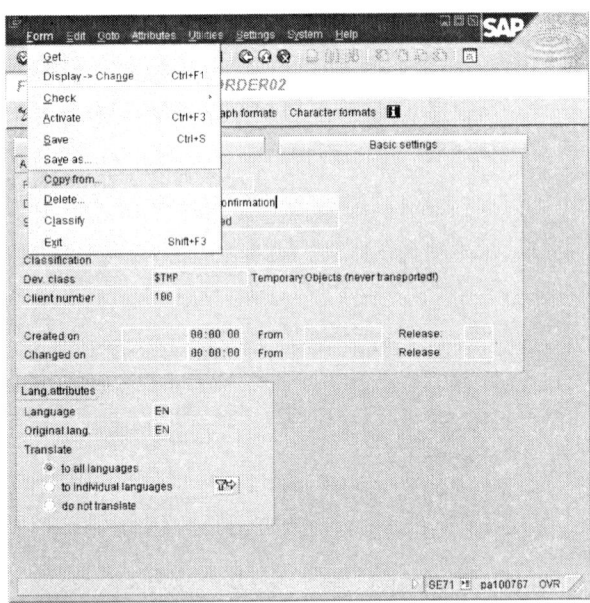

5. In the popup window:

   a. Enter `ZVORDER01` in the *Form* field.

   b. Enter `EN` in the *Language* field.

   c. Choose 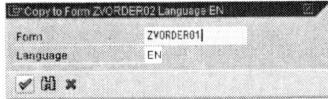.

6. On the *Form: Change Header: ZVORDER02* screen:

a. Save form *ZVORDER02*.

If your system is connected to the Change and Transport System (CTS), the new form must be written on a correction request. (The instructions for writing a correction request are not included in this guide.)

b. To activate the changes, choose 　.

c. Go *Back* to return to the SAP standard menu.

> If you activate the form, it is not necessary to save the form in step 6a, because the form is saved during activation in step 6b.

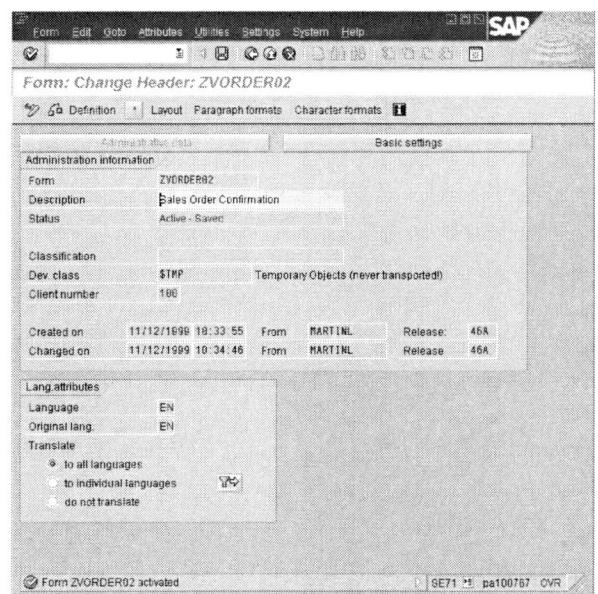

Tips & Tricks

> To test the form during sales order customizing, specify that form. ZVORDER02 should be used to print all sales order confirmations. For more information, see Chapter 6, "Customizing Sales and Distribution for Print Forms" on page 161.

4

Test Printing a Form

Test prints provide an easy way to check modified forms. On a test print, SAPscript prints a string of *X*s for all of the variables used in the form. For example, if a variable is 5 characters in length, SAPscript prints **XXXXX** in its place.

All windows, except *MAIN*, are printed as they appear in the actual output. *MAIN* contains a list of all defined text elements.

Task

Execute a print test of a form.

1. From SAP standard menu, choose *Tools → SAPscript → SE71 - Form*.

2. On the *Form Painter: Request* screen:

   a. Enter **ZVORDER02** in the *Form* field.

   b. From the menu bar, choose *Utilities → Test print*.

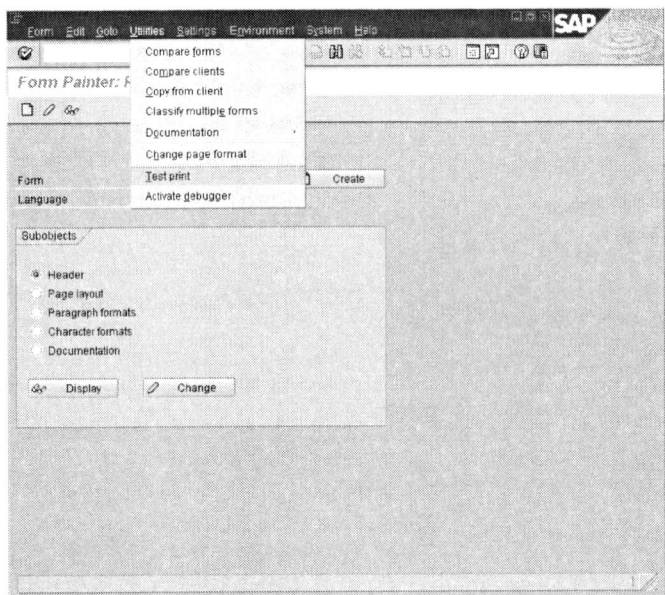

3. On the *Print* screen:

    a. Enter a printer name (for example, **LP01**) in the *OutputDevice* field.

    b. Select *Print immediately.*

    c. Choose 🖨 *Print.*

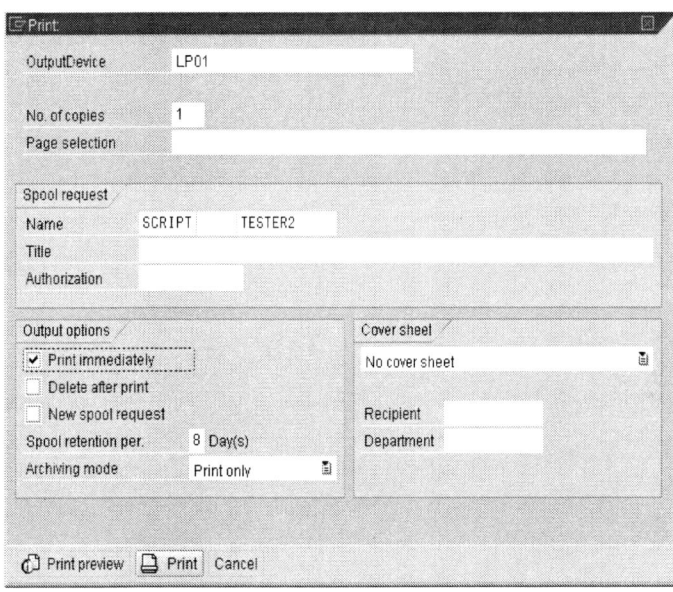

4. On the *Form Painter: Request* screen, go *Back* to return to the SAP standard menu.

Manipulating the Layout of a Form

Manipulation of the layout of a form can be subdivided into the following operations:

- Creating a new window

- Renaming a window

- Changing the position of a window

- Changing the size of a window

- Removing a window

- Aligning a window

> **Note**
>
> The following sections describe the manipulation of a form using the graphical Form Painter. It is always possible to manipulate the forms by conventional means in the *Administrative Screen*, that is, by specifying the coordinates of windows by numerical values. For instructions switching over to the graphical Form Painter, see "Activating the Graphical Form Painter and PC Editor" on page 34.

Creating a New Window

> **Task**
>
> Add a new window to a form.

1. From the SAP standard menu, choose *Tools → SAPscript → SE71 - Form*.

2. On the *Form Painter: Request* screen:

   a. Enter **ZVORDER02** in the *Form* field.

   b. Enter **EN** in the *Language* field.

   c. Select *Page layout*.

   d. Choose ✏ *Change*.

 The window can also be created by choosing *Edit → Windows → Create → Variables window* from the menu on the *Administrative Screen*.

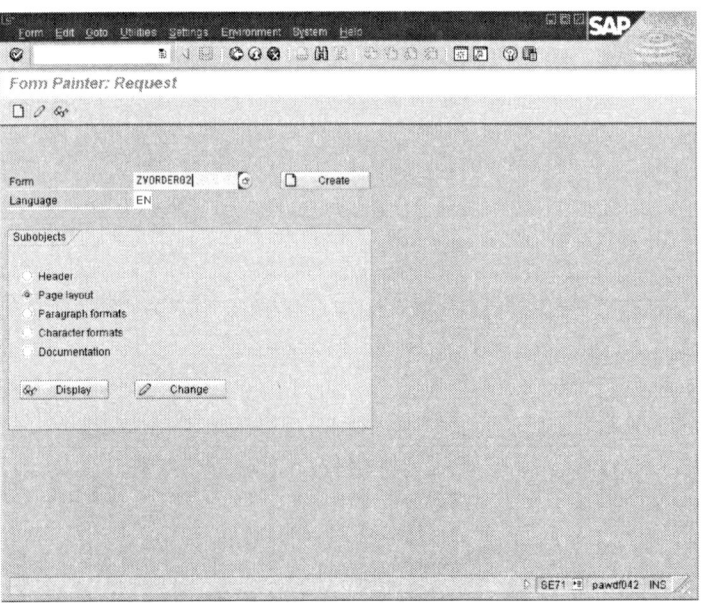

3. In the *Design Window,* right-click to access the form layout manipulation menu and choose *Create window*.

The new window is automatically named WINDOW1 and placed in the top left corner of the page.

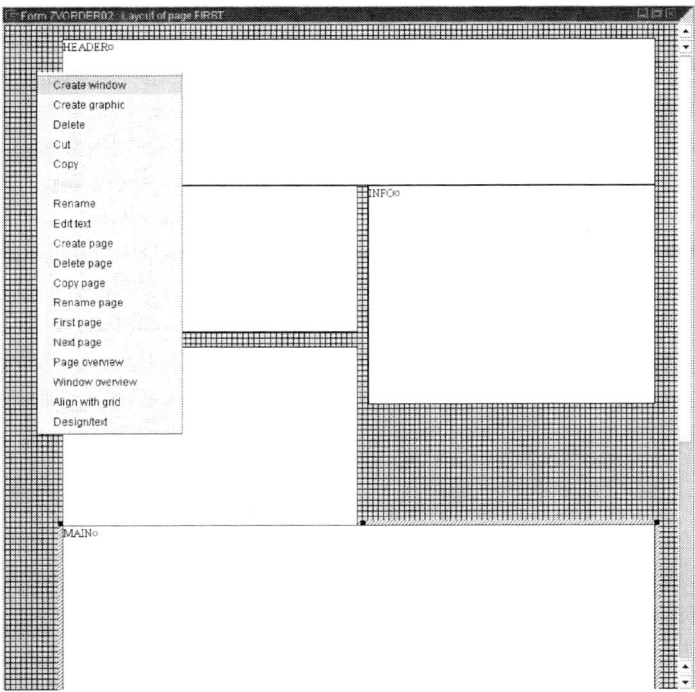

4. Click on the *Administrative Screen*.

5. To activate the changes, choose   .

In general, you will proceed with:

- Renaming the newly created window (see "Renaming a Window" on page 72)

- Changing the size of the newly created window (see "Changing Window Position or Size Using Design Window" on page 75)

- Changing the position of the newly created window (see "Changing Window Position or Size Using Design Window" on page 75)

4

Renaming a Window

Task

Change the name (and description) of the existing window (for example, WINDOW1 to ADDRESS2).

1. From the SAP standard menu, choose *Tools → SAPscript → SE71 - Form*.

2. On the *Form Painter: Request* screen:

   a. Enter **ZVORDER02** in the *Form* field.

   b. Enter **EN** in the *Language* field.

   c. Select *Page layout*.

   d. Choose 🖉 *Change*.

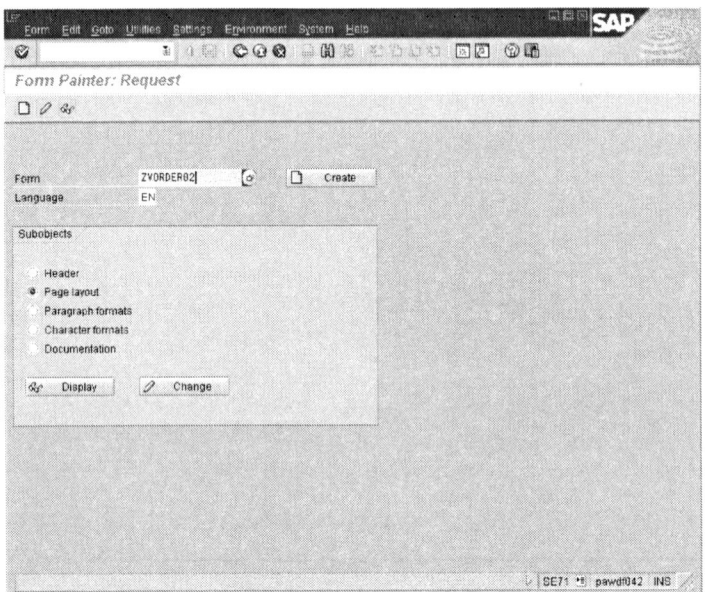

3. In the *Design Window:*

   a. Select *WINDOW1.*

   b. Right-click to access the form layout manipulation menu and choose *Rename.*

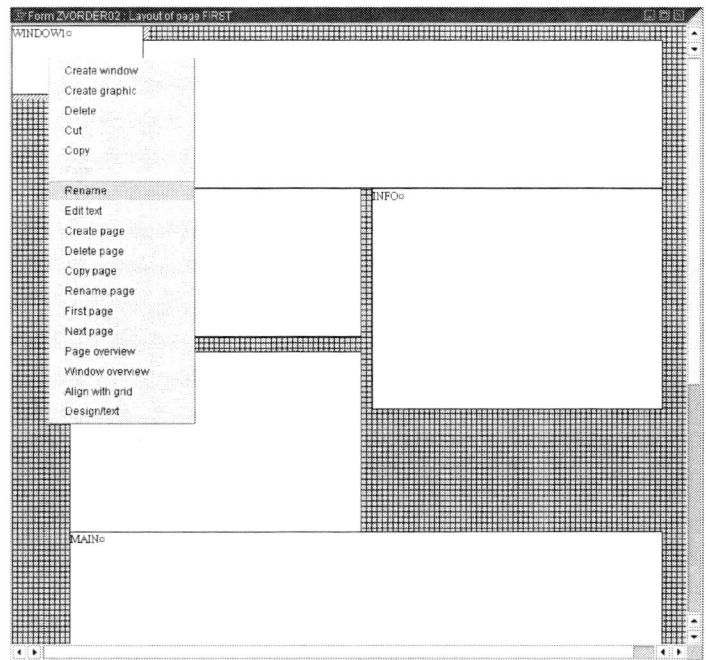

4. On the *Rename* window:

   a. Enter a name (for example, **ADDRESS2**) in the *to* field.

   b. Choose ✅ .

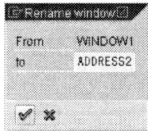

5. Click on the *Administrative Screen.*

4

The window can also be renamed by choosing *Edit → Windows → Rename* from the menu bar on the *Administrative Screen*.

6. On the *Administrative Screen*:

a. Enter a description for the renamed window (for example, `Shipping Address`) in the *Description* field.

b. To activate the changes, choose ▮ .

c. Go *Back* twice to return to the SAP standard menu.

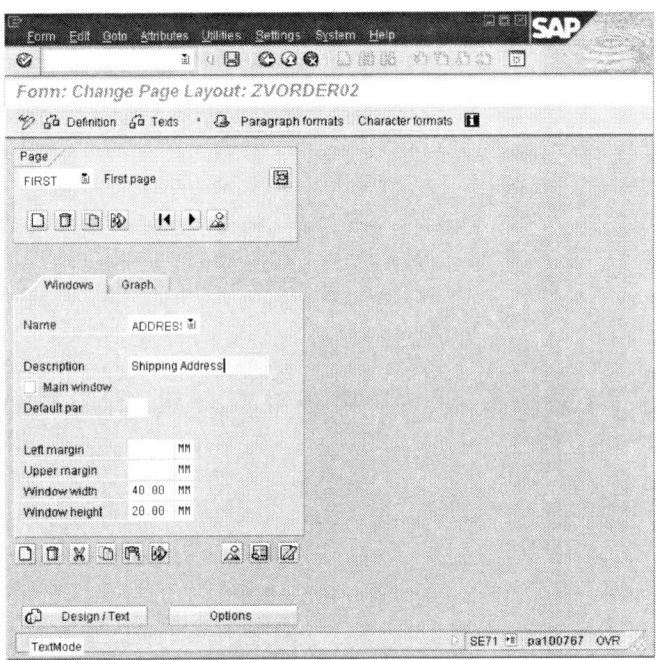

Changing Window Position or Size Using Design Window

Task

Enlarge or shrink the size of a window, or place a window at another position in the form.

1. From the SAP standard menu, choose *Tools → SAPscript → SE71 - Form*.

2. On the *Form Painter: Request* screen:

   a. Enter **ZVORDER02** in the *Form* field.

   b. Enter **EN** in the *Language* field.

   c. Select *Page layout*.

   d. Choose ⌀ *Change*.

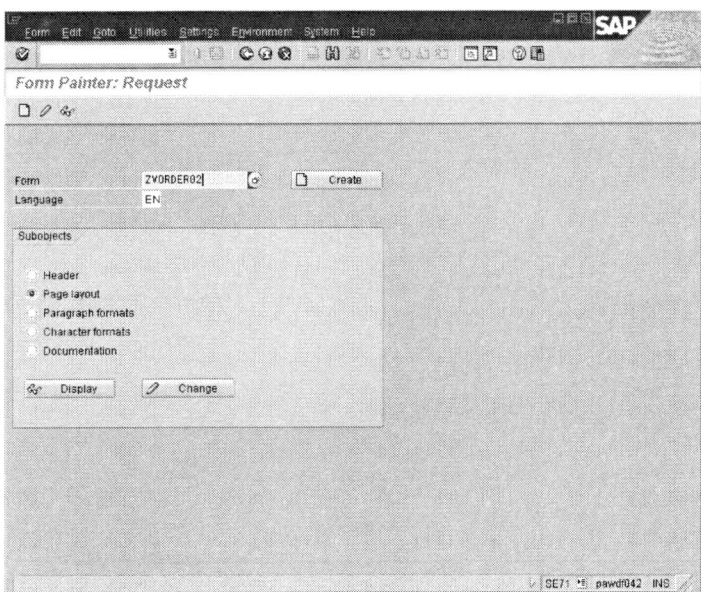

4

3. In the *Design Window*:

   a. To move a window, grab the window by pressing the left mouse button. Move the window to the new position while keeping the left mouse button pressed. Release the left mouse button at the new position.

   b. To change the size of a window, position the cursor on the corner or edge of the window and press the left mouse button. Keep the left mouse button pressed while changing the window size. Release the left mouse button when the new size is adjusted.

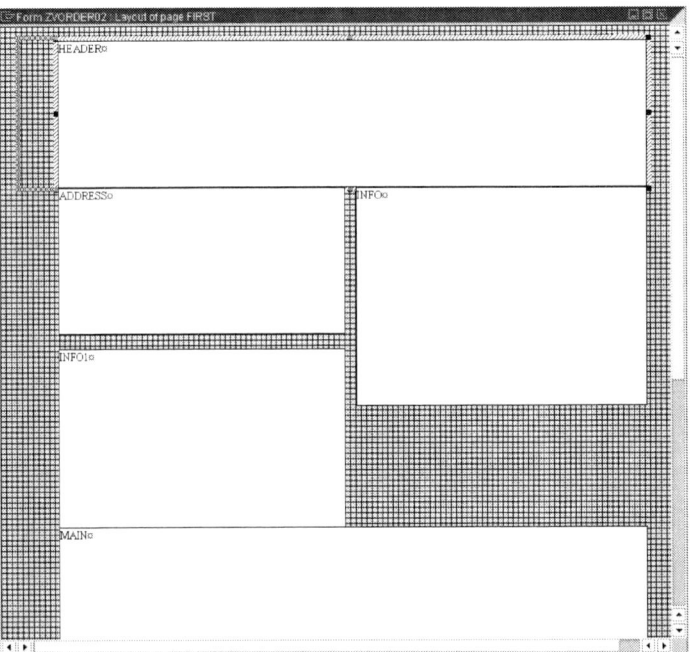

4. Click on the *Administrative Screen*.

   a. To activate the changes, choose ⬛.

   b. Go *Back* twice to return to the SAP standard menu.

Changing Window Position or Size Using Administrative Screen

Task

Change the position or size of a window by changing the margin position or the width and height of a window.

1. From the SAP standard menu, choose *Tools → SAPscript → SE71 - Form.*

2. On the *Form Painter: Request* screen:

    a. Enter **ZVORDER02** in the *Form* field.

    b. Enter **EN** in the *Language* field.

    c. Select *Page layout*.

    d. Choose ⌀ *Change*.

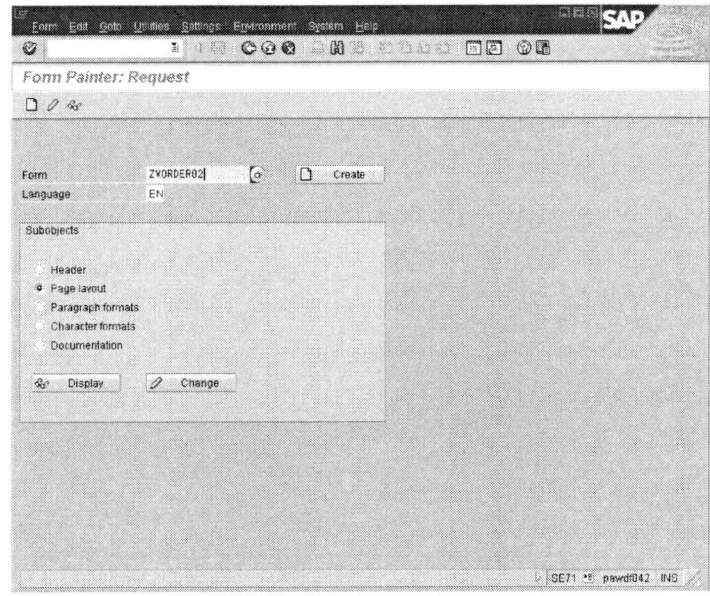

4

3. Click on the *Administrative Screen*.

4. In the *Windows* section of the *Administrative Screen*:

   a. Choose a window by clicking the arrow 🗐 in the *Name* field.

   b. Choose the desired window name.

   c. To change the position of the chosen window, change the values in the *Left margin* and *Upper margin* fields.

   d. To change the size of the chosen window, change the values in the *Window width* and *Window height* fields.

   e. To activate the changes, choose ▮ .

   f. Go *Back* twice to return to the SAP standard menu.

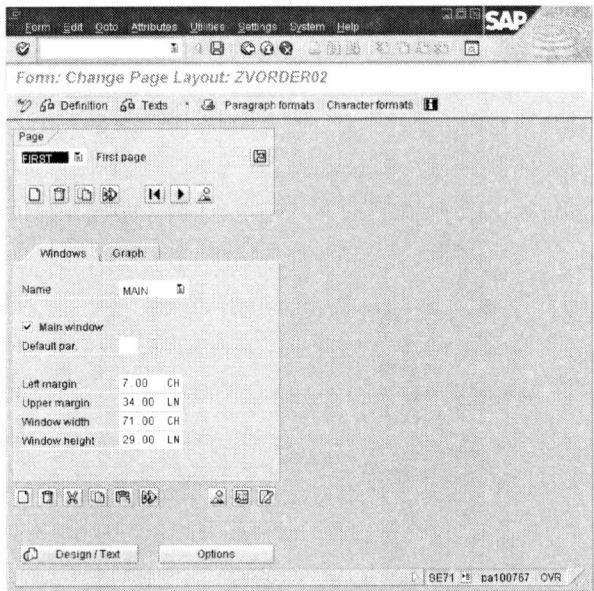

Removing a Window

Task

Delete the window ADDRESS2 from the form.

1. From the SAP standard menu, choose *Tools → SAPscript → SE71 - Form*.

2. On the *Form Painter: Request* screen:

   a. Enter **ZVORDER02** in the *Form* field.

   b. Enter **EN** in the *Language* field.

   c. Select *Page layout*.

   d. Choose *⌀ Change*.

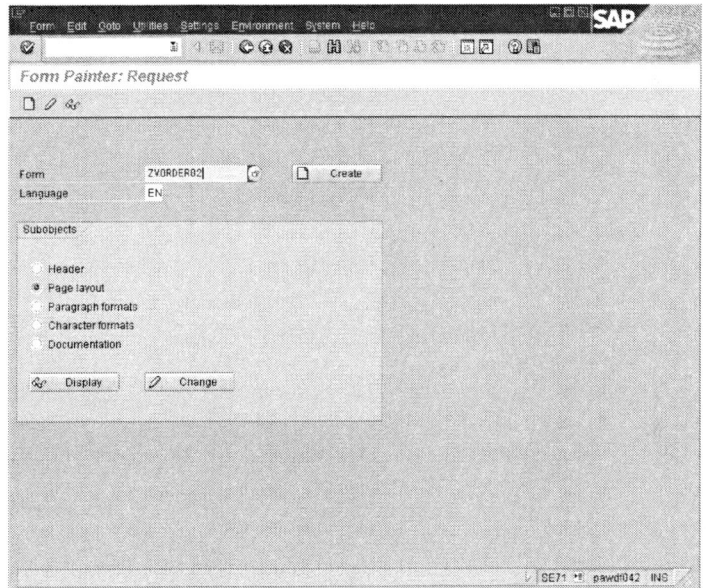

4

3. In the *Design Window:*

   a. Select *ADDRESS2.*

   b. Right-click to access the form layout manipulation menu and choose *Delete.*

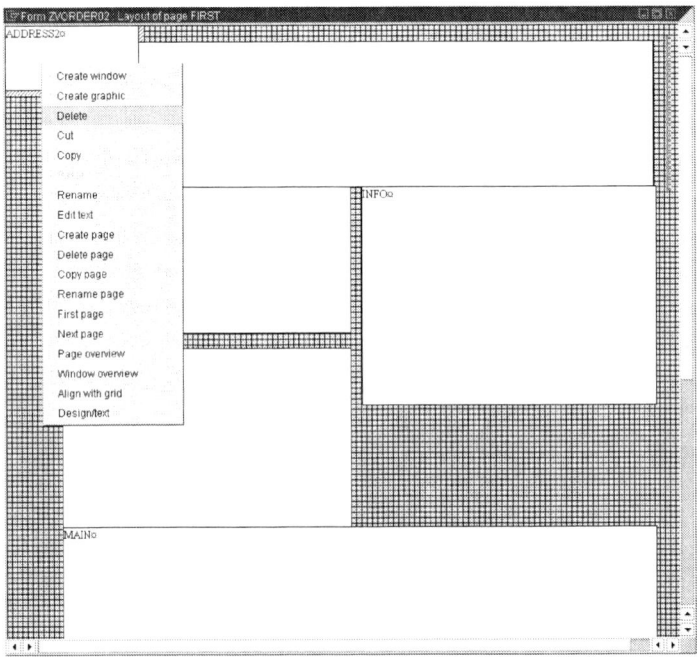

4. Click on the *Administrative Screen.*

5. On the *Administrative Screen*:

   a. To activate the changes, choose .

   b. Go *Back* twice to return to the SAP standard menu.

Aligning Windows to the Grid

You will notice a grid in the background of the *Design Window.* You can adjust the grid step size by specifying the step width (from 0 to 10) and the unit of measurement (for example, inches, millimeters, etc.). If you activate the automatic alignment in the Form Painter, the precise position or size of the windows will be defined by the grid.

Task

Adjust the grid step size of a form.

1. From the SAP standard menu, choose *Tools → SAPscript → SE71 - Form*.

2. On the *Form Painter: Request* screen:

   a. Enter **ZVORDER02** in the *Form* field.

   b. Enter **EN** in the *Language* field.

   c. Select *Page layout*.

   d. Choose ⧫ *Change*.

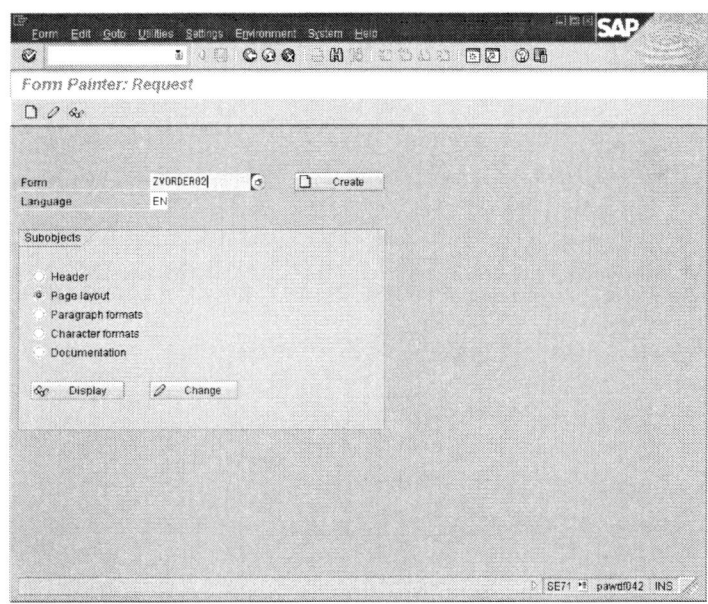

3. On the *Administrative Screen*, choose *Utilities → Options*.

4. In the *Options* window:

   a. Adjust the new *Step size* for the grid with a value between 0 (zero) and 10.

   b. Select *Align automatically to grid*.

   c. Choose ✅ .

The grid measurement unit can also be changed here (for example, in the *Unit of measure* field, change *MM* to *IN*).

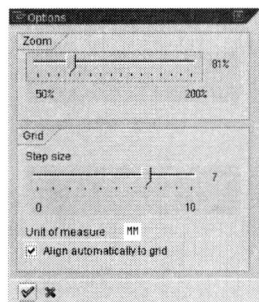

Note

You activated the *Align automatically to grid* option. Next time you change the position or size of a window, the system automatically aligns the window to the grid you defined in step 4a.

Manipulating Form Content

This section highlights the major features available for manipulating the content of a window, for example its text fields. The following functions will be described in detail:

- Moving a field

- Removing a field

- Looking up a field

- Adding a new field

- Adding a field to the print structure

Caution

The following sections describe how to manipulate the content of a window with the PC Editor. Of course, it is always possible to manipulate the content in the conventional way (that is, by specifying the position of a field with numerical values).

Moving a Field

Text appearing in the form output can be moved as follows:

- If it is the only text in a window, move the window (as described in "Changing Window Position or Size Using Design Window" on page 75).

- If it is positioned with a tab, move the tab.

- If it has to be moved vertically, insert or delete an empty line.

Moving a Tab

Task

In the table header of line items for an order confirmation, move the
text `Material` one character to the right.

Tips & Tricks

In this example, we move one word in the table header of line items in a sales
order one character to the right. The complete task would be also to move the
corresponding line item variable to match the columns for both the table header
and line items.

1. From the SAP standard menu, choose *Tools → SAPscript → SE71 -
Form.*

2. On the *Form Painter: Request* screen:

    a. Enter **ZVORDER02** in the *Form* field.

    b. Enter **EN** in the *Language* field.

    c. Select *Page layout.*

    d. Choose ⬦ *Change.*

4

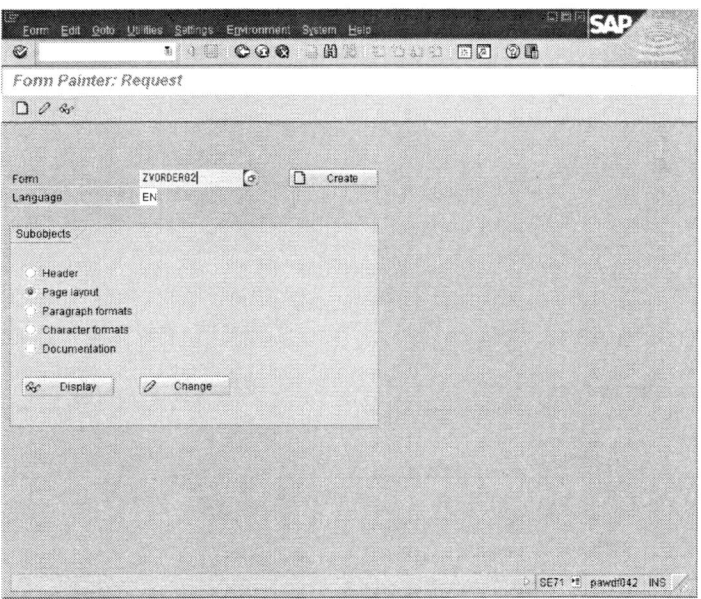

3. In the *Design Window:*

   a. Activate the *MAIN* window.

   b. Right-click to access the form layout manipulation menu and choose *Edit text.*

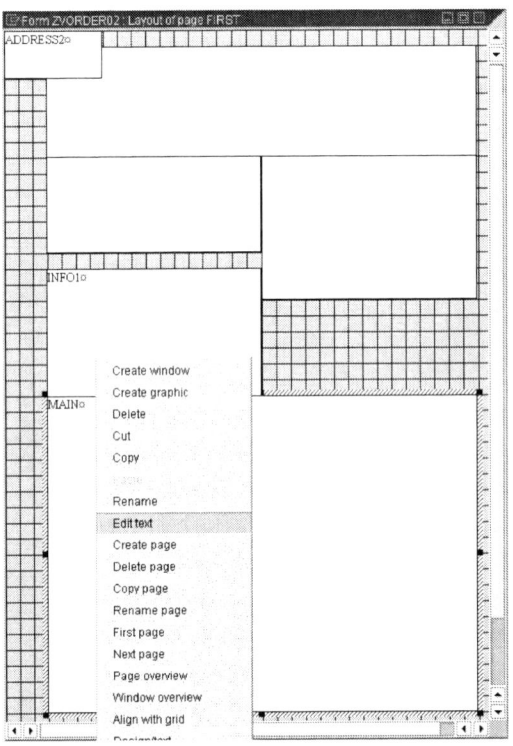

TechTalk

If any unknown paragraph formats are used in the window, the Form Painter cannot call the PC Editor; it launches the text editor instead. A message indicating the names of the unknown formats appears in the status line of the *Administrative Screen* where the text editor is located. In general, you should assign a paragraph format, which is already defined for the form, to each paragraph with an unknown paragraph format.

If a window uses an unknown paragraph format, the Form Painter can not call the PC Editor. You have the following alternatives:

- Work with the line editor as described in the example. This needs a little practice, because the technique is different from the way you work with the PC Editor.

- Create paragraph formats for the unknown formats.

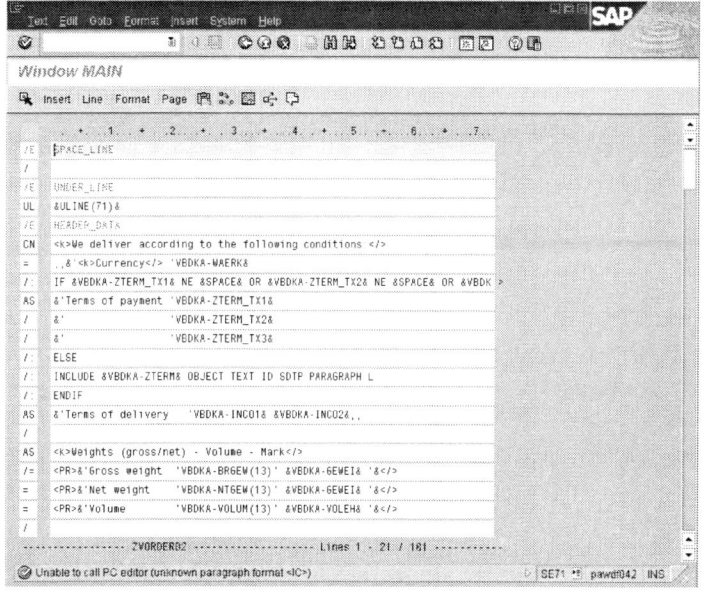

4. On the *Window MAIN* screen: **4**

   a. Scroll down until you see */E ITEM_HEADER*.

   b. Look at the line where *Material* is printed in paragraph format *IL*.

Material is printed after the first tab, which is represented by a set of double commas. To move the word one character to the right, you must increase the tab by 1.

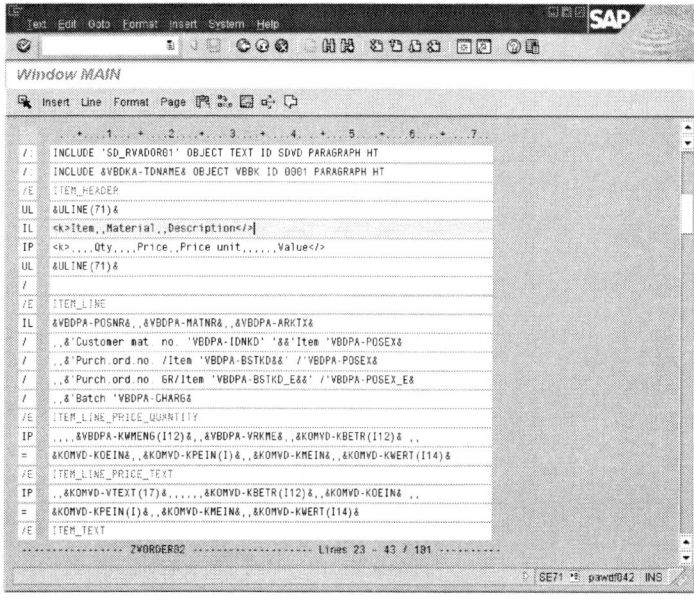

5. Go *Back* to return to the *Administrative Screen*.

6. On the *Administrative Screen*:

   a. Choose *Paragraph formats*.

   b. Select *IL* by double-clicking on its line. The paragraph format will be highlighted after selection.

   c. Choose *Tabs*.

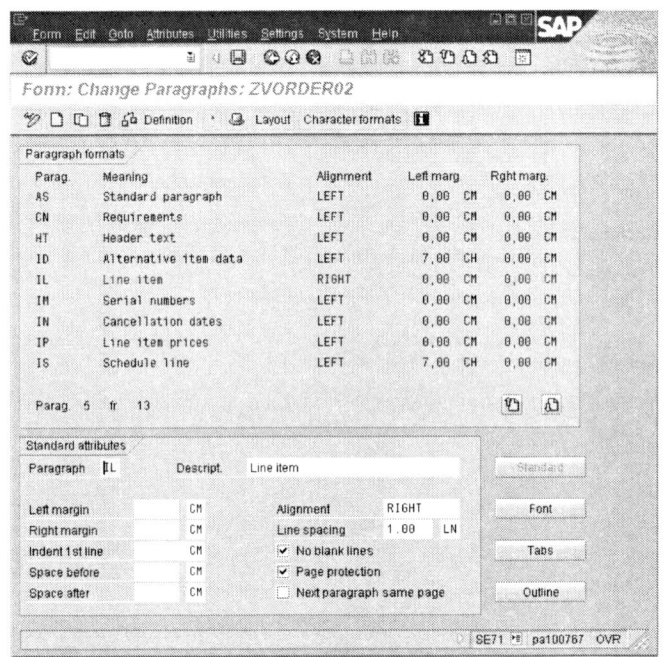

7. In the *Form: Change Paragraphs: ZVORDER02* window, in the *Tabs* block:

a. The first tab entry means that the first tab position is 7 characters from the left border of the form, and the corresponding text will be printed with left alignment.

b. To move *Material* one character to the right, increase the first tab by one and overwrite `7.00` with `8.00`.

c. To activate the changes, choose 📄 .

d. Go *Back* twice to return to the SAP standard menu.

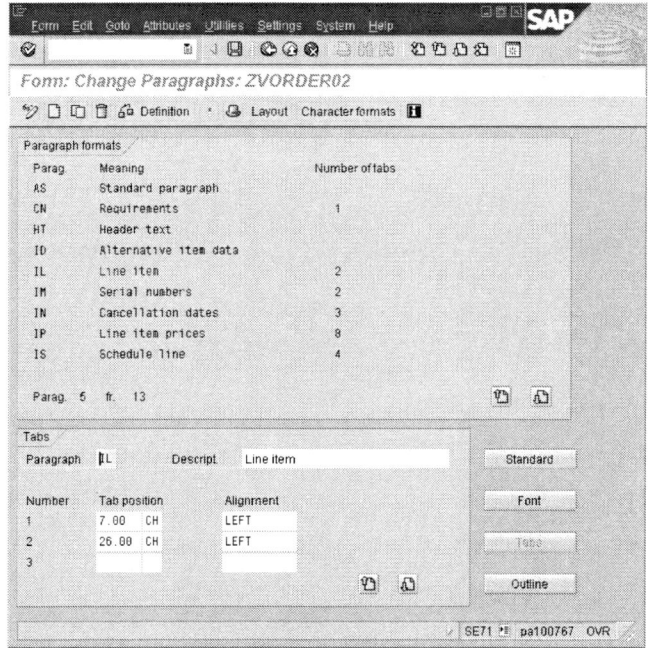

Inserting or Deleting a Line

Task

On an order confirmation, insert a blank line between "ship-to address" and "address."

1. From the SAP standard menu, choose *Tools → SAPscript → SE71 - Form.*

2. On the *Form Painter: Request* screen:

   a. Enter **ZVORDER02** in the *Form* field.

   b. Enter **EN** in the *Language* field.

   c. Select *Page layout.*

   d. Choose 🖊 *Change.*

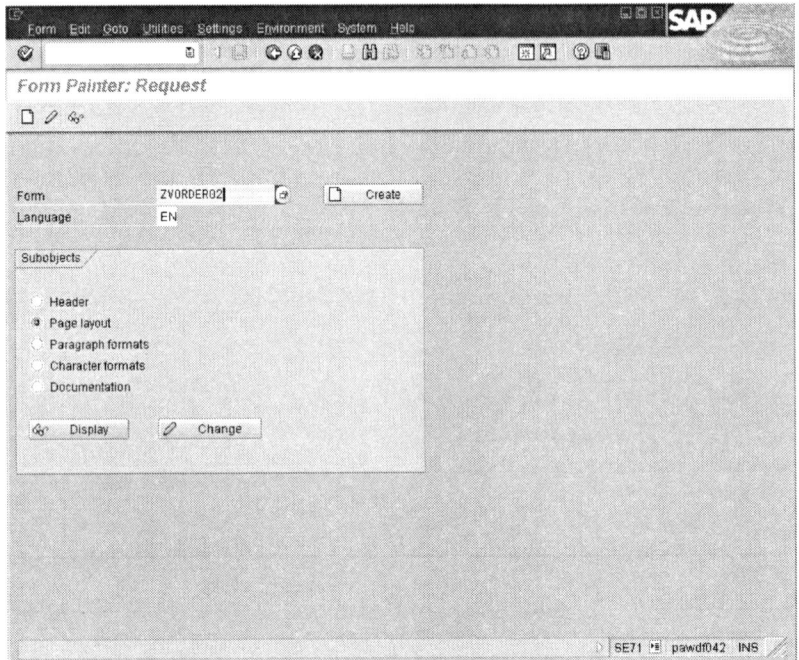

3. In the *Design Window*:

   a. Right-click the *INFO1* window.

   b. Right-click to access the form layout manipulation menu and choose *Edit text.*

   c. Position the cursor where you want to insert an empty line. In this example, it is following the *Ship-to address.*

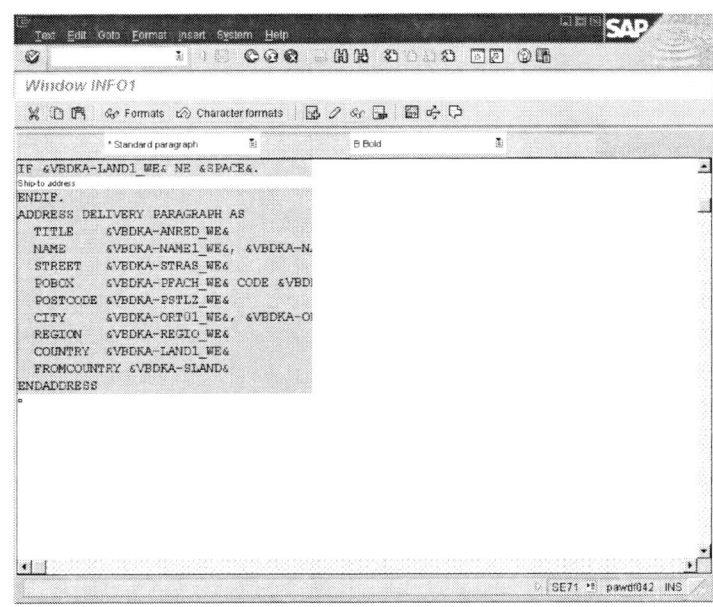

4. Press *Enter* on your keyboard.

A new line is inserted behind the cursor position as shown in the illustration below.

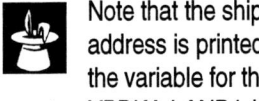 Note that the ship-to address is printed only if the variable for the ship-to country, *VBDKA-LAND1*, is filled. Character string **s** (small font) is used to print the *Ship-to address.*

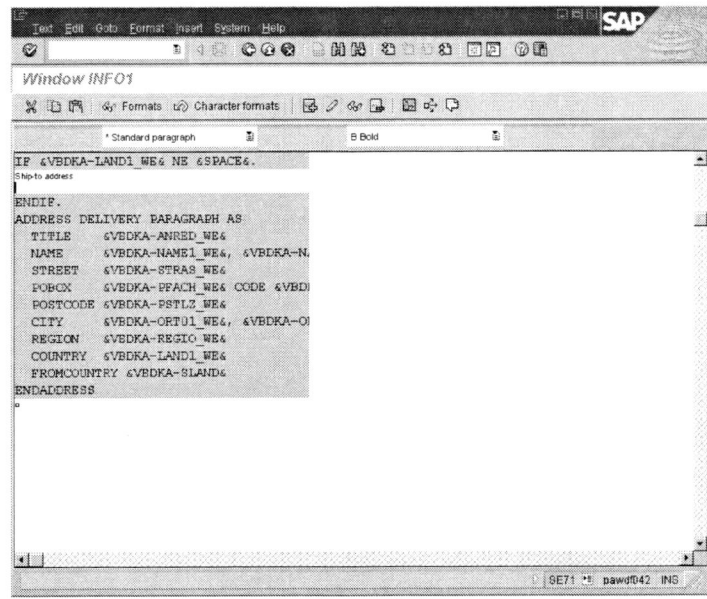

5. Go *Back* to return to the *Administrative Screen.*

6. To activate the changes, choose ▯ .

Deleting Window Text Using the PC Editor

- To delete the content of a line in a window, highlight and delete the content. Then place the cursor on the empty line and delete the line.

- To delete an entire block, highlight and delete the block.

Deleting Window Text using the Text Editor

After overwriting a line with spaces, do not choose *Enter* because it will insert an empty line. To exit the text editor, choose *Back*.

- To delete a line in a window, overwrite the line (including the format column) using spaces.

- To delete an entire block of lines, mark the block by double-clicking on the format columns of the first and last lines. Choose *Delete*.

Removing a Field

There are several different cases to consider when removing a field.

A command line is highlighted gray in the PC Editor.

Case 1: The field is not located with other fields in a command line. You can remove the field by deleting the command line.

Case 2: The field is located with other fields in a command line. Tabs do not separate the fields. You can remove the field by changing the command line. In the command line, highlight the field and delete it.

Case 3: The field is located in a line item table. Tabs separate the different table columns.

For example, to remove the item number from a sales order confirmation delete the text *ITEM* and the subsequent tab in the item header and move the text *Material* and *Description*. Next, delete the item number variable and move the material number and the description variables.

Task

Remove the item number from a sales order confirmation.

1. From the SAP standard menu, choose *Tools → SAPscript → SE71 - Form*.

2. On the *Form Painter: Request* screen:

   a. Enter **ZVORDER02** in the *Form* field.

   b. Enter **EN** in the *Language* field.

   c. Select *Page layout*.

   d. Choose ⌀ *Change*.

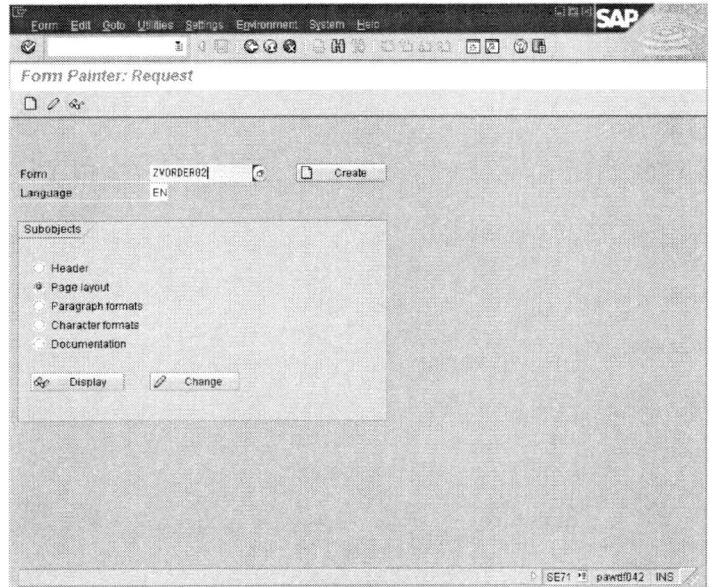

4

3. In the *Design Window*:

   a. Activate the *MAIN* window.

   b. Right-click to access the form layout manipulation menu and choose *Edit text*.

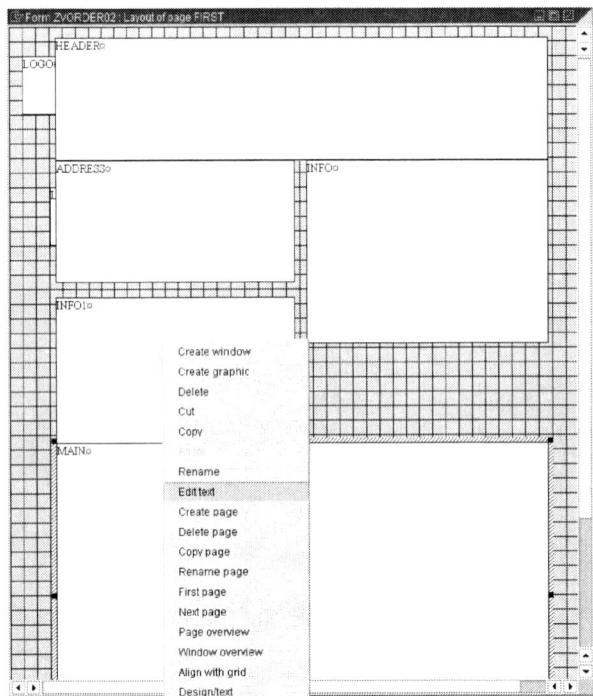

The PC Editor for the *MAIN* window is displayed on the *Administrative Screen*.

4. On the *Window MAIN* screen:

　a. Scroll down until you see the command line **ITEM_HEADER**.

　b. From the menu bar, choose *Format → Paragraph on/off* to display
　　the tabs in the PC Editor.

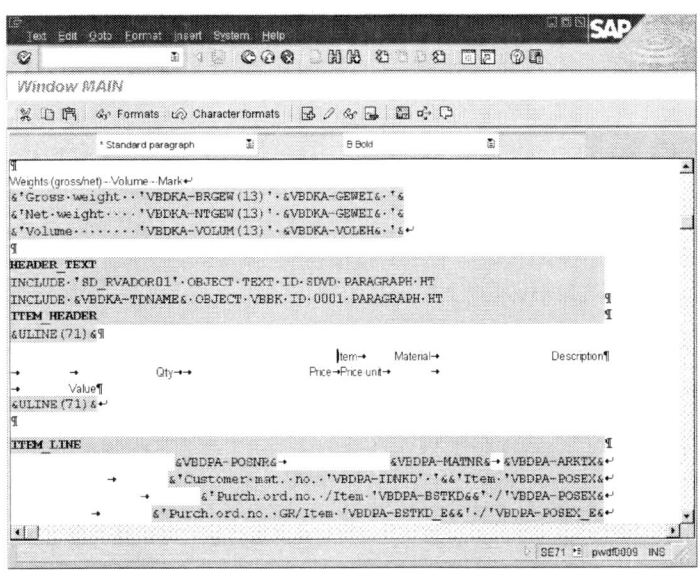

5. Highlight the text *Item* and the subsequent tab (represented by an
arrow) and delete both (press the *Delete* key on your keyboard).

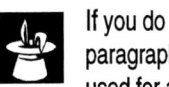 If you do not know the
paragraph format which is
used for a text element in
the PC Editor, you can display the
paragraph format by choosing
　Formats. For the first text
element displayed under the
command line &ULINE (71), the
paragraph format is IL (line item).

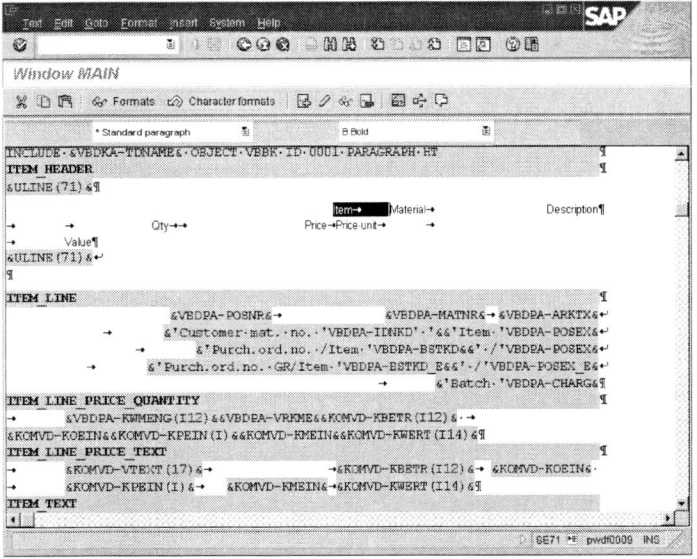

4

6. On the *Window MAIN* screen:

   a. Scroll down until you see the command line **ITEM_LINE**. All lines within this section have the paragraph format *IL* (line item).

   b. Click the variable *&VBDPA-POSNR&*.

   c. Choose ![delete] to delete the variable.

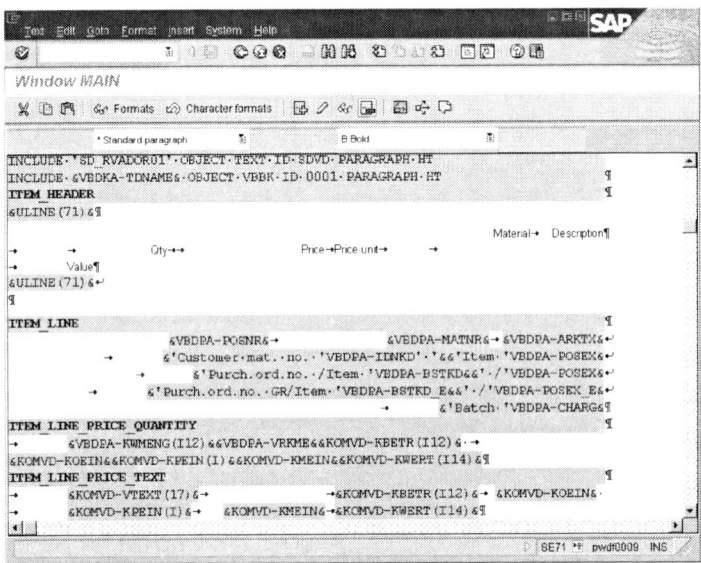

7. Delete the tab that follows *&VBDPA-POSNR&*.

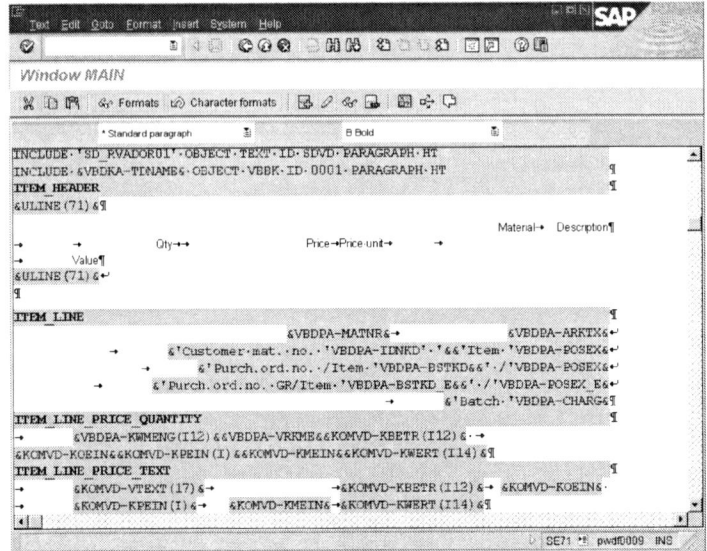

8. Delete the first tab in the four lines that follow.

The screenshot shows the result of the changes.

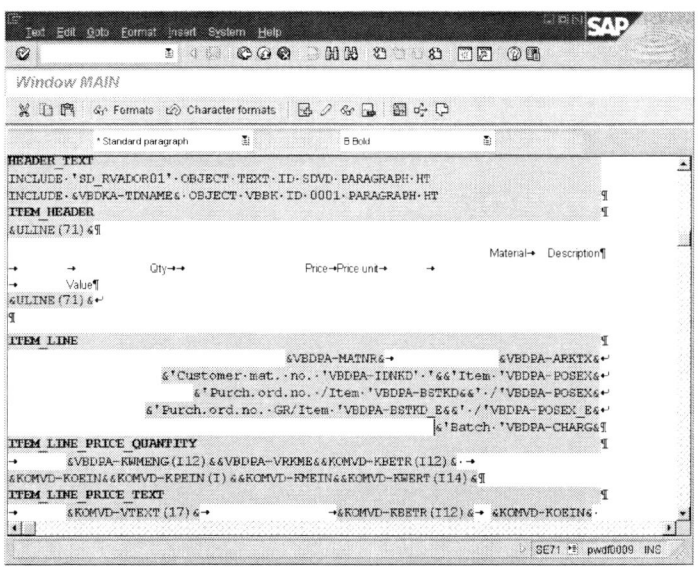

Since you deleted the first tab in the paragraph format *IL* (line item), you have to adjust the tabs for this paragraph format.

9. Go *Back* to return to the *Administrative Screen*.

10. On the *Administrative Screen*:

   a. Choose *Paragraph formats*.

   b. Double-click paragraph format *IL*.

   c. Choose *Tabs*.

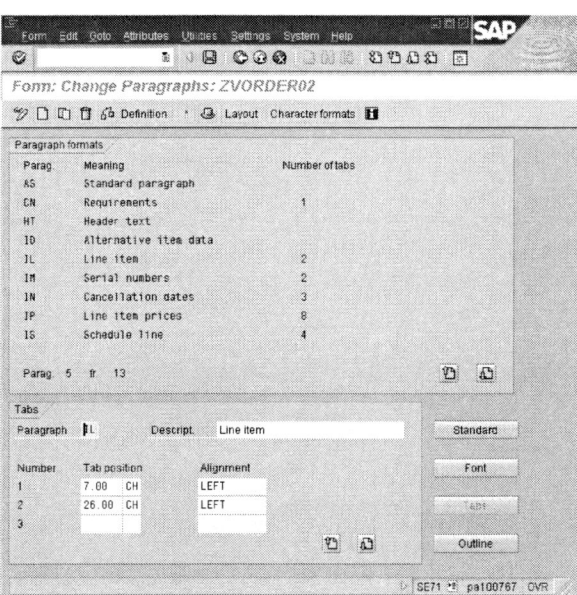

4

d. To delete the first tab you have to overwrite the first tab position
`7.00` with blanks.

e. To move the second tab to the left you have to adjust the second
tab position by overwriting `26.00` with `19.00`.

Since the first tab was positioned seven characters from the left,
the second tab has to be moved nineteen characters to the left (26
minus 7).

f. To activate the changes, choose ▯ .

g. Go *Back* twice to return to the SAP standard menu.

Note

The system automatically removes blank tab lines by shifting the entries of the
second tab line *(Number 2)* to the first tab line *(Number 1)*.

Looking Up a Field

To add a new field, first make sure that the new field is "printable."

Only data dictionary defined fields can be used as printable fields. So,
before adding a new field, determine whether the field name is part of
the data dictionary.

Tips & Tricks

All R/3 documents have at least two structures defined in the data dictionary.
These structures are used to print header and line item document data. The
fields of these structures can be used as variables in the layout set.

Some of the structures have user exits for additional to-be-printed
fields. Although it is sometimes enough to add the user exit field to
the structure, some ABAP programming may be necessary.

Task

Look up the "sales office" field in the data dictionary.

1. From the SAP standard menu choose *Logistics* → *Sales and Distribution* → *Sales* → *Order* → *VA02 - Change* to locate the *Sales office* field.

2. On the *Change Sales Order: Initial Screen*:

   a. In the *Order* field, enter a sales order (for example, 5040).

   b. Choose ⛰ *Sales*.

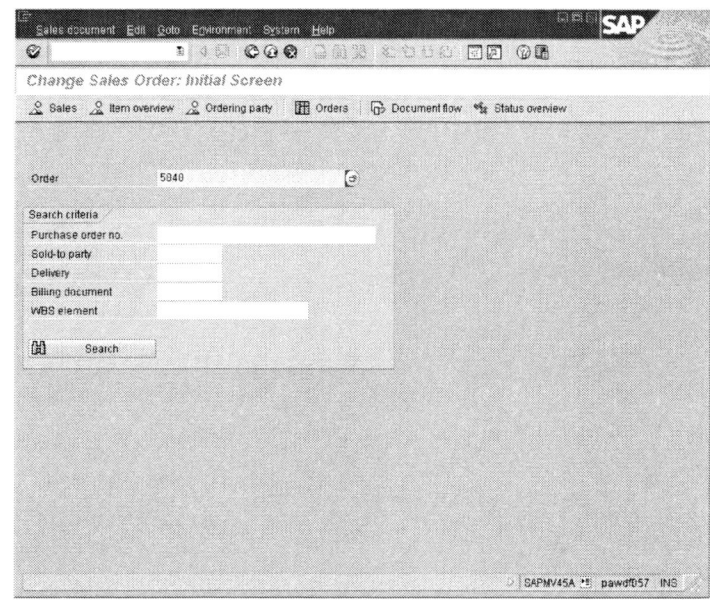

3. On the *Change OR Standard Order OR <...>: Overview* screen, choose *Goto* → *Header* → *Sales* from the menu bar.

4. On the *Change OR Standard Order OR <...>: Header Data* screen:

   a. Place the cursor in the field to determine that field's technical name (for example, *Sales office*).

   b. Press *F1* or *Help*.

5. On the *Help - Change OR Standard Order OR <...>: Header Data* window, choose *Technical info*.

4

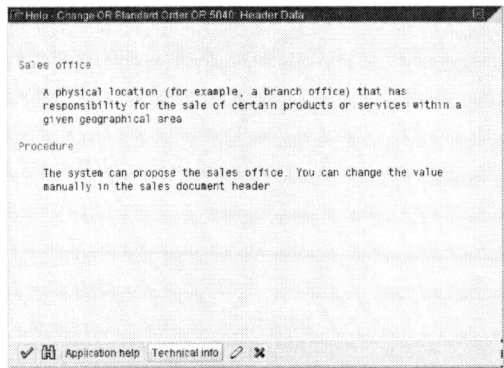

On the *Technical Information* window you find the technical name of the *Sales office* field in the Field name field. In our example the technical name is *VKBUR*.

The technical name of a field is displayed in the *Field name*.

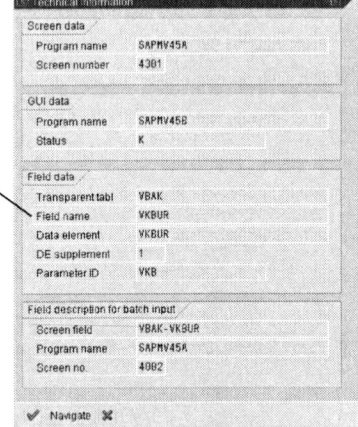

The next step is to decide if the field *Sales office* belongs to the document header or the document items. In this example, *Sales office* belongs to the header because it was accessed via the path *Goto →Header → Sales* on the *Change Standard Order: Overview* screen.

The next task is to find out if the field is designated for output. Table 4–1 shows the structures used to print header and item data. A field is flagged as an output field only if it is included in one of the structures shown in Table 4–1.

Table 4–1 Structures used to print header and item data

Item Data	Dictionary Structure
Sales Order Confirmation	VBDPA
Packing List	VBDPL
Picking List	VBLKP
Invoice	VBDPR
Purchase Order	EKPO
Prenumbered Check	REGUP
PP Goods Issue Slip	RESBD
PP Pick List	RESBD
PP Confirmation Slip	AFVGD
PP Time Ticket	AFVGD
PP Goods Receipt List	RESBD (In addition for co-products with settlement: AFPOD)
PP Operations Control Ticket	AFVGD
PP Object List	AFVGD
PP Kanban Card	KARTE

4

Note

The *Prenumbered Check* print program also provides *REGUD*, a structure for bank data.

Task

Determine whether the field VKBUR is included in the table VBDKA.

1. From the SAP standard menu, choose *Tools → ABAP Workbench → Development → SE11 - ABAP Dictionary.*

2. On the *Dictionary: Initial Screen*:

    a. Enter **VBDKA** in the *Database table* field.

    b. Choose ⚙ *Display*.

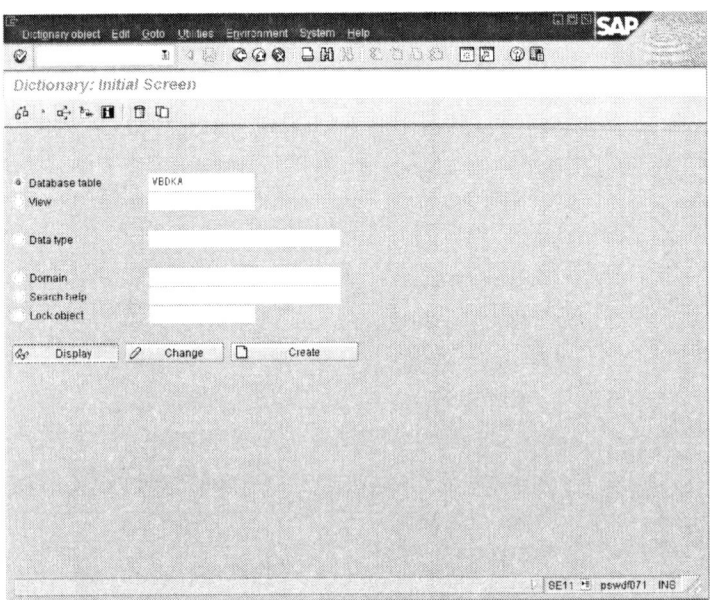

The result is a list of all fields in table *VBDKA*.

3. From the SAP standard icon bar, choose 🔲 .

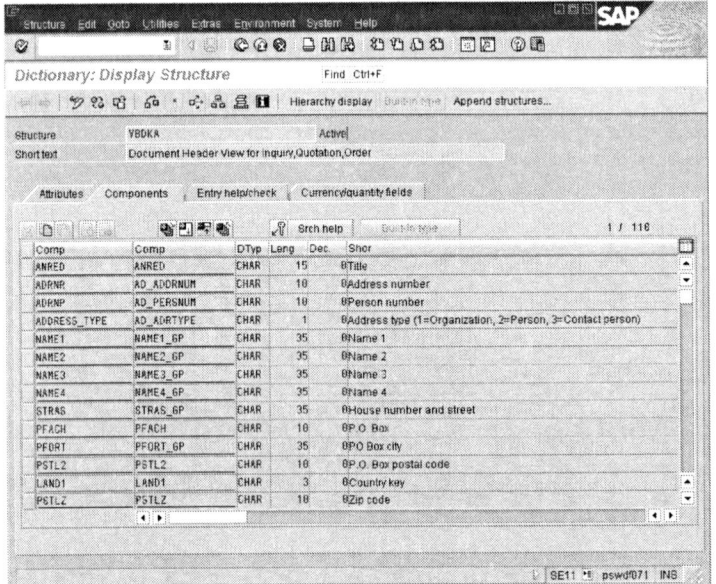

4. On the *Dictionary: Display Structure* dialog window:

  a. Enter **VKBUR**.

  b. Choose ✅ .

5. On the *Dictionary: Display Structure* screen, the cursor will be positioned automatically on the field name *VKBUR*.

If the field name is not found, the message *String '...' not found* appears.

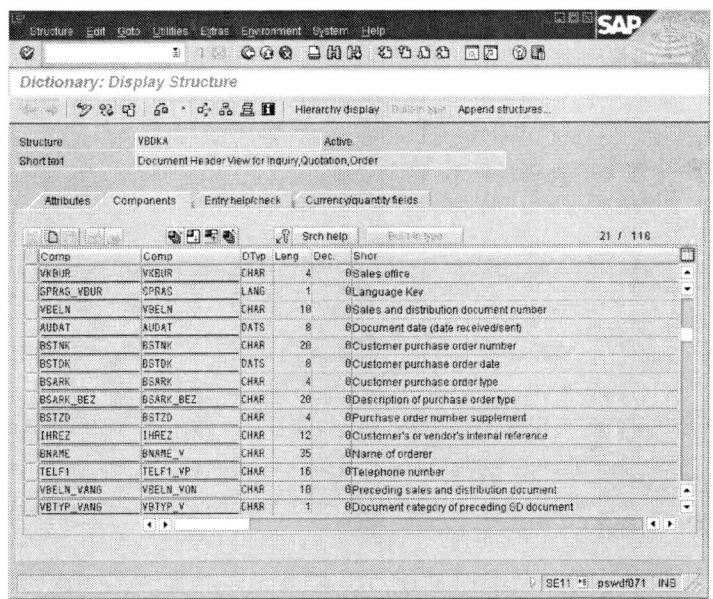

If the field name was found, follow the steps in "Adding a New Field" on page 102.

If the field name was not found, proceed to the "Adding a Field to the Print Structure" on page 106 and then follow the steps in the "Adding a New Field" on page 102.

Adding a New Field

Add the "sales office" field to the bottom of the INFO window.

1. From the SAP standard menu, choose *Tools → SAPscript → SE71 - Form*.

2. On the *Form Painter: Request* screen:

   a. Enter **ZVORDER02** in the *Form* field.

   b. Enter **EN** in the *Language* field.

   c. Select *Page layout*.

   d. Choose ⬦ *Change*.

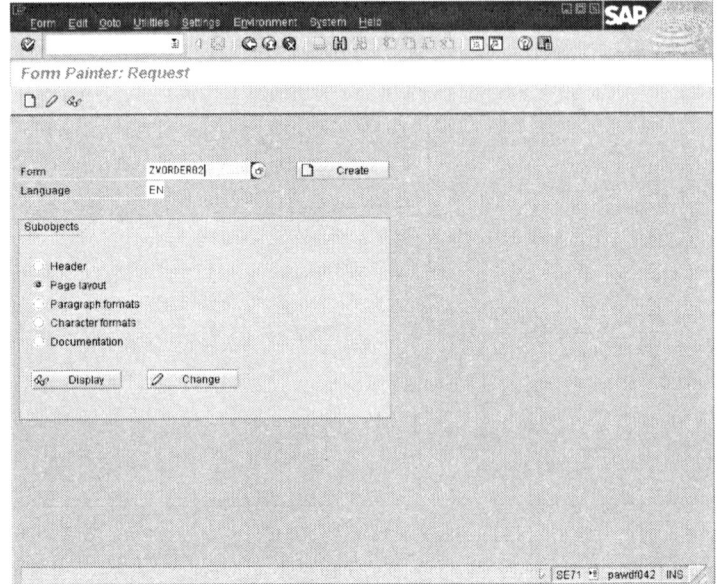

3. In the *Design Window*:

   a. Select *INFO*.

   b. Right-click to access the form layout manipulation menu and choose *Edit text*.

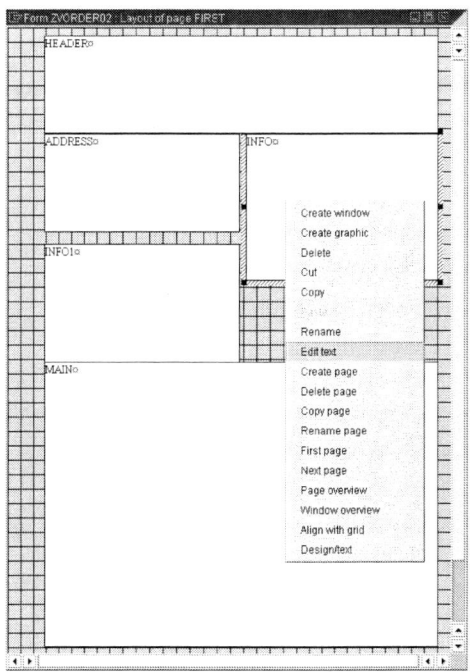

4. On the *Window INFO* screen:

   a. Scroll down to the last line, position the cursor behind the last character, and press *Enter* to create a new line.

   b. Enter `Sales Office` (the header of the new variable).

   c. Format the newly entered text by marking it.

   d. Choose the paragraph format *AS* (standard paragraph) and the character format *S* (small key word).

   e. Choose *Enter*.

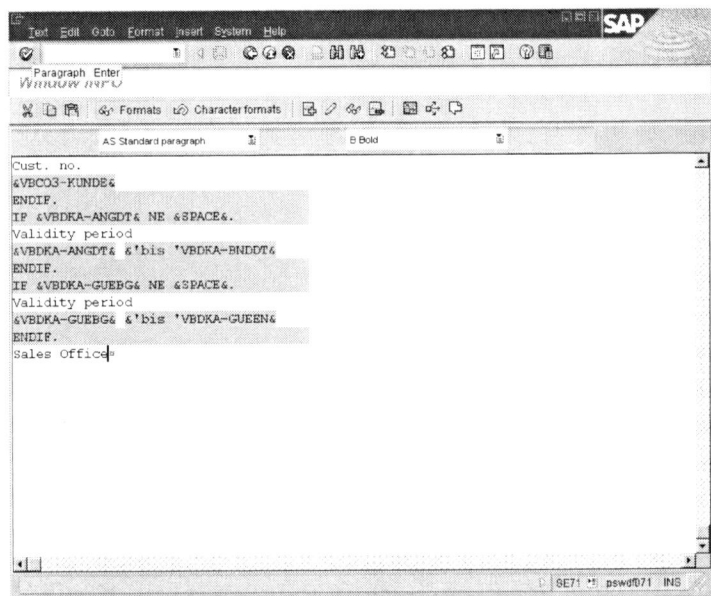

TechTalk

After creating the new line, the paragraph is automatically set to AS. This is the last paragraph used in this window. All headers are printed in a smaller font, defined with the character string S.

   f. Enter `&VBDKA-VKBUR&` (the variable name is enclosed in ampersands).

Tips & Tricks

A variable name is the name of the structure followed by a hyphen ("-") and the field name. Variable names must be enclosed in ampersands.

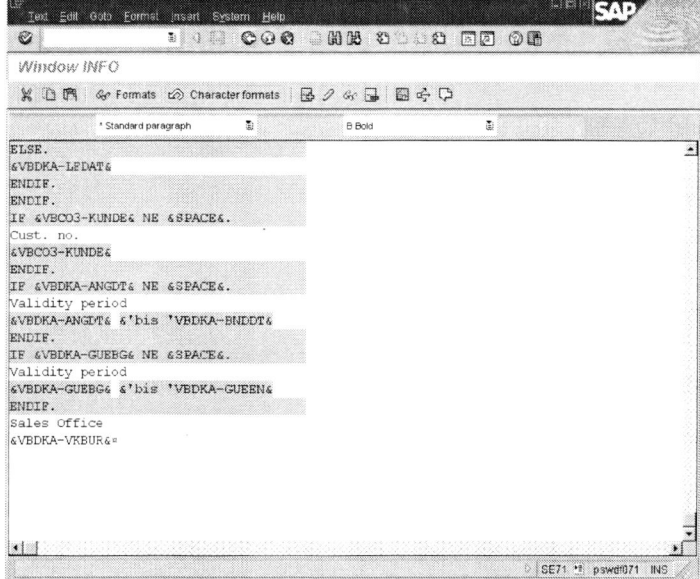

5. Go *Back* to return to the *Administrative Screen*.

6. On the *Administrative Screen*:

   a. To activate the changes, choose ▮ .

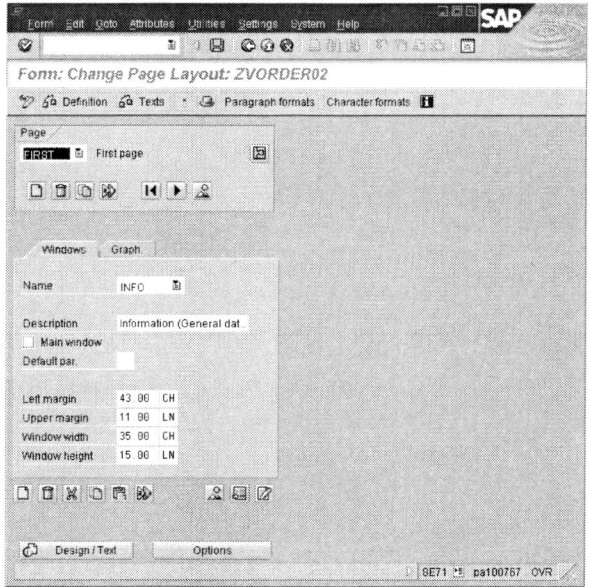

   b. Go *Back* twice to return to the SAP standard menu.

Adding a Field to the Print Structure

These steps only apply to SD documents. No steps exist for other documents. However, the structures for the other documents already contain most, if not all, of the required fields.

SD structures include substructures. By adding a field to a substructure and activating it, a field is automatically added to the structure. These substructures are treated as user exits, and SAP does not overwrite them during an upgrade.

This section provides directions on how to add a new field to a print structure. If a field is not included in a print structure, follow the step-by-step example in this section.

For example, field *XBLNR* is not included in the sales order header print structure. For more information, refer to the *Standard Order: Header → Business Data → Billing Details screen. XBLRN* is the *Reference No.* field in the *Financial Accounting* section.

The following table shows the names of structures that you can add field names to:

Table 4–2 Names of structures to which field names can be added

Document	Structure
Sales Order Header	VBDKAZ
Sales Order Item	VBDPAZ
Packing List Header	VBDKLZ
Packing List Item	VBDPLZ
Picking List Header	VBLKKZ
Picking List Item	VBLKPZ
Invoice Header	VBDKRZ
Invoice Item	VBDPRZ

If you want to include the field *XBLNR* to the sales order header add it to the substructure *VBDKAZ*.

Task

Add the XBLNR field to print structure VBDKAZ.

1. From the SAP standard menu, choose *Tools → ABAP Workbench → Overview → SE84 - Information System → ABAP Dictionary → Basic objs → Structures.*

2. On the *R/3 Repository Information System: Structures* screen:

   a. Enter **VBDKAZ** in the *Structure name* field.

   b. Choose ⊕ .

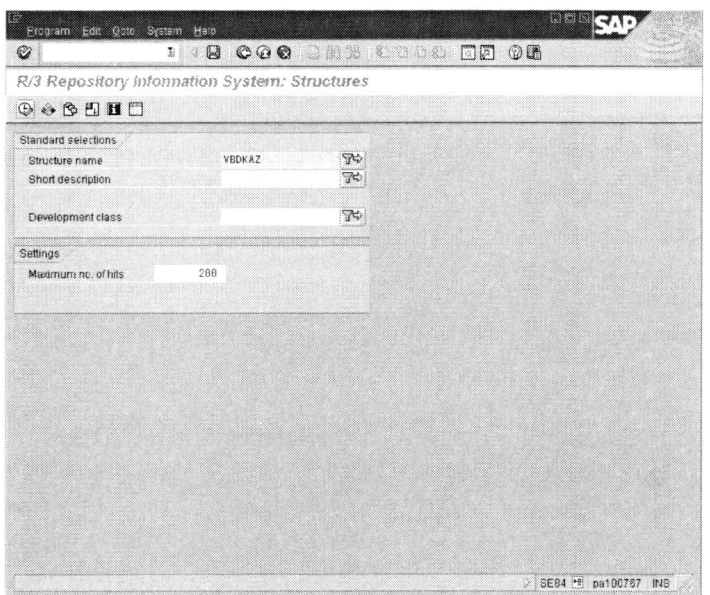

3. On the *Structures (1 Hits)* screen:

   a. Select the structure *VBDKAZ.*

   b. Choose ⌀ .

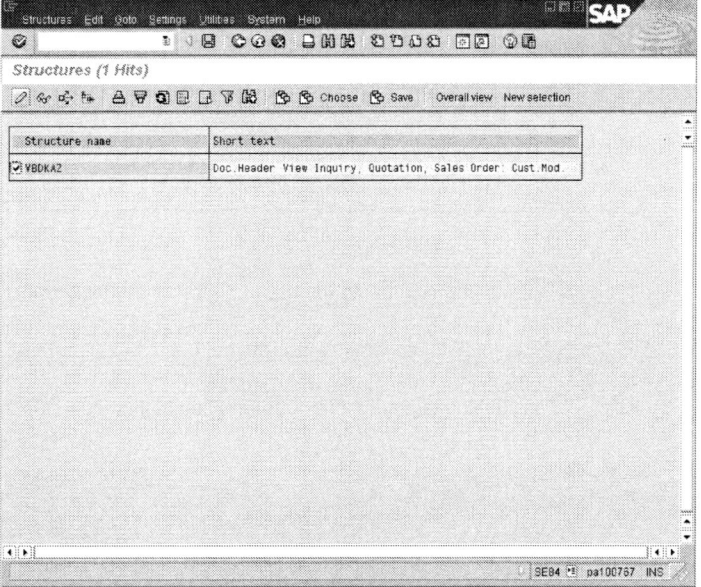

TechTalk

If the original language and the logon language are different a dialog window appears. You can maintain the structure *VBDKAZ* in its original language or in the logon language.

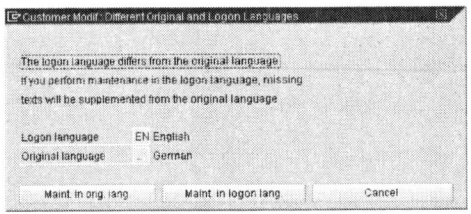

If you do not know where to get this object access key or you are not familiar with the object reparation procedure, see your system administrator.

4. A 20-digit object access key must be specified to register the object as *modified*.

Next, proceed with the whole object reparation procedure. During the procedure, you must specify the object you want to modify. In this example, you must enter **R3TR TABL VBDKAZ** in the *Object registration* screen.

5. On the *Dictionary: Maintain Structure* screen:

   a. Choose a blank line.

   b. Enter **XBLNR** in the first *Comp* field. In this example, the field represents the object's field name.

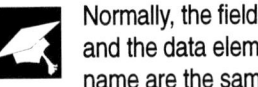

Normally, the field name and the data element name are the same.

   c. Enter **XBLNR** in the second *Comp* field. In this example, the field represents the object's data element name.

   d. To activate the changes, choose   ▯   .

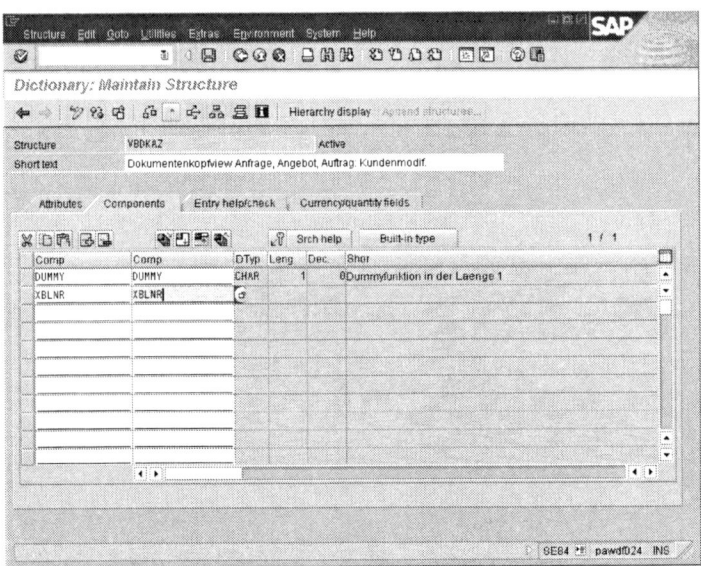

Now *VBDKA-XBLNR* is a valid variable that can be added to the form. Note that the name of the structure is still *VBDKA*, not *VBDKAZ*.

The next step is to find out whether or not additional ABAP programming is needed to fill the variable, or if the new variable has been automatically filled in. When you look up the field name, notice the table name where the field is stored. For *XBLNR*, the table is *VBAK*.

Table 4–3 shows the name of all tables where no additional ABAP programming is necessary:

Table 4–3 Tables that do not require ABAP programming

Document	Tables
Sales Order Header	VBAK
Sales Order Item	VBAP
Packing List Header	LIKP
Packing List Item	LIPS
Picking List Header	LIKP
Picking List Item	LIPS
Invoice Header	VBRK
Invoice Item	VBRP

If additional ABAP programming is necessary, the following programs have been provided to fill the variables. However, this guide does not provide programming instructions.

Table 4–4 shows the user exit program names:

Table 4–4 User exit program names

Document	Program
Sales Order	V05DZZEN
Packing List	V05OZZEN
Picking List	V05AZZEN
Invoice	V05NZZEN

In the sales order print program, the header data is collected in *VBDKA*. The item data structure is *POS*.

4

Example

This is an example for a sales order user exit, where data was first selected to be added to the header and then to be added to the items.

```
* Select field1 from dbtab1 and put it into newfield1 in
vbdka
  Select single * from dbtab1 where vbeln = vbdka-vbeln.
  If sy-subrc = 0.
    Vbdka-newfield1 = dbtab-field1.
  Endif.
* Select field2 from dbtab2 and put it into newfield2 in
vbdpa
  Loop at pos.
    Select single * from dbtab2 where vbeln = vbdka-vbeln
                              And   posnr = pos-posnr.
    If sy-subrc = 0.
      Pos-newfield2 = dbtab2-field2.
      Modify pos.
    Endif.
  Endloop.
```

- In the packing list print program, the header data is collected in *VBDKL*. The structure for the item data is *VBDPL_TAB*.

- In the picking list print program, the header data is collected in *VBLKK_WA*, and the item data structure is *VBLKP_TAB*.

- In the invoice print program, the header data is collected in *VBDKR*, and the item data structure is *LVBDPR*.

4

Modifying SAPscript Forms: Advanced Topics

Overview

This chapter builds further on what you learned in the previous chapter. This chapter covers the following topics:

- Printing company logos (in Windows BMP and TIFF 6.0 format)
- Inserting bar code information
- Adding a box with shading
- Printing text vertically
- Calling ABAP subroutines (using the PERFORM command)

Caution

To make a system upgrade easier and smoother, do not modify the standard forms or the preconfigured forms. Copy these forms and modify the copies.

Printing a Company Logo (Windows BMP Format)

Starting with Release 4.6, SAPscript offers you a new tool for importing graphics —in the Windows bitmap format—into your forms (for example, logos). Called SAPscript Graphic Management, this new solution:

- Gives you more flexibility in creating graphics
- Helps you manage your graphics with ease
- Helps you easily include graphics in forms
- Updates the former complex process for importing graphics

The SAPscript Graphic Management can also manage graphics saved as Baseline TIFF 6.0 format. Although we highly recommend using the new process, the processes for Baseline TIFF 6.0 format are still available. We describe these in the section "Printing a Company Logo (Baseline TIFF 6.0 Format)" on page 124.

TechTalk

The SAPscript Graphic Management Tool supports Windows bitmap format (*.bmp) and Baseline TIFF 6.0 format (*.tif). Make sure that you save graphics in these formats.

Caution

> SAPscript enables you to import graphics in the Windows bitmap format into your forms. To make this process independent of any graphics tool and ensure flexibility, no graphic tool is included with SAPscript itself. Therefore, you cannot modify graphics within SAPScript. Graphics modifications have to be executed with a graphics tool that allows you to save your graphic in the Windows bitmap format.

To include a graphic in your form, perform the following steps:

1. Import the graphic into the document server.
2. Preview the graphic printout.
3. Include the graphic in a form.

Step 1: Import the Graphic into the Document Server

Task

Make a graphic (BMP format) available on the document server by importing the graphic.

1. From the SAP standard menu, choose *Tools → SAPscript → Administration → SE78 - Graphic.*

2. From the workplace menu, choose *Stored on document server → GRAPHICS → BMAP.*

5

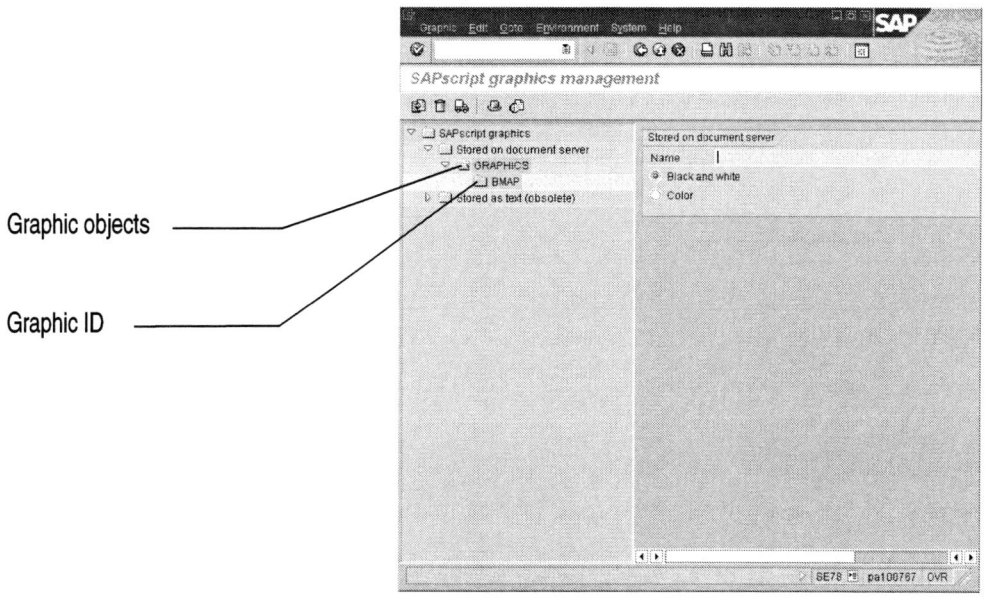

Graphic objects

Graphic ID

Tips & Tricks

Graphics stored in the document server are separated into graphic objects and graphic IDs. In the example, only the graphic object GRAPHICS and the graphic ID BMAP are available. You can create new graphic objects and IDs (see "Creating Graphic Objects and Graphic IDs" on page 120).

3. On the *SAPscript graphics management* window, choose 📝 .

4. On the *Import graphic* window:

    a. In the *File name* field, enter the file location (on your presentation server) where the import program can find the graphic (for example, **C:\SAPlogo.bmp**).

Note

You will refer to this name, if you include the graphic in a form (as described in "Step 3: Include the Graphic in a Form" on page 118).

    b. In the *Name* field, enter a name for the graphic (for example, **LOGO_01**).

    c. In the *Description* field, enter a description (for example, **COMPANY LOGO**).

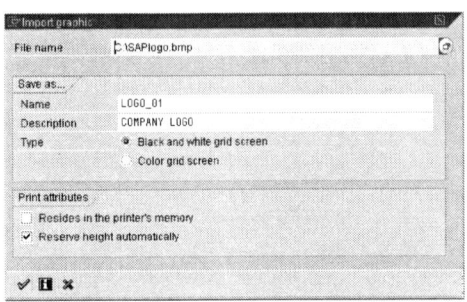

    d. Choose ✔ .

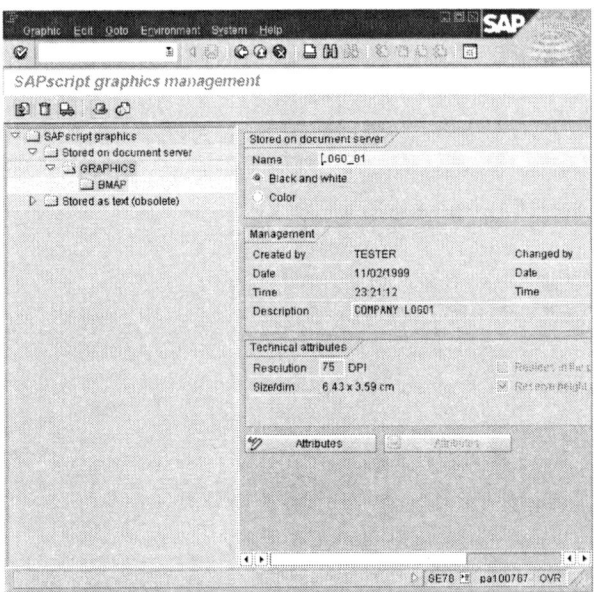

5. Choose *Exit* to return to the SAP standard menu.

Caution

You may want to insert a graphic from other documents (for example, your company web side) into a form by using a copy and paste approach. SAPscript does **not** support this technique.

You must copy the graphic to your local drive, import the graphic into the document server as describe in this task, and include the graphic in the form (as described in step 3 (see page 118).

Step 2: Preview the Graphic Printout

Task

Preview the graphic printout (on the document server).

1. From the SAP standard menu, choose *Tools → SAPscript → Administration → SE78 - Graphic.*

2. From the workplace menu, choose *Stored on document server → GRAPHICS → BMAP.*

3. On the *SAPscript graphics management* screen:

   a. Enter the graphic name in the *Name* field (for example, LOGO_01).

   b. To preview the graphic, choose 🗋.

5

The graphic is displayed in the workplace area.

 A color graphic can be viewed only in color.

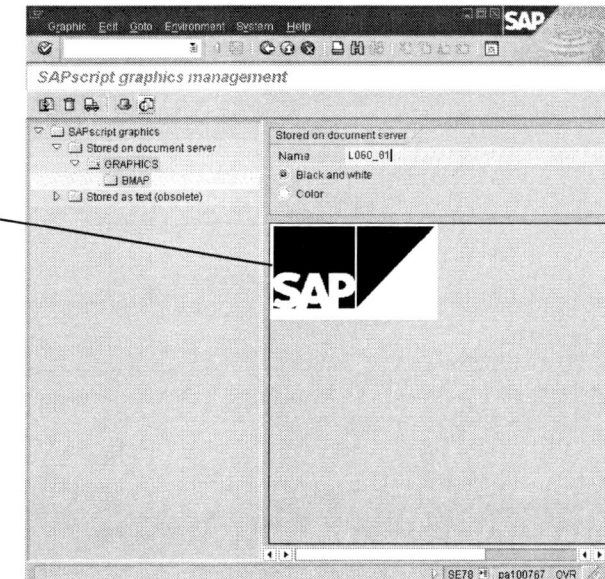

   c. Choose *Exit* to return to the *SAP Easy Access* screen.

Step 3: Include the Graphic in a Form

To include your company logo in a form, you must create a graphic. SAPscript creates a new window and places it automatically on the top left corner of the page.

Task

Include a graphic in a form by creating a graphic window.

1. From the SAP standard menu, choose *Tools → SAPscript → SE71 - Form*.

2. In the *Form Painter: Request* screen:

   a. Enter **ZVORDER02** in the *Form* field.

   b. Enter **EN** in the *Language* field.

   c. Select *Page layout*.

   d. Choose 🖉 *Change*.

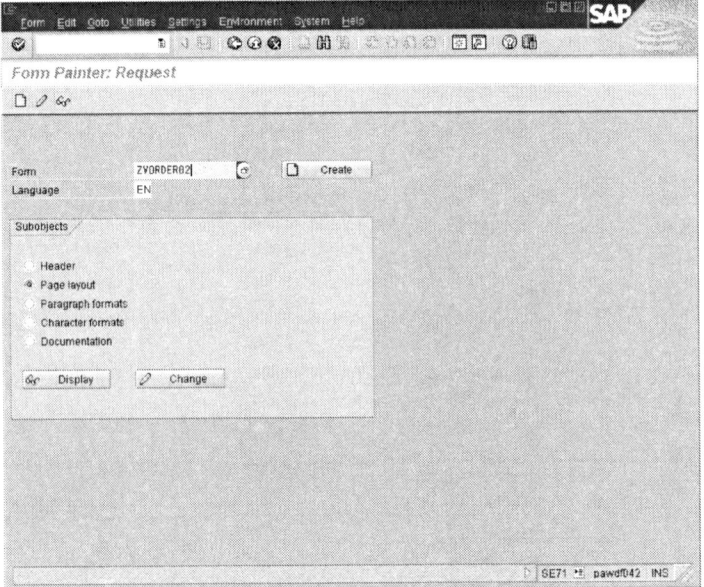

3. In the *Design Window,* right-click to access the form layout manipulation menu and choose *Create graphic.*

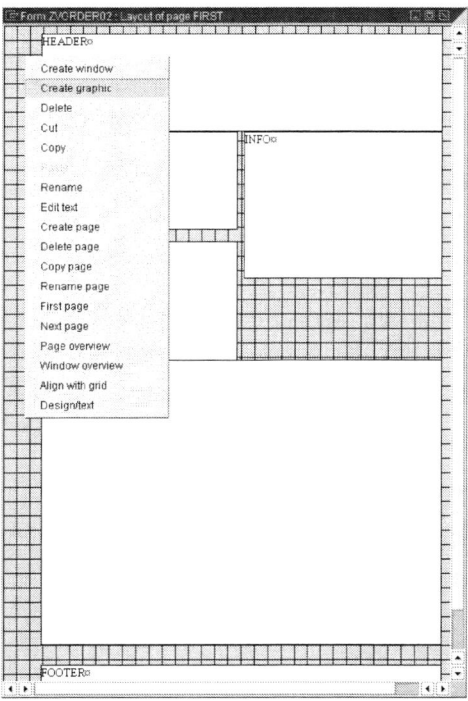

4. On the *Include graphic* screen:

You can specify the resolution of the graphic by entering the number of dots per inch (dpi).

The ratio between the resolution you entered and the original resolution in which the graphic was scanned determines the printed size of the graphic on the form.

Example

The graphic was originally scanned with a resolution of 300 dpi. If you enter a resolution of 150 dpi, the width and height of the graphic will be doubled. If you enter a resolution of 600 dpi, the graphic's width and height will be halved.

a. Enter the name of the graphic (for example, **LOGO_01**).

The name of the graphic is the name you defined when you imported the graphic onto the document server (see "Step 1: Import the Graphic into the Document Server" on page 115).

b. Choose ✅ .

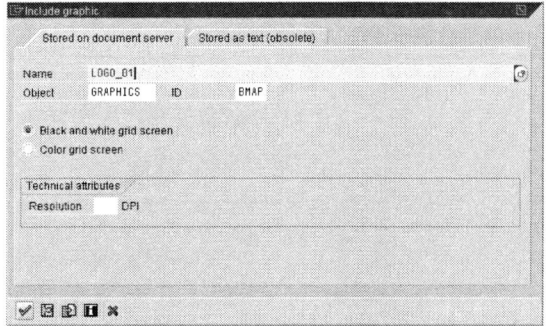

5

The new graphic is always positioned in the top left corner of the form.

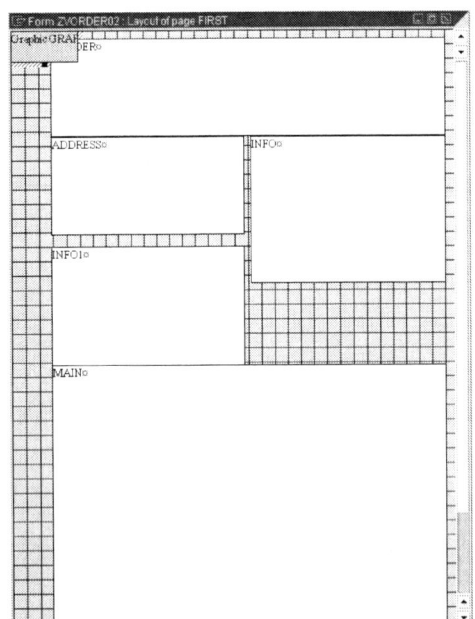

 You can move the graphic window easily using the drag-and-drop technique, but you cannot resize the graphic within SAPscript. You have to resize the graphic using a graphics tool outside SAPscript. You must then import the graphic onto the document server and include it in your form.

Tips & Tricks

5. Select the *Administrative Screen*.

6. On the *Administrative Screen*:

   a. To activate the changes, choose ⬛ .

   b. Go *Back* twice to return to the SAP standard menu.

Creating Graphic Objects and Graphic IDs

You can easily create your own object structure on the document server by defining your own graphic objects and graphic IDs.

Task

Create a new graphic object and graphic ID using SAPscript settings.

1. From the SAP standard menu, choose Tools → *SAPscript* → *Administration* → *SE75 - Settings*.

2. On the *SAPscript Settings* screen:

   a. Select *Graphical objects and IDs*.

   b. Choose ✎ *Change*.

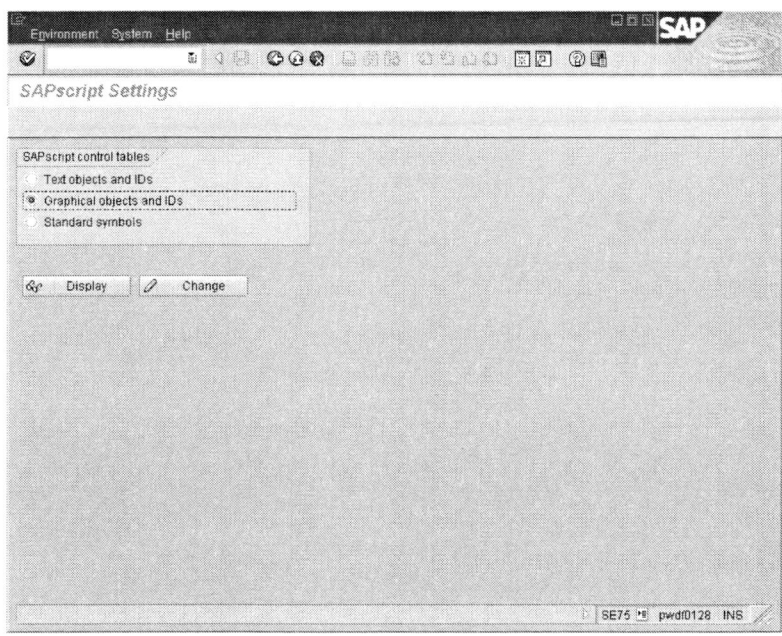

3. On the *Information* window, choose ✔ .

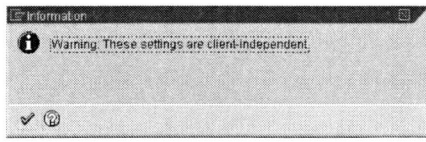

4. On the *Change graphics IDs* screen, choose ▯ .

5. On the *Create Object* dialog window:

> **Note**
>
> Make sure your graphic object names begin with a Y or Z.

   a. In the *Graphic object* field, enter a name for the object (for example, **Z_GRAPHIC**).

   b. Enter a description.

   c. Choose ✔ .

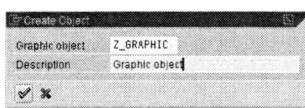

The new object is displayed in the list of all available graphic objects.

5

6. On the *Change graphics IDs* screen, double-click on the object Z_GRAPHIC to open the object's graphic IDs.

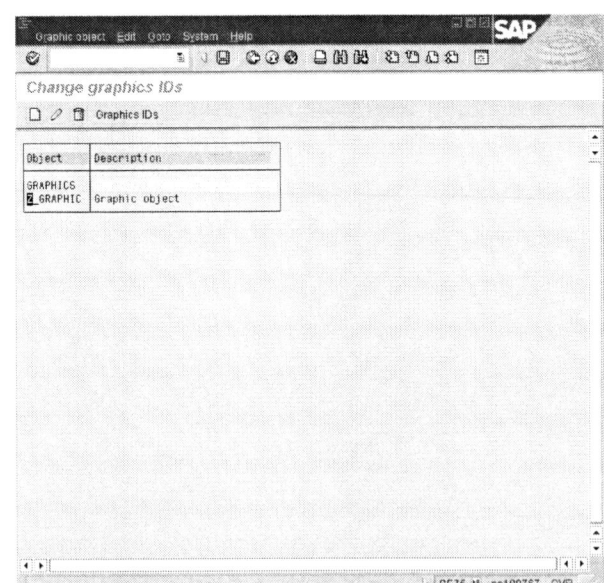

7. On the *Change graphics IDs for object <...>* screen, choose ☐ .

8. On the *Create ID* dialog window:

   a. In the *Graphic ID* field, enter the ID's name (for example, **ZLOG**).

   b. Enter a description.

   c. Choose ✓ .

<table>
<tr><td>Note</td></tr>
</table>

Make sure your graphic ID names begin with a Y or Z.

9. On the *Change graphics IDs for object <...>* screen, save the graphic ID.

The graphic object will also be saved.

If you use the CTS, specify a transport request after saving.

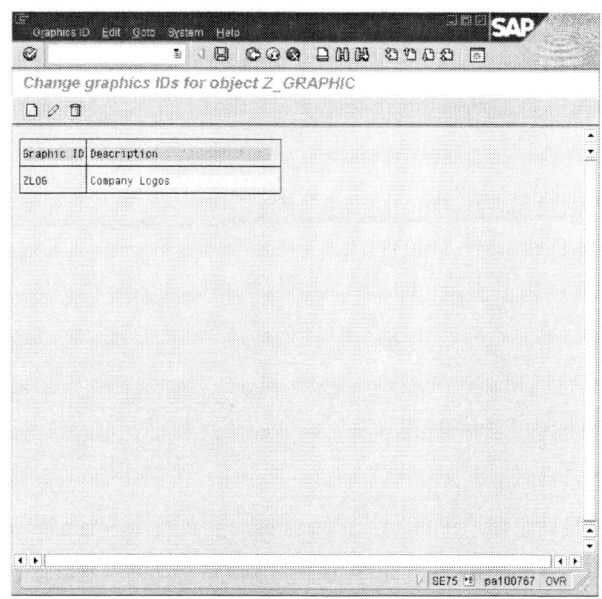

10. Go *Back* three times to return to the SAP standard menu.

11. Choose *Tools → SAPscript → Administration → SE78 - Graphic*.

12. On the SAPscript graphics management screen, in the workplace menu, expand *Stored on document server*.

5

The graphic object *Z_GRAPHIC* is displayed.

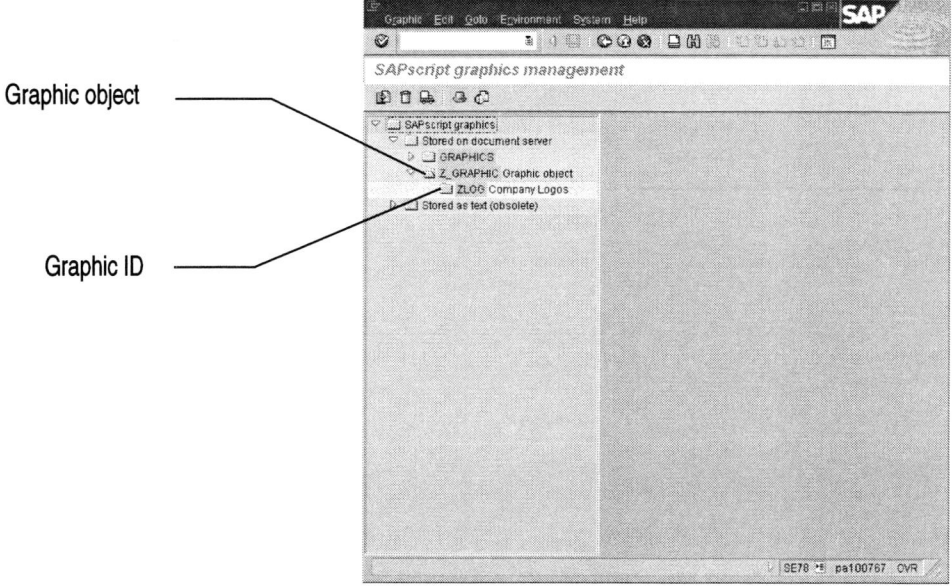

Printing a Company Logo (Baseline TIFF 6.0 Format)

To print a company logo, either include it in the form or as a macro on a PCL-5 printer. The following rules help you to determine which method is most appropriate.

Note

Many paint programs support the Baseline TIFF 6.0 format.

- If you cannot provide your logo in the Baseline TIFF 6.0 format, the company logo should be a macro on the printer (see "Including the Company Logo as a Macro on PCL-5 Printers" on page 132").

- If you do not have a PCL-5 printer, include the company logo in the form (see "Including the Company Logo on the Form" below).

- In all other cases, include the company logo in the form (see "Including the Company Logo on the Form" below).

Tips & Tricks

If you followed the directions exactly and no logo is printed, the format of the logo file format is probably not Baseline TIFF 6.0. SAPscript does not give an error message if an incorrect file format is used.

The following procedures are also documented in the SAPNet Frontend notes 39031, 18045, and 5995.

Including the Company Logo on the Form

Create your company logo with a graphic program and save it in the Baseline TIFF 6.0 format. To include your company logo in a form, first convert your Baseline TIFF 6.0 file into SAPscript standard text. Next, include the standard text in the form (see "Including Standard Text in a Form" on page 127).

Converting Baseline TIFF 6.0 Format to SAPscript Standard Text

Task

Convert your Baseline TIFF 6.0 format company logo into SAPscript standard text.

1. From the SAP standard menu, choose *Tools → ABAP Workbench → Development → SE38 – ABAP Editor.*

2. On the *ABAP Editor: Initial Screen*:

    a. Enter **RSTXLDMC** in the *Program* field.

    b. Choose ⊕ .

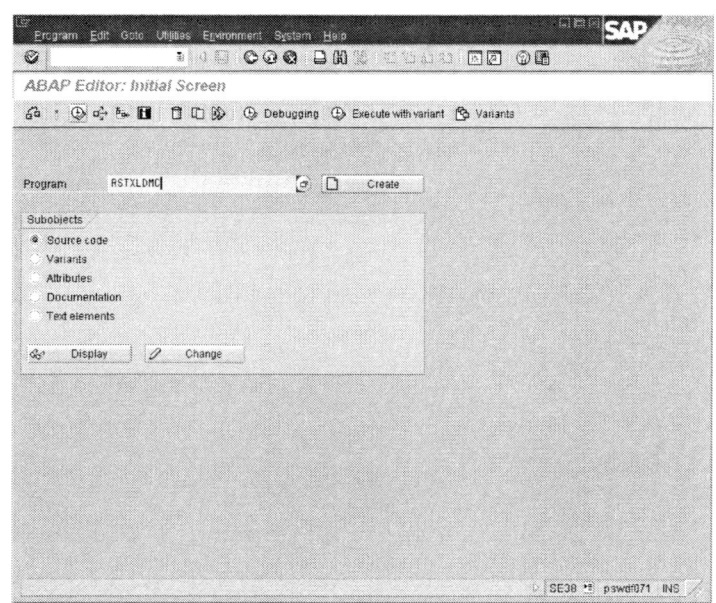

3. On the *Upload TIFF files to SAPscript texts* screen:

    a. In the *File name* field, enter the filename and its path (for example, **C:\SAPlogo.tif**).

    b. In the *Type* field, enter the appropriate type of raster image.

       • **BMON** stands for a black and white raster image. Use **BMON** for monochrome printers because they normally do not perform a gray-level conversion.

       • **BCOL** stands for a color raster image with up to 256 colors.

Note

UNIX file names are case-sensitive.

5

c. Enter a name for the standard text in the *Text name* field.

The name must begin with the prefix *ZHEX-MACRO-*, which is the default value for the field (for example, **ZHEX-MACRO-LOGO**).

d. Choose 🕒 .

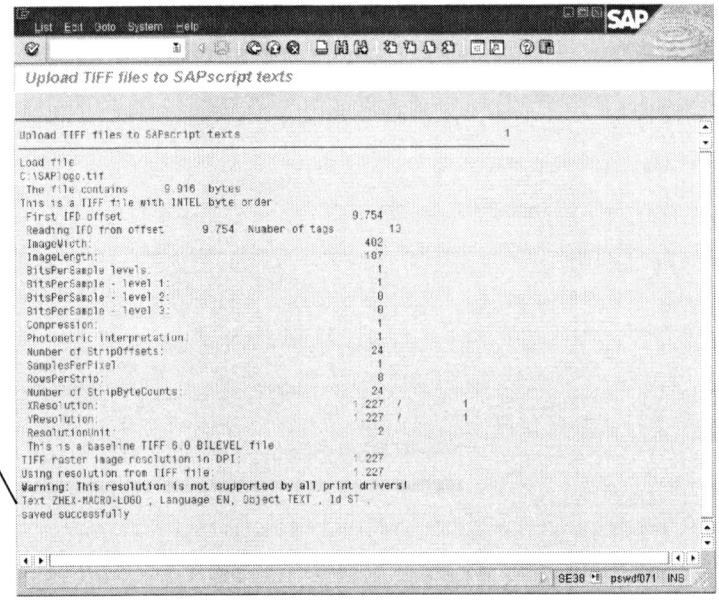

File name: enter the filename and its path as it appears on the *C* or *A* drive.

Text name: ZHEX-MACRO is the technical name under which the logo is stored. You can freely define the name of the file by adding some characters (for example, ZHEX-MACRO-TEST).

The filename and text name do not have to be the same.

The upload may take some time. The result should be a protocol as shown.

At the end of the protocol, the *Text ZHEX-MACRO-LOGO, Language EN, Object TEXT, Id ST saved successfully* message indicates that the standard text was created.

4. Go *Back* four times to return to the SAP standard menu.

Tips & Tricks

You can easily display the created standard text.

1. From the SAP standard menu, choose *Tools → SAPscript → SO10 Standard Text.*

2. In the *Text name* field, enter **ZHEX-MACRO-LOGO**.

3. Choose *Display.*

The print preview does not display the logo.

TechTalk

For additional information about report *RSTXLDMC*, access the report documentation:

1. From the SAP standard menu, choose *Tools → ABAP Workbench → Development → SE38 - ABAP Editor.*

2. In the *Program* field, enter **RSTXLDMC**.

3. Select *Documentation.*

4. Choose *Display.*

Including Standard Text in a Form

5

Task

Include the standard text ZHEX-MACRO-LOGO in the sales order confirmation form ZVORDER02.

1. From the SAP standard menu, choose *Tools → SAPscript → SE71 - Form.*

2. On the *Form Painter: Request* screen:

   a. Enter **ZVORDER02** in the *Form* field.

   b. Enter **EN** in the *Language* field.

   c. Select *Page layout*.

   d. Choose ✐ *Change*.

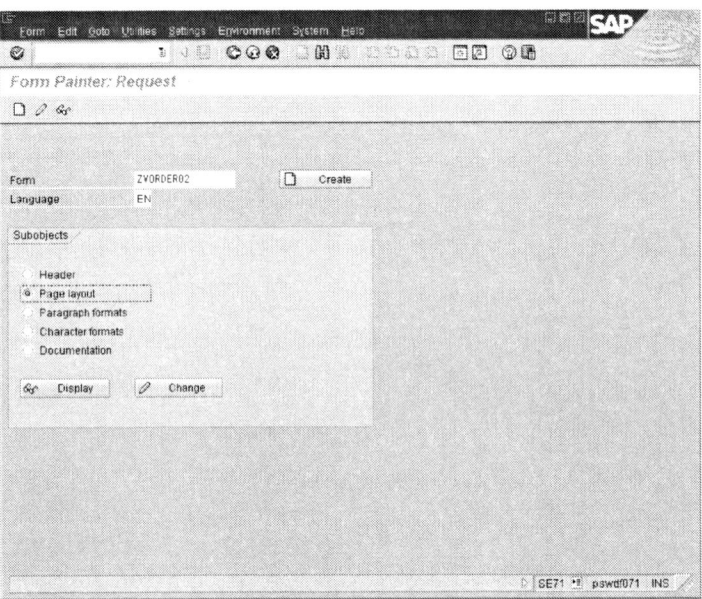

3. In the *Design Window*, right-click to access the form layout manipulation menu and choose *Create window*.

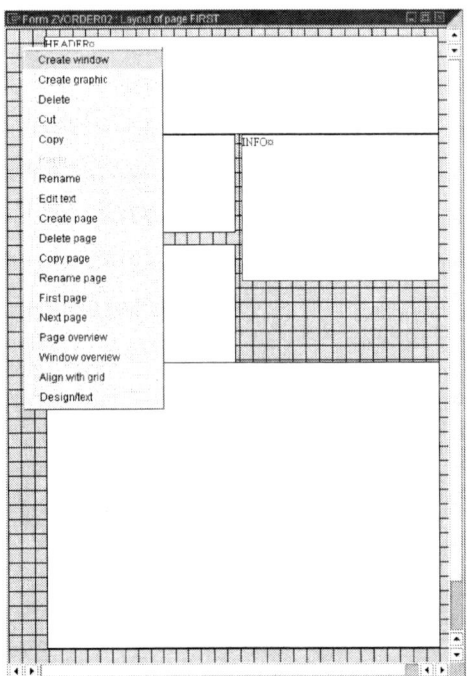

The new window is automatically named *Window1*.

4. In the *Design Window:*

    a. Select *Window1.*

    b. Right-click to access the form layout manipulation menu and choose *Rename.*

The new window is automatically named *Window1.*

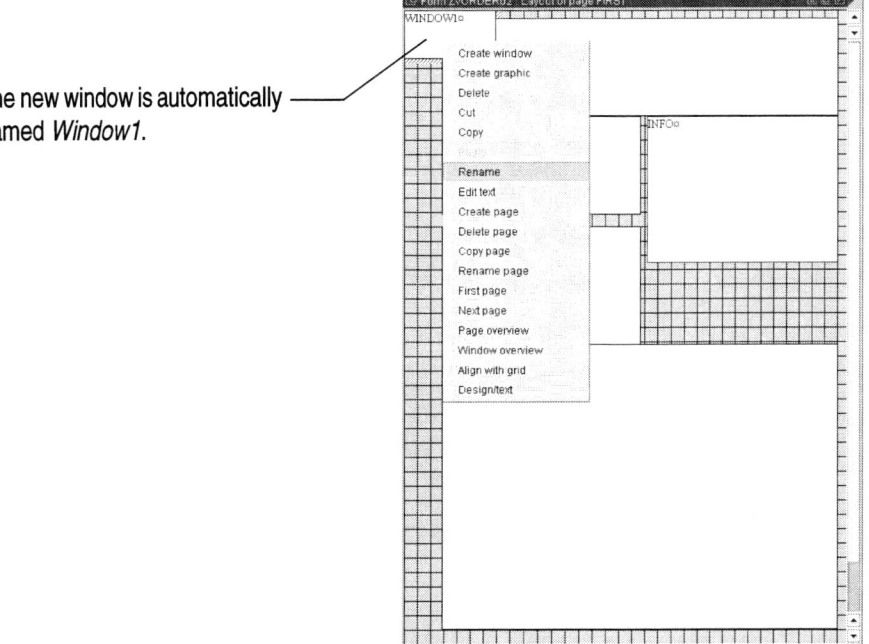

5. On the *Rename window:*

    a. Enter a new name for the window (for example, **LOGO**).

    b. Choose ✔ .

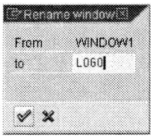

6. Define the position of the new window *LOGO* using the graphical Form Painter.

TechTalk

> With graphics or macros, the system considers only the window position, not the window size. The *Left margin* must be specified in **CH** (characters) and the *Upper margin* must be specified in **LN** (lines).

5

7. In the *Design Window:*

   a. Select *LOGO* window.

   b. Right-click to access the form layout manipulation menu and choose *Edit text*.

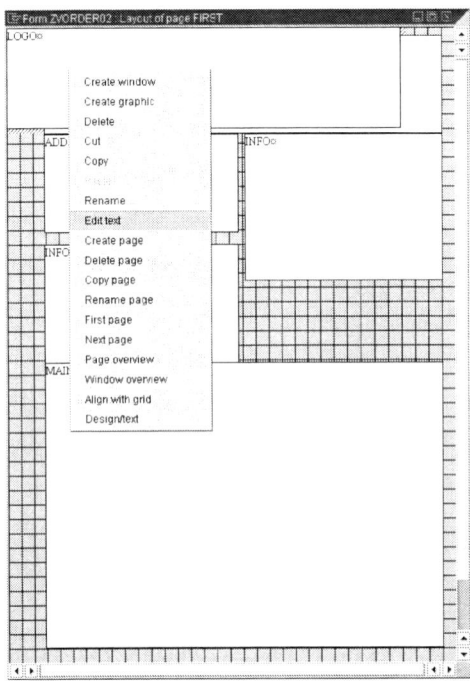

The PC Editor for the *LOGO* window appears.

8. From the PC Editor tool bar, choose [icon].

9. On the *Creating Additional Information* screen:

   a. Select *Command*.

   b. Enter **INCLUDE ZHEX-MACRO-LOGO OBJECT TEXT ID ST** in the *Command* line.

   c. Choose [icon].

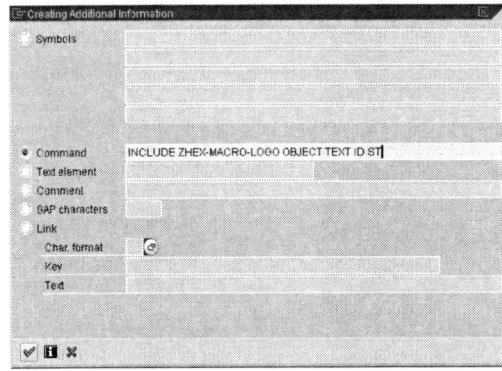

The new command line
appears in the PC Editor.

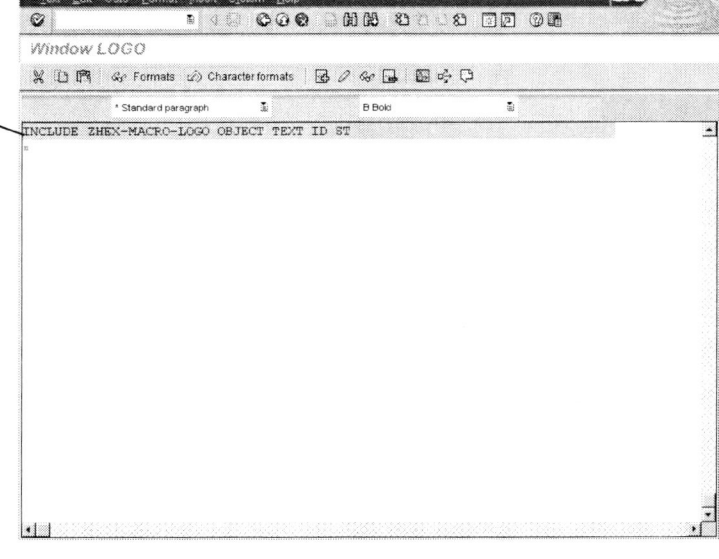

10. Go *Back* to return to the *Administrative Screen*.

The text changes are automatically transferred by the system.

11. On the *Administrative Screen*:

a. In the *Description* field, enter a short explanation text for the window *LOGO* (for example, **Company Logo**).

b. To activate the changes, choose ⚓ .

5

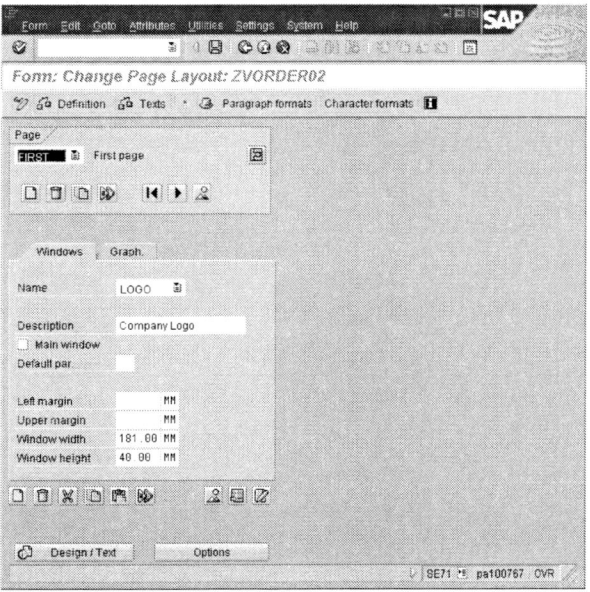

Tips & Tricks

Your company logo appears on the first page of form ZVORDER02 using the standard text ZHEX-MACRO-LOGO and the LOGO window for the print output. To display the company logo on subsequent pages, you must copy the LOGO window to page NEXT.

You must repeat the following procedure for all defined pages:

1. On the *Administrative Screen,* choose the *LOGO* window.

2. Copy the window.

3. Choose page *NEXT.*

4. Insert the window.

   The position and size of the *LOGO* window defined for page *FIRST* apply to the other pages.

5. Activate the form.

Including the Company Logo as a Macro on PCL-5 Printers

Including a company logo as a macro works only on a PCL-5 printer.

To include a company logo as a macro on a PCL-5 printer:

1. Copy a standard printer type to modify it (see "Copying a Standard Printer Type" on page 133).

2. Define a print control for the macro (see "Defining a Print Control for the Macro" on page 135).

3. Include the print control in a form (see "Including the Print Control in the Form" on page 138).

TechTalk

In R/3, the following printer types (or a copy of the printer type) represent PCL-5 printers:

- HPLJIIID

- HPLJ4

- HPLJ5SI

- HPLJMI

- IBMAFP

- IBMAFP3

- IBMEFP

- IBMEFP3

- LX4039

- SNI20XX8

Note

Several third parties offer logos as a PCL-5 macro and describe how to bring the logo to the printer.

TechTalk

The macro file can be loaded onto the printer by printing the file once from the operating system level (for example, using UNIX command *lp*). The disadvantage is that macros are lost when you turn off the printer. To avoid this, load the macro onto a Flash-Memory cartridge.

Copying a Standard Printer Type

Task

Copy a standard printer type for modification.

1. To determine the device type to use, from the SAP standard menu choose *Tools → CCMS → Spool → SPAD - Spool administration*.

2. On the *Spool Administration: Initial Screen*, choose the *Devices / servers* tab and choose the *Output devices* button.

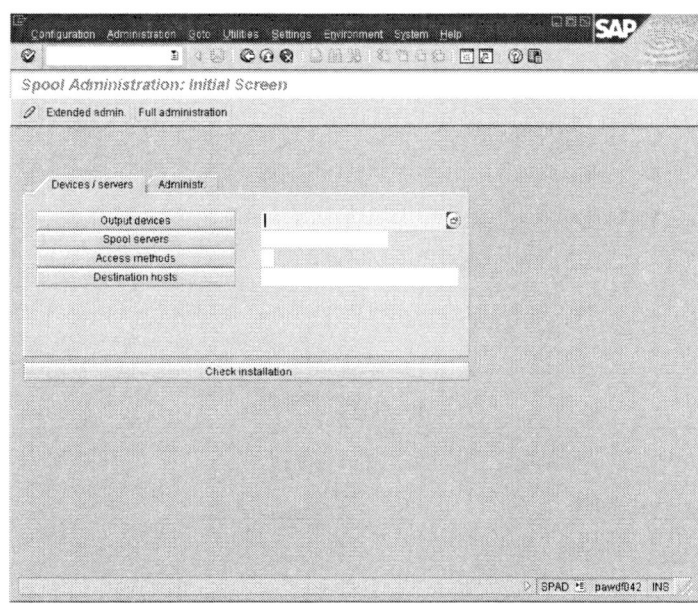

A list of all available output devices appears.

5

3. Each printer name has a corresponding device type name.

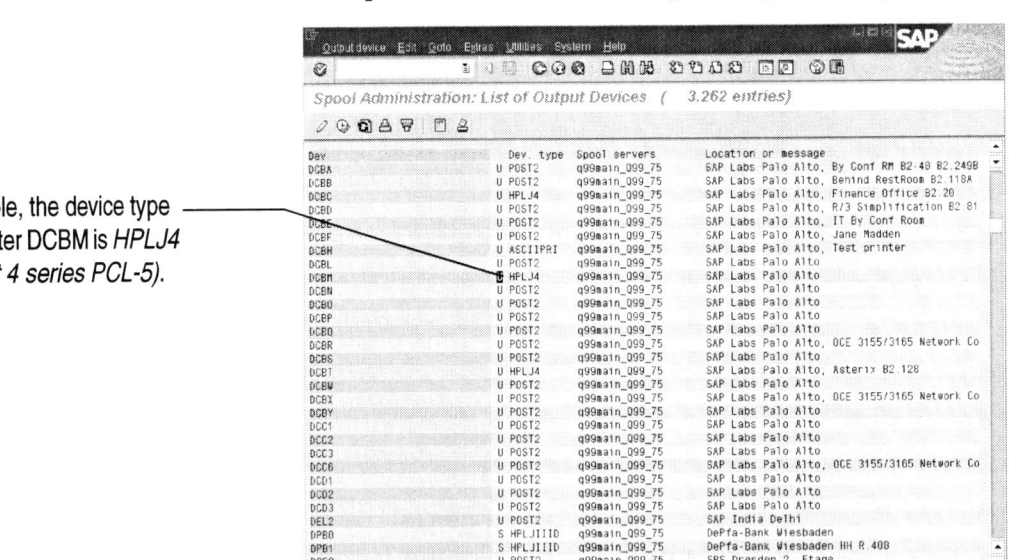

In this example, the device type name for printer DCBM is *HPLJ4* (*HP Laserjet 4 series PCL-5*).

4. Go *Back* to return to the *Spool Administration: Initial Screen*.

5. From the *Spool Administration: Initial Screen*, choose *Utilities* → *For device types* → *Copy device type*.

6. On the *Copy device type* screen:

    a. Enter the name of the device type in the *Copy device type* field (for example, **HPLJ4**).

    b. Enter the name for copied device type in the *to device type* field (for example, **Z_HPLJ4**).

    c. Choose ⊕.

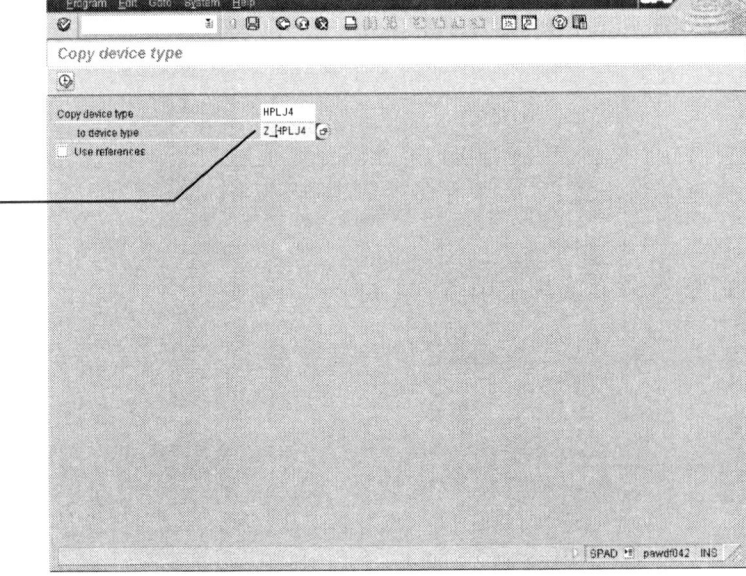

Make sure the name of the copied device type starts with Y or Z (customer name range)

Although you are free to define the name of the copied device type, we recommend using a name that is as close as possible to the original name.

7. Confirm all the subsequent popup windows.

If you use the Change and Transport System (CTS), specify a transport request.

The result is shown on the *Copy device type* screen.

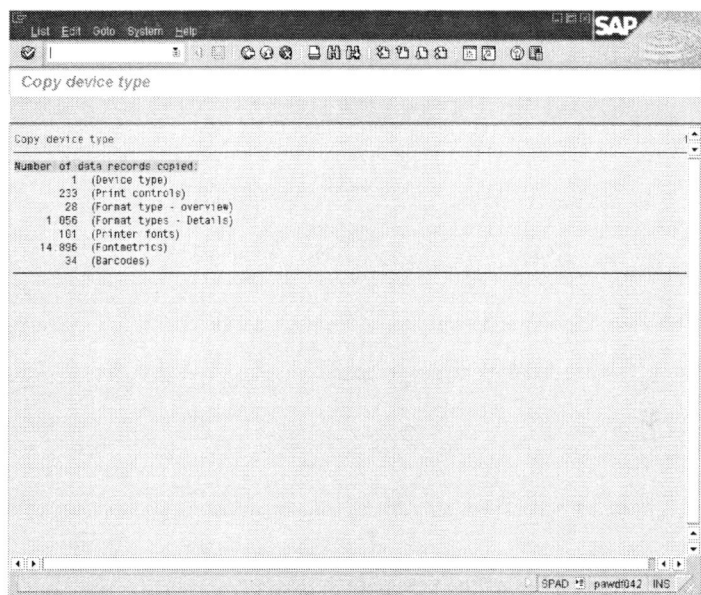

8. Go *Back* three times to return to the SAP standard menu.

5

Defining a Print Control for the Macro

Task

Define a print control for your macro.

1. From the SAP standard menu, choose *Tools* → *CCMS* → *Spool* → *SPAD - Spool administration*.

Note

In our example, the macro has a macro ID of 100. The macro ID, which is set when you bring the macro to the printer, must be between 100 and 999.

To get your ID, ask your system administrator.

2. On the *Spool Administration: Initial Screen,* choose *Full administration.*

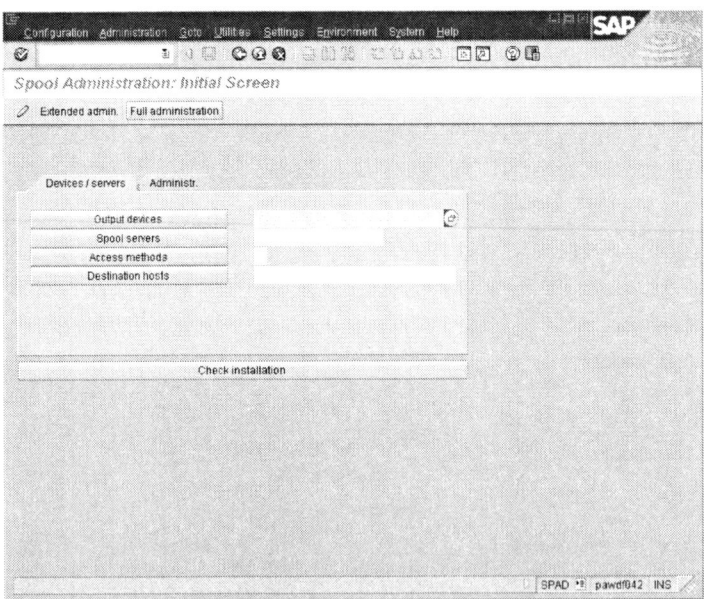

3. On the *DeviceTypes* tab, click on *Device types.*

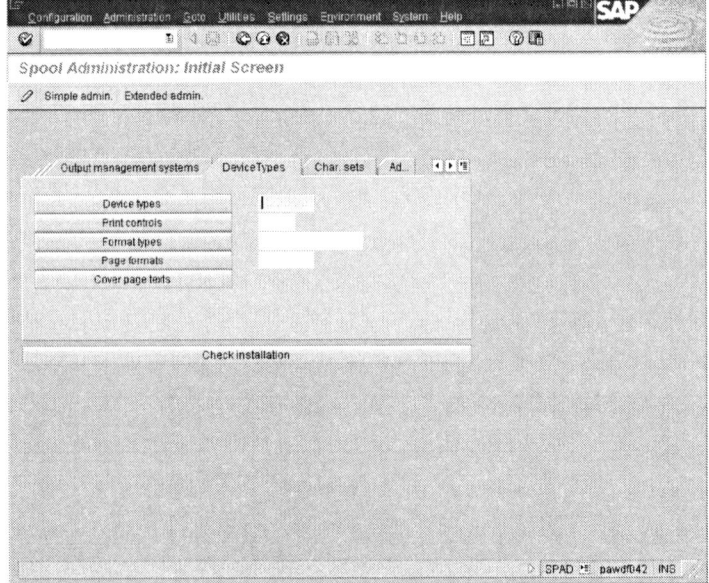

4. On the *Spool Administration: List of Device Types* screen:

    a. Scroll down until you find the desired device type (for example, *Z_HPLJ4*).

    b. Select the device type.

    c. Choose ▦ *Print Controls*.

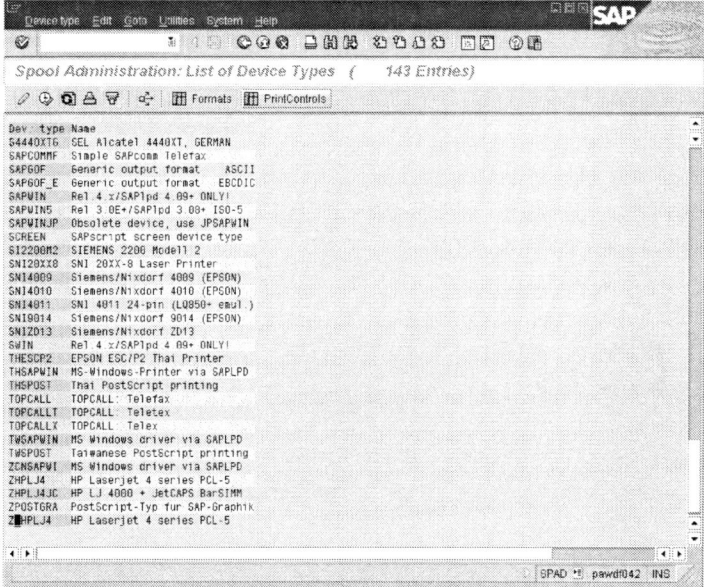

5

5. On the *Spool Administration: Edit Print Controls* screen:

a. Choose 🖉 .

Since the system switched to the change mode, the icons displayed on the screen changed.

Make sure your print control starts with Y or Z. We recommend that the macro ID is also part of the name.

b. Overwrite the first row of the *PrCtl* column with the newest print control (for example, **ZM100**).

c. Overwrite the first row of the *Control character sequence* column with the control character sequence (for example, **1B2666313030793358**).

 The **control character sequence** contains the macro ID in hexadecimal representation. The sequence is 1B2666...793358, where the three dots are the hexadecimal representations of the macro ID letters. In general, the hexadecimal representations for 0 to 9 are 30 to 39.

The sequences are printer dependent. You will find the sequences in your printer manual.

Example

If the macro ID is 100, the three dots will be 313030.

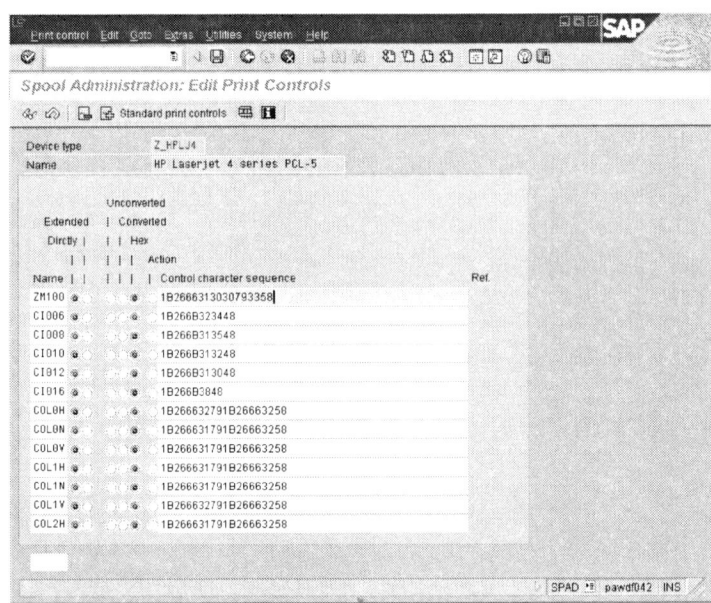

d. Save the new print control.

6. Go *Back* four times to return to the SAP standard menu.

Including the Print Control in the Form

Task

Include the print control (for example, **ZM100**) in the sales order confirmation form **ZVORDER02**.

1. From the SAP standard menu, choose *Tools → SAPscript → SE71 - Form.*

2. On the *Form Painter: Request* screen:

   a. Enter **ZVORDER02** in the *Form* field.

   b. Enter **EN** in the *Language* field.

   c. Select *Page layout*.

   d. Choose ✎ Change.

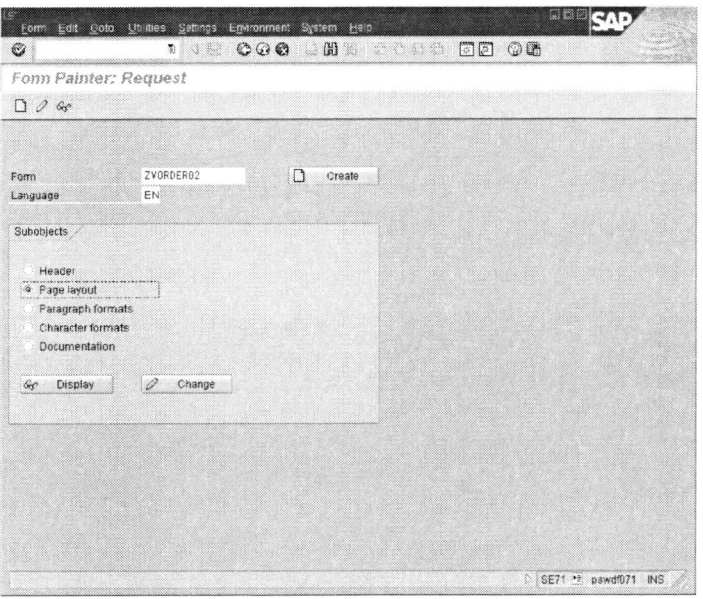

3. In the *Design window*, right-click to access the form layout manipulation menu and choose *Create window*.

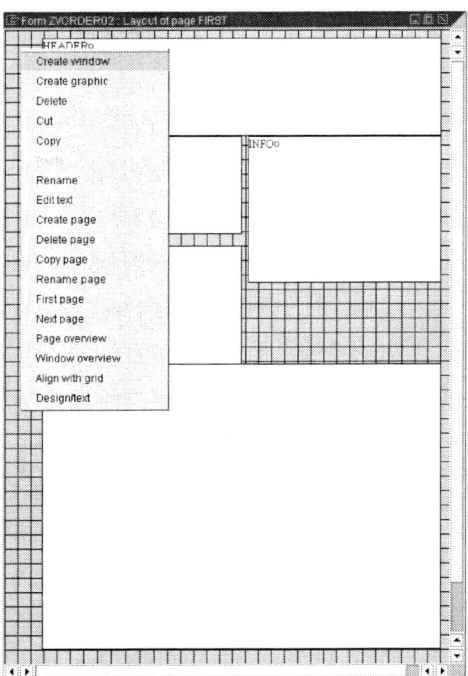

5

4. In the *Design Window:*

a. Select *Window1.*

b. Right-click to access the form layout manipulation menu and choose *Rename.*

The new window is automatically named *Window1.*

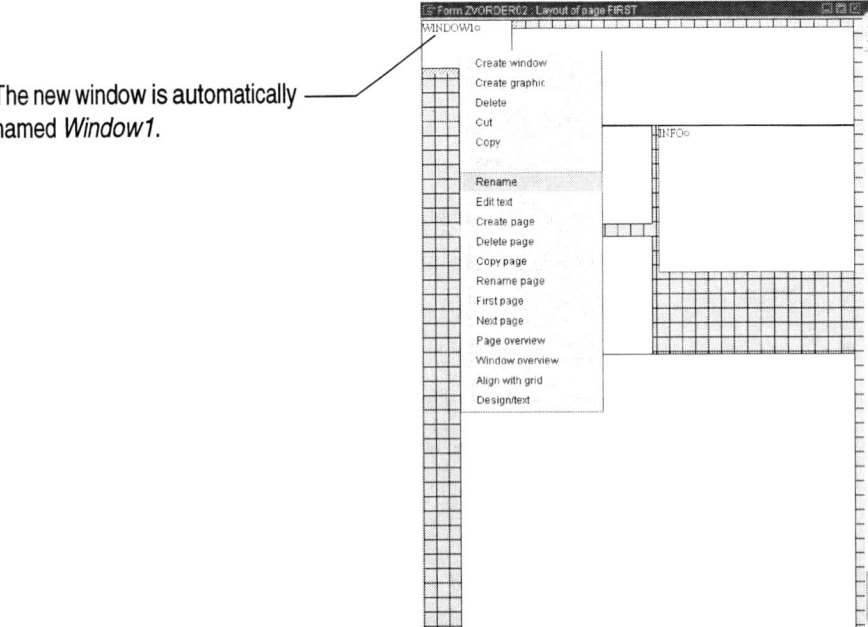

5. On the *Rename window:*

a. Enter a new name for *Window1* (for example, **LOGO**).

b. Choose ✓ .

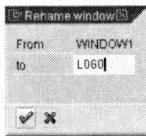

With graphics or macros, the system considers only the window position, but not the size. The left margin must be specified in CH (characters) and the upper margin must be specified in LN (lines).

6. Define the position of the *LOGO* window using the graphical Form Painter.

7. In the *Design Window.*

   a. Select the *LOGO* window.

   b. Right-click to access the form layout manipulation menu and choose *Edit text.*

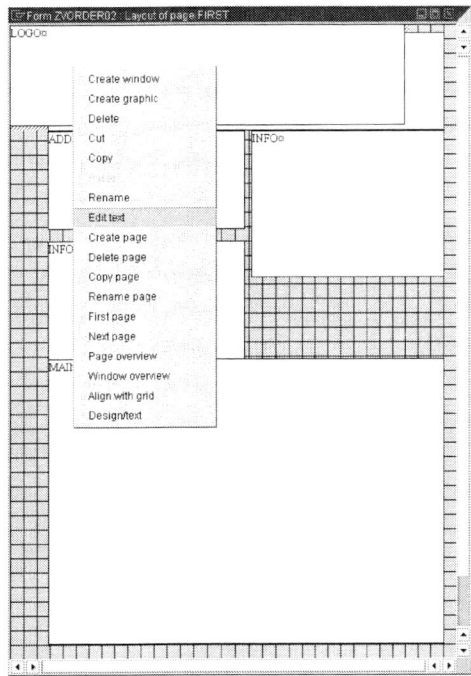

The PC Editor for the *LOGO* window appears.

8. From the PC Editor tool bar, choose [icon].

9. On the *Creating Additional Information* screen:

   a. Select *SAP characters.*

   b. Enter **32** in *SAP characters.*

   c. Choose [icon].

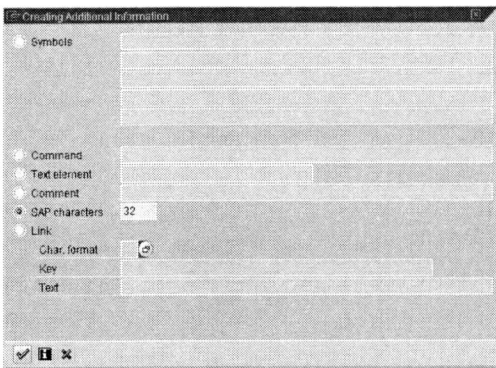

10. From the PC Editor tool bar, choose [icon].

5

11. On the *Creating Additional Information* screen:

    a. Select *Command*.

    b. Enter **PRINT-CONTROL ZM100** in the *Command* line.

    c. Choose ✅ .

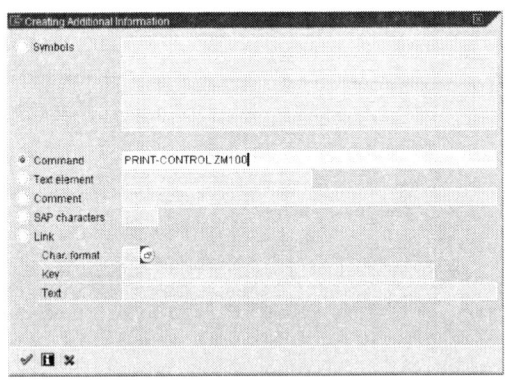

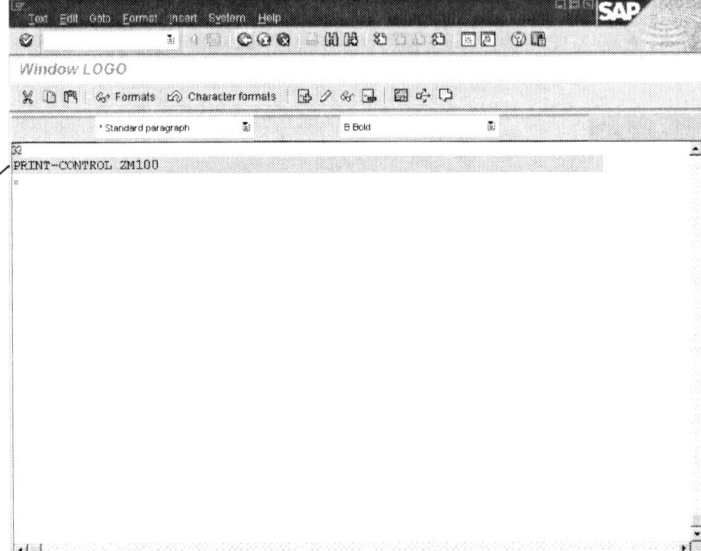

The new command lines appear in the PC Editor.

12. Go *Back* to return to the *Administrative Screen*

The text changes are automatically transferred by the system.

13. On the *Administrative Screen*:

    a. In the *Description* field, enter a short explanation text for the window *LOGO* (for example, **Company Logo**).

    b. To activate the changes, choose   .

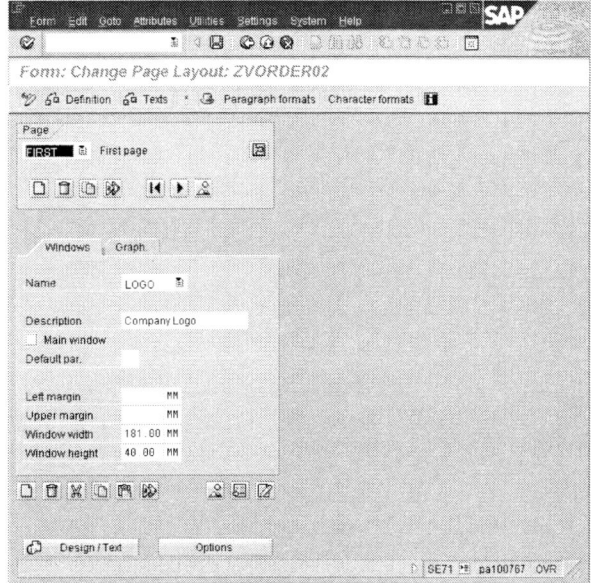

Tips & Tricks

Your company logo appears on the first page of form *ZVORDER02* using the print control *ZM100* and the *LOGO* window for the print output. If the company logo should be displayed on the subsequent pages, you must copy *the LOGO* window to page *NEXT*.

You have to repeat the following procedure for all defined pages:

1. On the *Administrative Screen*, choose the *LOGO* window.

2. Copy the window.

3. Choose page *NEXT*.

4. Insert the window.

    The position and size of the *LOGO* window defined for page FIRST apply to the other pages.

5. Activate the form.

5

Printing Bar Codes

The easiest way to print bar codes is to use a Kyocera laser printer because you do not need additional hardware or software. You just add the bar code to the form.

With an HP laser printer, the solution is also simple — it is basically a "plug-and-play." Add the JetCAPS BARSIMM to an HP Laserjet 4 or 5 printer and then add the bar code to the form.

Most other solutions require more work. To keep bar code printing easy, this guide covers only Kyocera and HP laser printers. For HP laser printers, insert the *SIMM* into your HP Laserjet 4 or 5 and make sure that your printer is an HPLJ4 in R/3. If you do not know your printer type, ask your system administrator.

Tips & Tricks

> With the *SIMM,* you receive a list of print controls that tell you how to switch the bar codes on and off. These print controls are already defined for the HPLJ4.

Task

Define the material numbers on the sales order confirmation ZVORDER02 as a "3 of 9" bar code with a check digit.

1. From the SAP standard menu, choose *Tools → SAPscript → SE71 - Form.*

2. On the *Form Painter: Request* screen:

   a. Enter **ZVORDER02** in the *Form* field.

   b. Enter **EN** in the *Language* field.

   c. Select *Character formats.*

   d. Choose ⊘ *Change.*

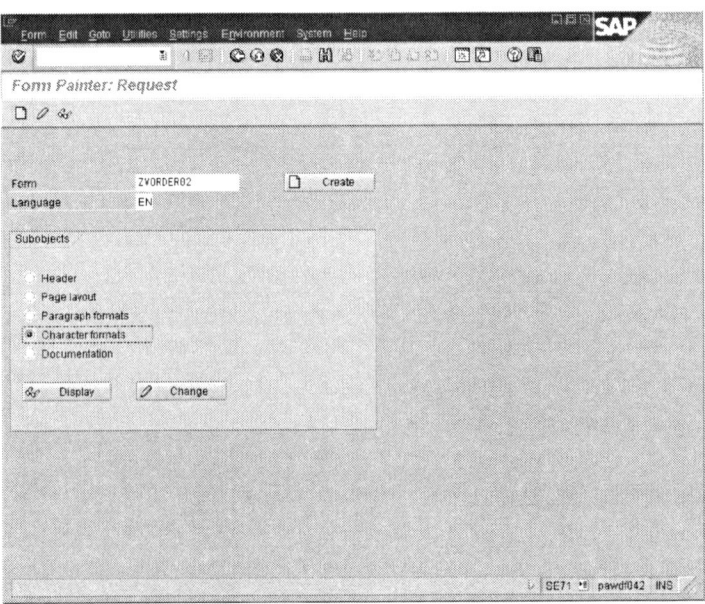

3. On the *Form: Change Character Strings: ZVORDER02* screen, choose *Edit → Create Element.*

4. On the *Create Element* screen:

   a. Enter a name for the character format (for example, **B3**).

   b. Enter a description (for example, **Bar code 3 of 9 w/check**).

   c. Choose ✅ .

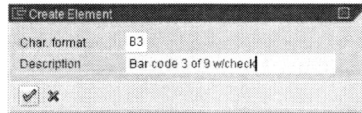

5. On the *Form: Change Character Strings: ZVORDER02* window:

   a. In the *Standard attributes* section, enter a description in the *Description* field (for example, **Bar code 3 of 9 w/check**).

   b. In the *Bar code* field, choose 🔲 .

The new character format appears in the *Character formats* section.

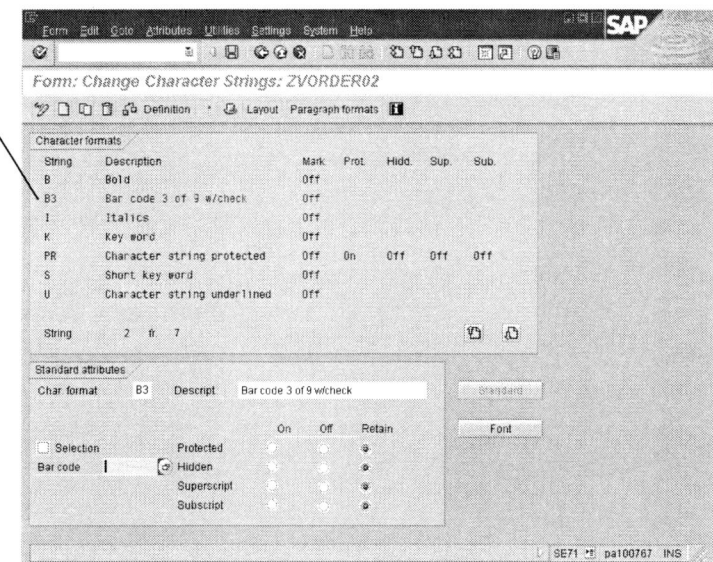

5

If you want to print a bar code vertically, you can choose a SAP bar code that has been defined for vertical bar code printing. You will recognize such a bar code on the rotation parameter. The rotation parameter has the value 090.

Rotation values of 000, 090, 180, and 270 degrees are possible values for this parameter, however, the value 090 is delivered for several SAP standard bar codes.

Bar codes are rotated in a counter-clockwise direction. If, for example, a bar code is rotated by 90 degrees, it is tilted to the left when printed.

6. From the *Name of an SAP bar code* screen:

   a. Select the desired bar code (for example, *BC_CD39C*).

   b. Choose ✅ .

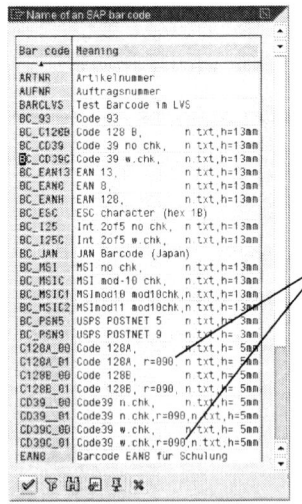

For example, r=090 indicates a rotation value of 90 degrees.

7. On the *Form: Change Character Strings: ZVORDER02* window:

   a. Save the new character format.

   b. Choose *Layout*.

A character format *B3* for the bar code format *BC_CD39C* is now defined and can be used.

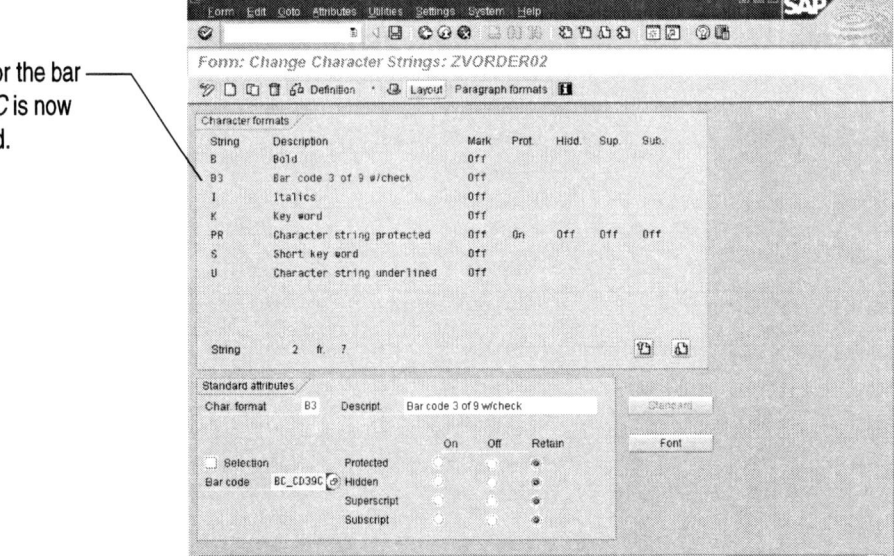

8. In the *Design Window:*

a. Select the *Main* window.

b. Right-click to access the form layout manipulation menu and choose *Edit text*.

9. On the PC Editor for the *Window MAIN* window:

a. Scroll down until you see the *ITEM_LINE* section (highlighted gray).

b. In the first line of the *ITEM_LINE* section, place the cursor on the symbol *&VBDPA-MATNR&* and mark it.

Make sure the symbol is marked (it must not blink).

c. In the list box for character formats, choose *B3 Bar code 3 of 9 w/check*.

Note

Next, we have to adjust the output of the MAIN window. In the example you assign the new character format B3 to the symbol &VBDPA-MATNR& in the ITEM LINE section.

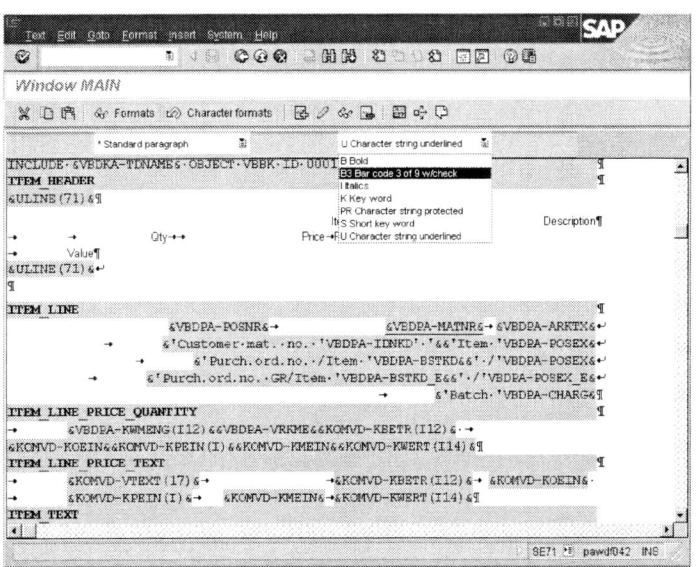

Tips & Tricks

You can check the assigned formats for the symbol *&VBDPA-MATNR&* by clicking on the symbol and choosing 🔍 *Formats*. The *Formats* window appears and shows the assigned formats.

Paragraph format	IL	Line item
Character format	B3	Bar code 3 of 9 w/check

Choose ✔ to close the *Formats* window.

10. Go *Back* to return to the *Administrative Screen*.

11. On the *Administrative Screen*, choose ░ to activate the changes.

5

Tips & Tricks

Some of the bar codes are higher than one line, which may cause the previous lines to overlap. To avoid overlapping, add blank lines before the line with the bar code. Assign a paragraph format to the blank lines. Make sure the paragraph format is not defined to automatically suppress or compress blank lines.

To check the paragraph settings, go to standard attributes and ensure that the *No blank lines* checkbox is deselected.

TechTalk

It is not possible to change the height of a bar code within a form. To change the height of a bar code you have to define your own bar code. To define your own barcode, you can use the font maintenance transaction *SE73*. Your barcodes must begin with Y or Z.

For more information, see the R/3 online documentation (*Basis → BasisService/Communication Interfaces → SAPscript.*

TechTalk

In our example, notice the bar code, which reserves space for the entire material number field (this field is 18 characters long). If you do not use all 18 characters and do not want to waste space, delimit the field length by using the output length formatting option. The symbol definition should be `&VBDPA-MATNR(8)&`

In a numerical bar code, some scanners cannot read special characters. For these scanners, omit the special characters inserted by SAPscript during formatting. An example of a special character is the delimiter for "Thousands" that is used for some numerical fields. For more information on formatting options, see "Overview of Formatting Options" on page 222 and "Syntax of Formatting Options" on page 249.

Adding a Box with Shading

In this section, we want to have a box around an entire window and to shade the first line of this window.

Draw a box around the ship-to address and shade the ship-to address on the sales order confirmation output.

1. From the SAP standard menu, choose *Tools → SAPscript → SE71 - Form.*

2. On the *Form Painter: Request* screen:

   a. Enter **ZVORDER02** in the *Form* field.

   b. Enter **EN** in the *Language* field.

   c. Select *Page Layout.*

   d. Choose ✐ *Change.*

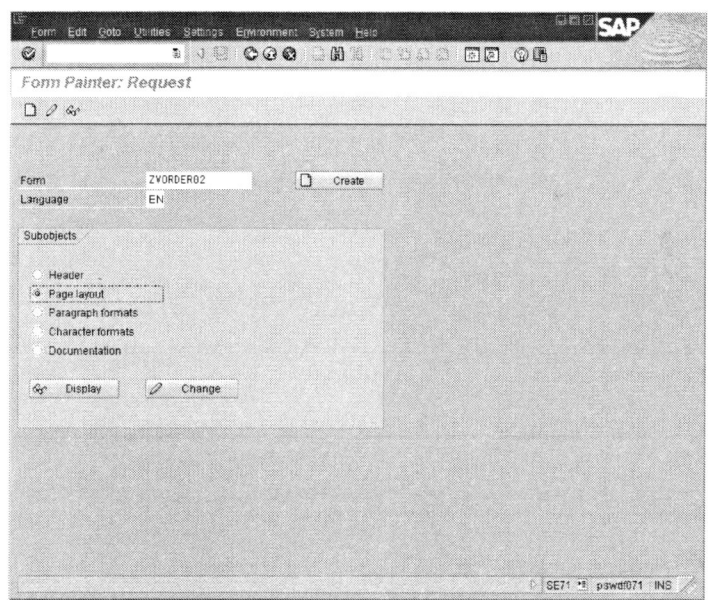

5

For more information, see the R/3 online documentation (*Basis → Basis Service/Communication Interfaces → SAPscript.*

3. In the *Design Window:*

   a. Select the *INFO1* window.

   b. Right-click to access the form layout manipulation menu and choose *Edit text*.

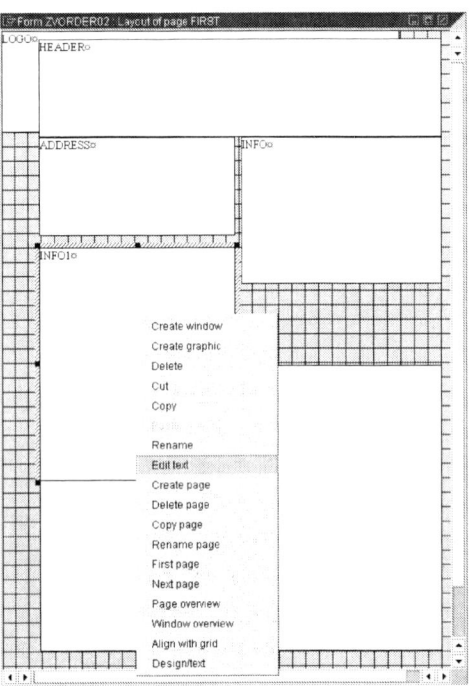

4. With the PC Editor on the *Window INFO1* screen:

   a. Position the cursor at the end of the first line.

   b. Choose .

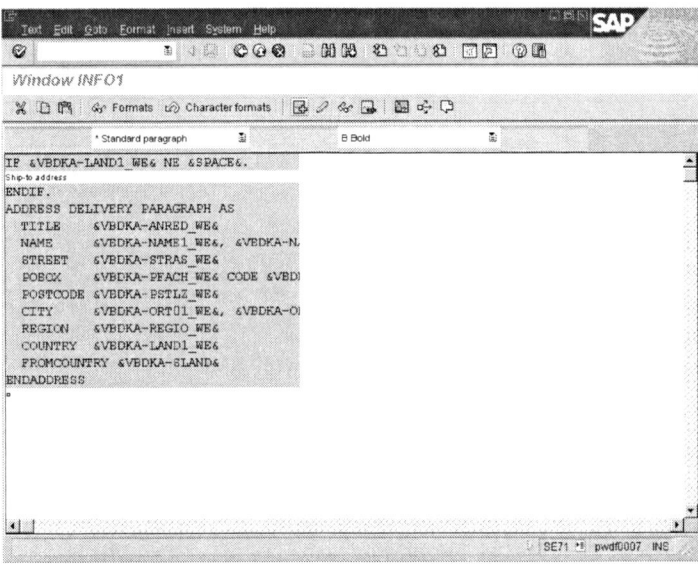

Only if the variable *VBDKA-LAND1_WE* is filled, will the *INFO1* window be printed in the output. Likewise, the box and shading will only be printed if this variable is filled. (We will insert the box and shading commands between the first and second line of the PC Editor.)

5. On the *Create Additional Information* window:

   a. Select *Command*.

   b. Enter **POSITION XORIGIN '-0.5' CH YORIGIN '-0.25' LN** in the *Command* line.

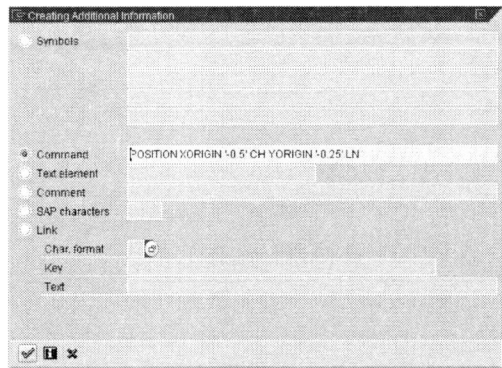 This command positions the cursor a half character and a quarter line off the upper left corner of the window. This is the starting point for the next command, which will be the sizing of the box. Place the cursor off the window to avoid overwriting the window's content with the box.

   c. Choose ✓ .

6. In the PC Editor on the *Window INFO1*, choose ⊞ .

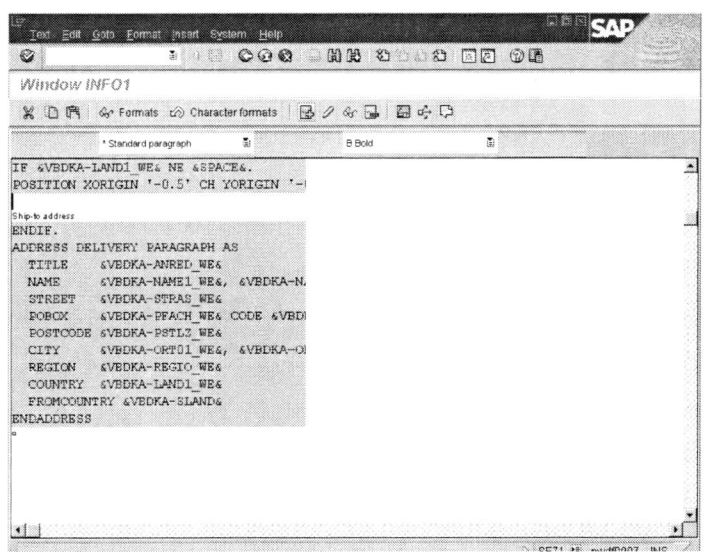

This command defines a new window one character wider and half a line higher than the window. Size the box bigger than the window to avoid overwriting the window's content with the box.

The line inserted in step 7b creates a new window, which overlaps the INFO1 window by half a character on the left and right sides and by a quarter line on the top and bottom of the window.

7. On the *Creating Additional Information* window:

   a. Select *Command*.

   b. Enter `SIZE WIDTH '+1' CH HEIGHT '+0.5' LN` in the *Command* line.

   c. Choose ✅ .

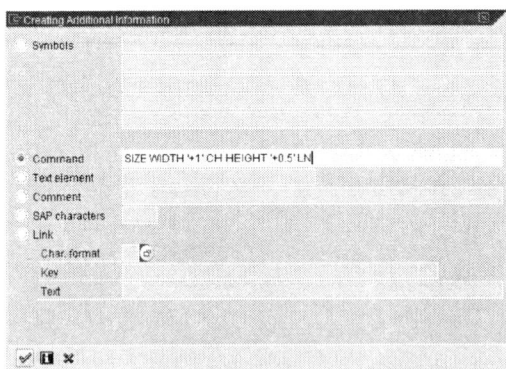

8. In the PC Editor on the *Window INFO1,* choose 🔲 .

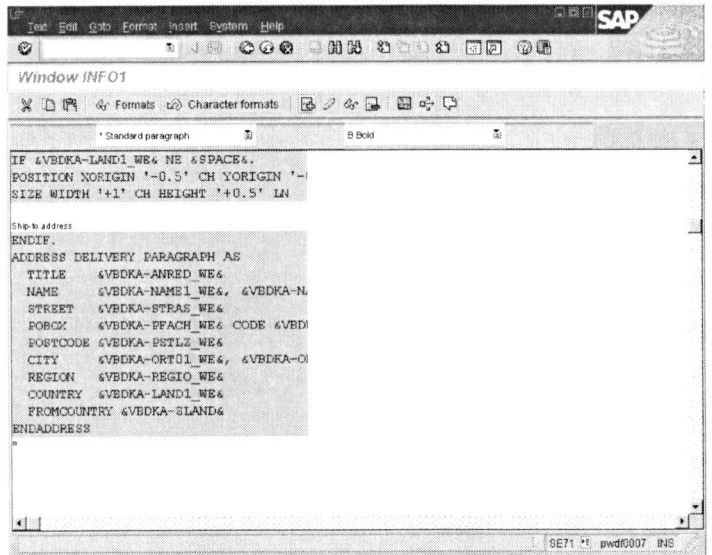

9. On the *Creating Additional Information* window:

  a. Select *Command*.

 This command paints the box in the previously defined size. The box line thickness is specified as 10 twips (one-twentieth of a point).

  b. Enter **BOX FRAME 10 TW** in the *Command* line.

  c. Choose ✓ .

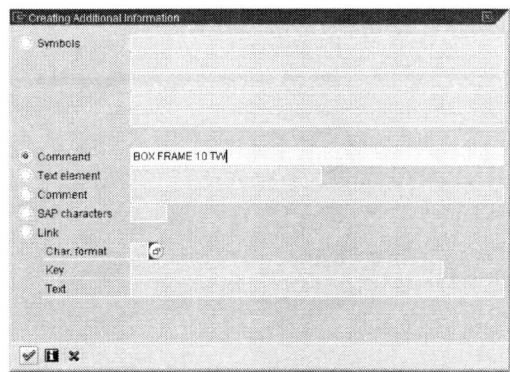

In the PC Editor on the *Window INFO1*, choose 🔲 .

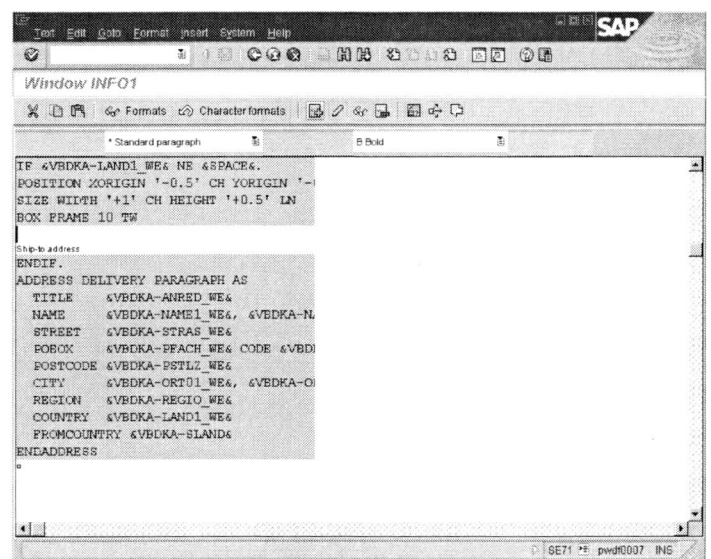

10. On the *Creating Additional Information* window:

   a. Select *Command*.

   b. Enter **BOX HEIGHT '1.5' LN INTENSITY 20** in the *Command* line.

   c. Choose ✓ .

This command shades the first one and a half lines of the box with the intensity of 20% gray. Shading more than one line is necessary because the box begins a quarter line above the window. With a shading level of 1.5 lines, the first line of the window, a quarter line above the first line, and a quarter line below the first line are shaded.

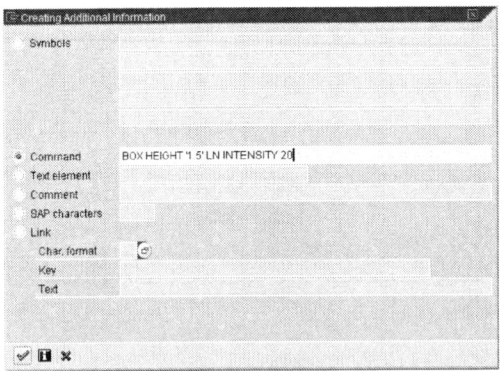

The PC Editor for the *Window INFO1* appears.

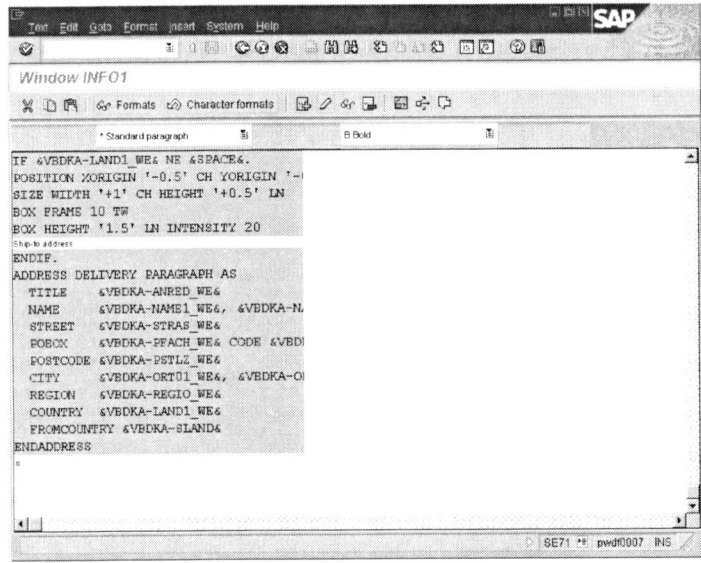

11. Go *Back* to return to the *Administrative Screen*.

12. To activate the changes, choose 🛈 .

Creating Multiple Boxes

By default, a box is oriented to the window coordinates. Therefore, you should create a new window for every box you want to include in the output. Instead of creating boxes for just parts of a window, the box should fill out the entire window. If you want multiple boxes on a page, you do not have to create a window for every box.

The following example shows how to create multiple boxes in one window.

Example

The following is a simple example of multiple boxes on one window:

```
/: POSITION WINDOW
/* First Box
/* POSITION XORIGIN '+0' CH YORIGIN '+0' LN "This is the
default
/: SIZE WIDTH '2'CH HEIGHT '4' LN
/: BOX FRAME 4 TW
/* Second Box
/: POSITION XORIGIN '+0' CH YORIGIN '+4' LN
/: SIZE WIDTH '10'CH HEIGHT '2' LN
/: BOX FRAME 4 TW
/* Third Box
/: POSITION XORIGIN '+10' CH YORIGIN '+2' LN
/: SIZE WIDTH '2'CH HEIGHT '2' LN
/: BOX FRAME 4 TW
```

This code will generate three boxes relative to the size of the page window.

Here is one possible configuration based on the example above:

Page

Box1
+0,+0
2 x 2

Box 2
+0,+4
2 x 10

Box1
+0,+0
2 x 2

Window

Left Margin	1 CH
Upper Margin	1 LN
Width	14 CH
Height	12 LN

5

Printing Text Vertically

Sometimes you may want to print text vertically. SAPscript itself is not able to print text vertically, but you can inform the printer to do this. To rotate the window during the printing, you need two separate print controls. You have to include the print controls so that they enclose the content (text, bar codes, graphics) you want to print vertically.

The content of the window should have the following structure.

```
PRINT-CONTROL ZM200
...
... Text to print vertical
...
PRINT-CONTROL ZM300
```

The print control *ZM200* informs the printer to print the following text vertically. The print control *ZM300* informs the printer to return to horizontal printing.

The specific print sequences for the print controls can be found in the documentation of your printer type.

SAPscript, however, interprets the window's content as horizontal text. Therefore, if you execute the test printing function in SAPscript, the text will be printed horizontal. To check the printout, you have to print the form starting the print program from the application.

To print text vertically, perform the following steps in the recommended order:

1. If necessary, copy a standard printer type (see "Copying a Standard Printer Type" on page 133).

2. Create the print control that informs the printer to print vertically (see "Defining a Print Control for the Macro" on page 135).

3. Create the print control that informs the printer to return to horizontal printing (see "Defining a Print Control for the Macro" on page 135).

4. Create a new window for vertical printing.

   Make sure that the window does not overlap with other windows or stand out of the page during the printing.

5. Include the print controls in the new window (see "Including the Print Control in the Form" on page 138).

Note

Make sure your print control starts with Y or Z. We recommend that the macro ID is also part of the name.

Calling ABAP Subroutines Using the PERFORM Command

In SAPscript, you can use the PERFORM command in a window to call an ABAP subroutine to:

- Obtain data from the database that is needed at print time

- Carry out complex ABAP calculations

- Format data

Often, without modification, the above operations cannot be executed by the print program assigned to your form. Instead of modifying the print program, you can use the PERFORM command to execute additional operations during the printing. Calling an ABAP subroutine from a SAPscript form causes a slight drop in performance during the printing. The delay depends on the complexity of the operations executed in the called subroutine.

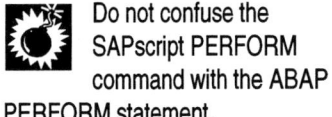 Do not confuse the SAPscript PERFORM command with the ABAP PERFORM statement.

The PERFORM command is executed when the form is formatted for printing. Communication between the called ABAP subroutine and the form is by the way of symbols whose values are set in the ABAP subroutine.

Syntax of the PERFORM statement in a form window.

```
PERFORM <form> IN PROGRAM <prog>
USING &INVAR1&
USING &INVAR2&
...
CHANGING &OUTVAR1&
CHANGING &OUTVAR2&
...
ENDPERFORM
```

5

INVAR1 and *INVAR2* are variable symbols and may be any of the four SAPscript symbol types. You can use as many symbols as you want. All symbols that are transferred from the SAPscript form to the ABAP subroutine are listed in the PERFORM command using the keyword *USING*.

OUTVAR1 and *OUTVAR2* are local text symbols and must, therefore, be character strings. The restriction to text symbols avoids the unintentional change of system symbols. Parameters transferred back to SAPscript forms from internal tables in subroutines are received by the PERFORM command as text using the keyword *CHANGING*.

The ABAP subroutine **<form>** called via the PERFORM command must be defined in the ABAP program **<prog>** as follows:

You can only use internal tables of structure ITCSY in the form routine. The structure is composed of two fields, *NAME* and *VALUE*. Text fields are transferred into the *NAME* field and text field contents into the *VALUE* field.

Create the subroutine in your customer namespace.

Syntax of the ABAP subroutine <form>.

```
FORM <form> TABLES IN_TAB STRUCTURE ITCSY
OUT_TAB STRUCTURE ITCSY
...
ENDFORM
```

Example

In the example, we will retrieve a customer name from table *SCUSTOM*. We assume this table is not defined in the print program. The SAPscript form calls the subroutine *GET_NAME* in the ABAP program *ZREADCUSTOM*.

```
<form> = GET_NAME
<prog> = ZREADCUSTOM
&INVAR1& =&CUST&
&OUTVAR1& = &NAME&
IN_TAB = INTTAB
OUT_TAB = OUTTAB
```

Coding in the SAPscript form window:

```
PERFORM GET_NAME IN PROGRAM ZREADCUSTOM
USING &CUST&
CHANGING &NAME&
ENDPERFORM
...
&NAME&
```

Coding in the ABAP program:

```
REPORT ZREADCUSTOM.
TABLES: SCUSTOM.

*&---------------------------------------------*
*&                  Form GET_NAME
*&---------------------------------------------*
FORM GET_NAME TABLES INTTAB STRUCTURE ITCSY
                     OUTTAB STRUCTURE ITSCY.

* read first line of inttab
READ TABLE INTTAB INDEX 1.

*select from scustom and modify outtab with new data
SELECT SINGLE* FROM SCUSTOM
 WHERE ID = INTTAB-VALUE.

IF SY-SUBRC = 0.
  READ TABLE OUTTAB INDEX 1.
  MOVE SCUSTOM-NAME TO OUTTAB-VALUE.
  MODIFY OUTTAB INDEX SY-TABIX.

ELSE.
  READ TABLE OUTTAB INDEX 1.
  MOVE 'no name' TO OUTTAB-VALUE.
  MODIFY OUTTAB INDEX SY-TABIX.

ENDIF.
ENDFORM
```

PART THREE

Customizing Applications for SAPscript Forms

Customizing Sales and Distribution for Print Forms

Overview

Before you can use print forms with your application, certain customizing steps may be needed.

This chapter covers the following two activities related to customizing Sales and Distribution (SD) for print forms:

■ How to use a modified form instead of a standard form

■ How to get printing results that cannot be achieved by modifying the form

Accessing the IMG

Since customizing is done through the Implementation Guide (IMG), it serves as the starting point for chapters 6 through 8.

All of the IMG-related procedures in this guide begin with the *Display IMG* screen for the *SAP Reference IMG*.

Tips & Tricks

Usually you use a current *Project IMG* instead of the *SAP Reference IMG*. A *Project IMG* is a subset of the *SAP Reference IMG* or the *Enterprise IMG*. Depending on your customizing projects you may see fewer topics on your screen.

Task

Access the SAP Reference Display IMG screen.

1. From the SAP standard menu, choose *Tools* → *AcceleratedSAP* → *Customizing* → *SPRO Edit Project*.

   The *Customizing: Edit Project* screen appears and displays all of the customizing projects defined in your system.

2. On the *Customizing: Edit Project* screen, choose &ℰ *SAP Reference IMG*.

The *Display IMG* screen appears and displays the *SAP Reference IMG*. The sample *Display IMG* screen below shows how to execute an IMG activity. For example, to execute *Configure transaction-related display characteristics for fields*, you start at the *Display IMG* screen. Next, you choose *General Settings → Field Display Characteristics → Configure transaction-related display characteristics for fields*.

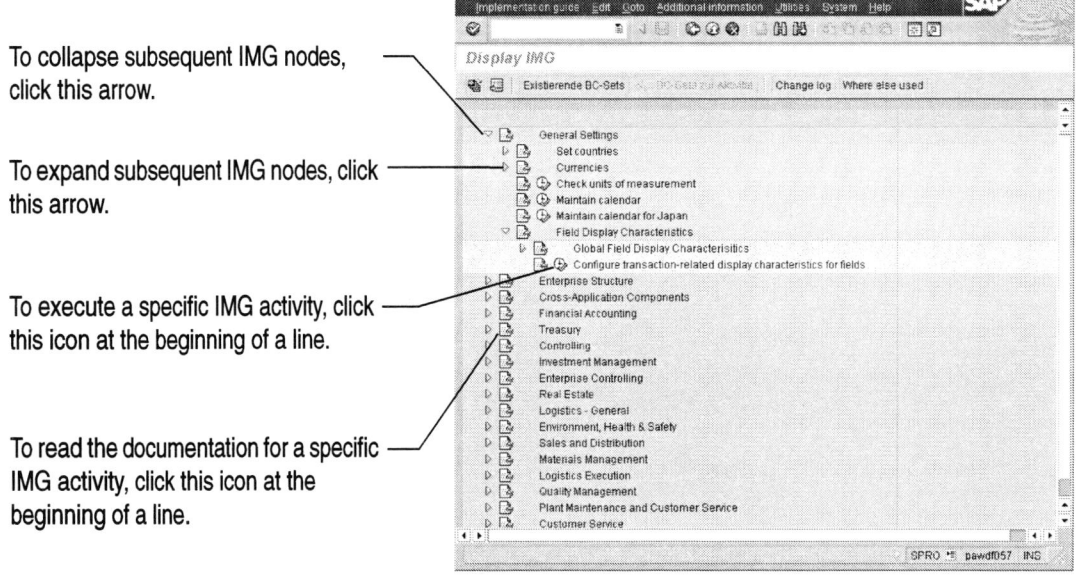

To collapse subsequent IMG nodes, click this arrow.

To expand subsequent IMG nodes, click this arrow.

To execute a specific IMG activity, click this icon at the beginning of a line.

To read the documentation for a specific IMG activity, click this icon at the beginning of a line.

Tips & Tricks

When expanding the IMG structure, not all nodes may be visible on the *Display IMG* screen. If the expanded list becomes too long, you may need to scroll up or down to view the nodes that are no longer on the screen.

6

Assigning Print Programs and Forms to Sales Documents

Before you can use your modified form for printing, you must assign it to the print program. If you do not assign your modified form, the system will use the standard form for printing.

In this section you will learn how to:

- Access the relevant customizing activity for sales documents

- Assign a modified form to a sales order confirmation

You may change the print program used to collect and print data but it is not mandatory. You can also specify the print program and form for each output type and medium.

You can use the standard form *RVORDER01* for inquiry, quotation, sales order confirmation, contract, and scheduling agreement.

Tips & Tricks

> Instead of the SAP standard form *RVORDER01*, you may want to use the preconfigured form *YPPC_ORDCONF* for the U.S. and Canadian markets. You can use *YPPC_ORDCONF* for inquiry, quotation, sales order confirmation, contract, and scheduling agreement confirmation.

Task

Assign a new form to sales documents.

1. Access the *SAP Reference IMG* (see "Accessing the IMG" on page 162).

2. On the *Display IMG* screen, choose *Sales & Distribution → Basic Functions → Output Control → Output Determination → Output Determination Using the Condition Technique → Maintain Output Determination for Sales Documents → Maintain Output Types.*

3. On the *Display View "Output Types": Overview* screen, choose ✏️ to switch to the *Change Mode.*

4. On the *Change View "Output Types": Overview* screen:

   a. Select an output type in the *Output Types* table (for example, *BA00 Order Confirmation*).

   b. From the workplace menu, double-click *Processing routines.*

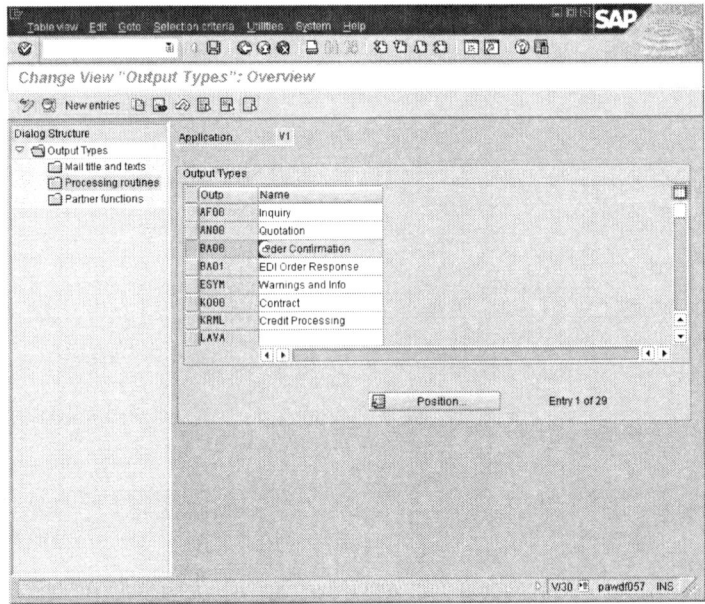

TechTalk

This step-by-step guide shows sales order confirmation output only. However, the standard form, *RVORDER01*, or the form, *YPPC_ORDCONF_STD*, can be used for all other output types.

5. On the *Change View "Processing routines": Overview* screen:

a. Enter the form name (for example, **ZVORDER02**) for the medium you want to use.

b. Save the changed processing routine.

If you use the Change and Transport System (CTS) specify a transport request after saving.

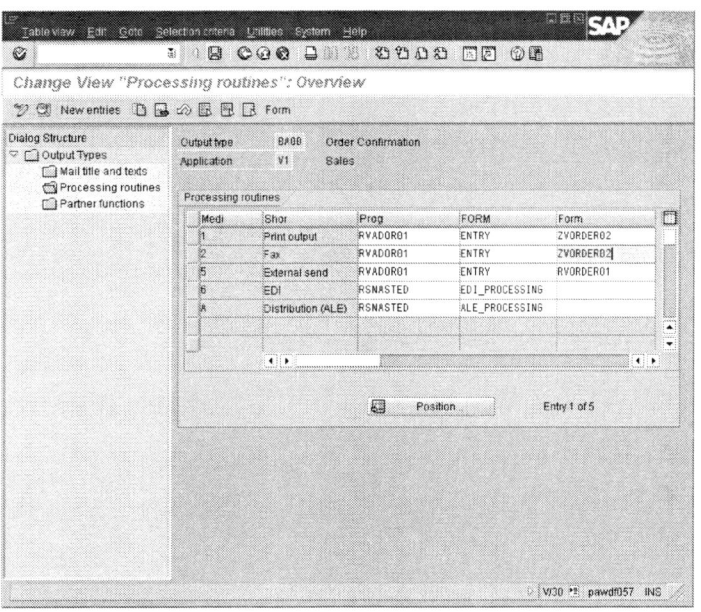

c. Go *Back* twice to return to the *Display IMG* screen.

Assigning Print Programs and Forms to Shipping Documents

Now you will see similar customizing steps for other SD documents, such as delivery notes (packing lists) and picking lists. You will find these forms now in the section *Logistics Execution*. The most important output types are *LD00* (delivery note/packing list) and *WMTA* (automatic TA/picking list).

Since Release 4.5, the output type EK00 (picking list) has been replaced with the output type WMTA (automatic TA).

6

Task

Assign a new form for packing list (delivery note) to shipping documents.

1. Access the *SAP Reference IMG* (see "Accessing the IMG" on page 162).

2. Choose *Logistics Execution → Shipping → Basic Shipping Functions→ Output Control → Output Determination → Maintain Output Determination for Outbound Deliveries → Maintain Output Types.*

3. On the *Display View "Output Types": Overview* screen, choose ✎ to switch to the *Change Mode.*

4. On the *Change View "Output Types": Overview* screen:

   a. In the *Output Types* table, select the output type *LD00.*

   b. From the workplace menu, double-click *Processing routines.*

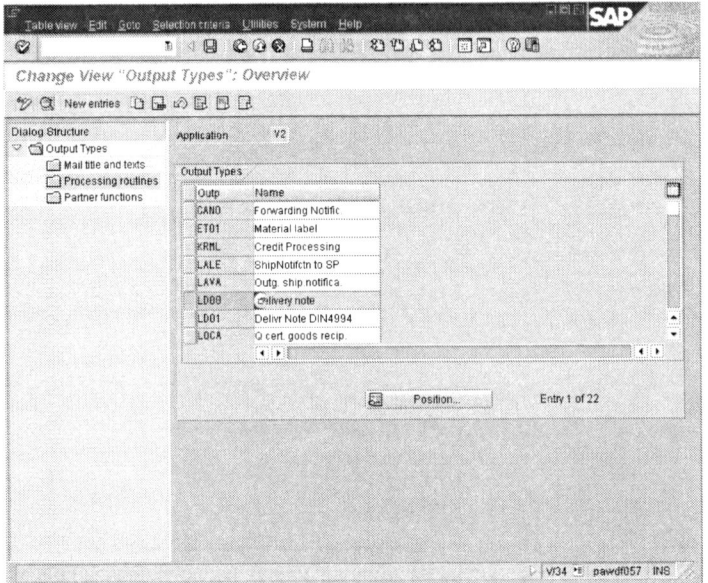

5. On the *Change View "Processing routines": Overview* screen:

a. In the *Form* field, enter the form name for the medium you want to use.

b. Save the changed processing routine.

If you use the Change and Transport System (CTS), specify a transport request after saving.

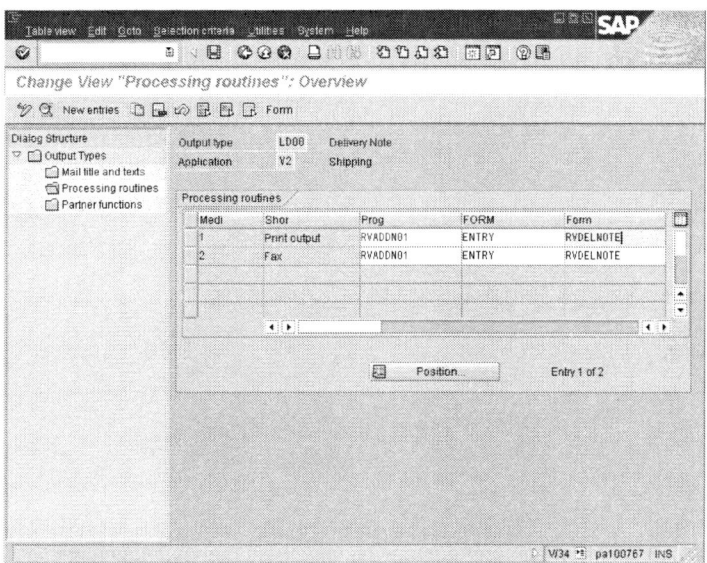

c. Go *Back* twice to return to the *Display IMG* screen.

Task

Assign a new form for picking list to shipping documents

6

1. Access the *SAP Reference IMG* (see "Accessing the IMG" on page 162).

2. Choose *Logistics Execution → Shipping → Basic Shipping Functions→ Output Control → Output Determination → Maintain Output Determination for Outbound Deliveries → Maintain Output Types*.

3. On the *Display View "Output Types": Overview* screen, choose ✐ to switch to the *Change Mode*.

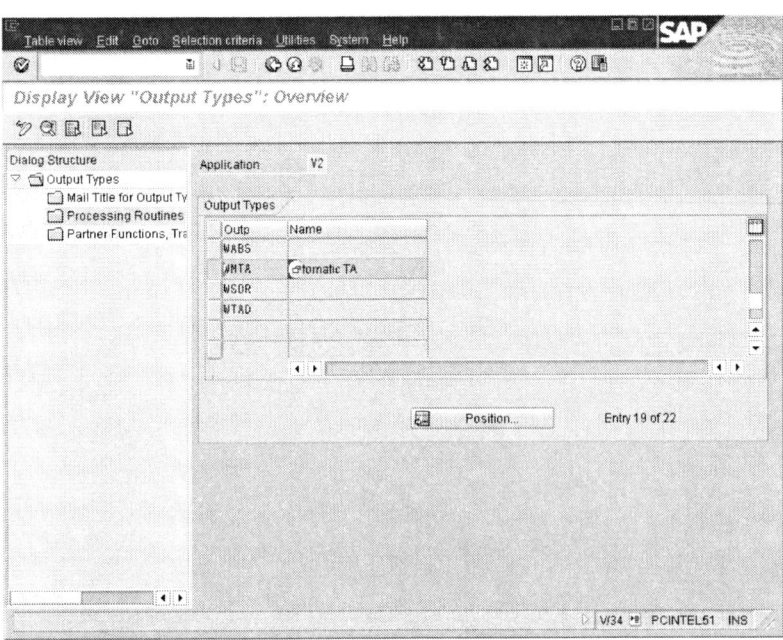

4. On the *Change View "Output Types": Overview* screen:

  a. In the *Output Types* table, select the output type *WMTA (Automatic TA)*.

  b. From the workplace menu, double-click *Processing routines*.

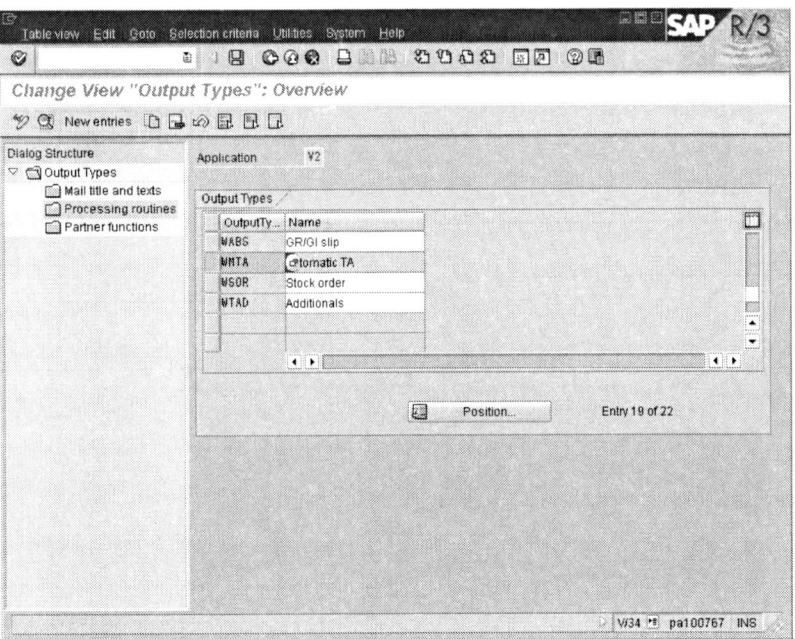

5. On the *Change View "Processing routines": Overview* screen:

a. Enter the form name for the medium you want to use.

b. Save the changed processing routine.

If you use the Change and Transport System (CTS), specify a transport request after saving.

Note

If only one processing routine is defined, the *Change View "Processing routines": Details* screen is displayed immediately.

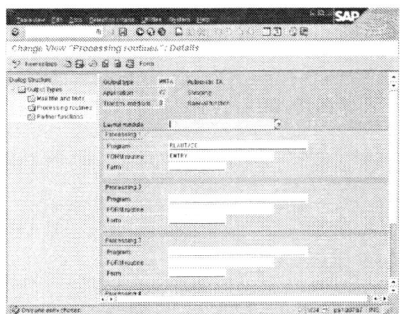

Go *Back* to return to the *Change View "Processing routines": Overview* screen.

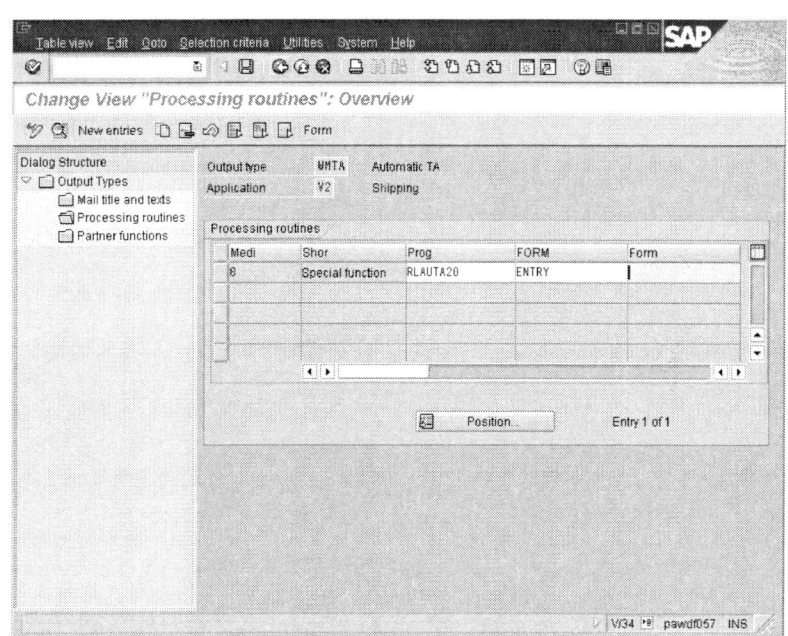

c. Go *Back* twice to return to the *Display IMG* screen.

Assigning Print Programs and Forms to Billing Documents

6

Task

Assign a new form for invoices to billing documents.

1. Access the *SAP Reference IMG* (see "Accessing the IMG" on page 162).

2. Choose *Sales & Distribution → Basic Functions → Output Control → Output Determination → Output Determination Using the Condition Technique → Maintain Output Determination for Billing Documents → Maintain Output Types*.

3. On the *Display View "Output Types": Overview* screen, choose ✐ to switch to the *Change Mode*.

4. On the *Change View "Output Types": Overview* screen:

    a. In the *Output Types* table, select the output type *RD00 (Invoice).*

    b. From the workplace menu, double-click *Processing routines.*

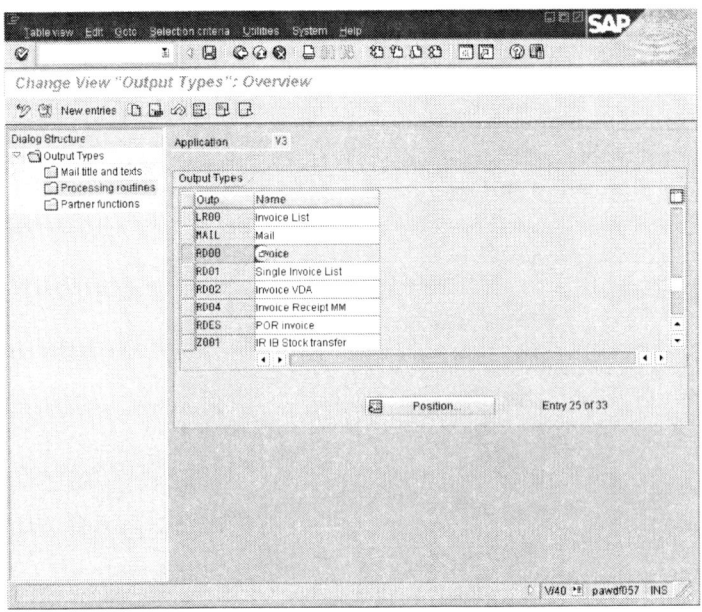

5. On the *Change View "Processing routines": Overview* screen:

    a. Enter the form name (for example, **YPCC_INVOICE_STD**) for the medium you want to use.

    b. Save the changed processing routine.

       If you use the CTS, specify a transport request after saving.

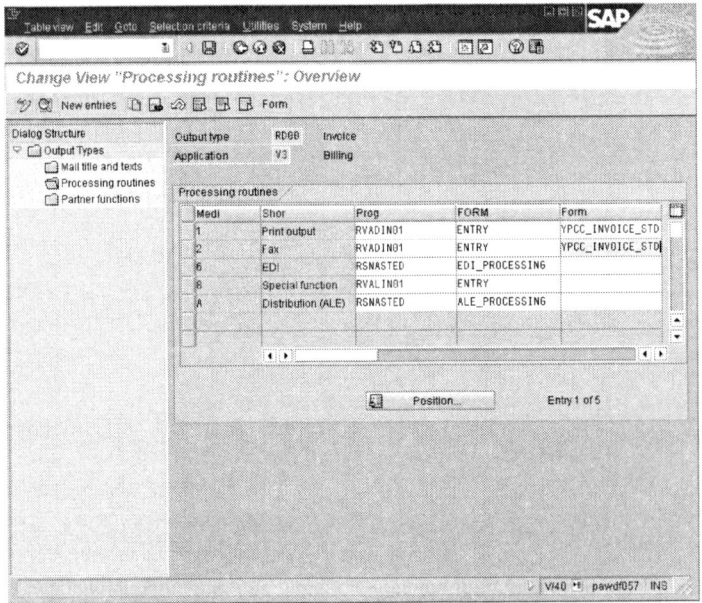

    c. Go *Back* twice to return to the *Display IMG* screen.

Specifying Standard Text for Sender, Header, and Footer

Standard text can be selected as output. The forms are configured to print standard text as headers, footers, and mailing addresses. The mailing address is printed above the greeting; the header and footer are printed at the top and bottom of the page respectively.

Sales order confirmations, packing lists, and invoices use different standard text for each sales organization, and picking lists use different standard text for each shipping point.

If you do not specify standard text, or if the specified standard text does not exist, there is no resulting error.

Specifying Standard Text per Sales Organization

Task

Assign standard text for sender, header and footer per sales organization.

1. Access the *SAP Reference IMG* (see "Accessing the IMG" on page 162).

2. Choose *Sales and Distribution → Basic Functions → Output Control → Output Determination → Process Output and Forms → Assign Form Texts.*

3. To specify the standard text for sales order confirmations, packing lists, and invoices, double-click on *Assign form texts per sales organization.*

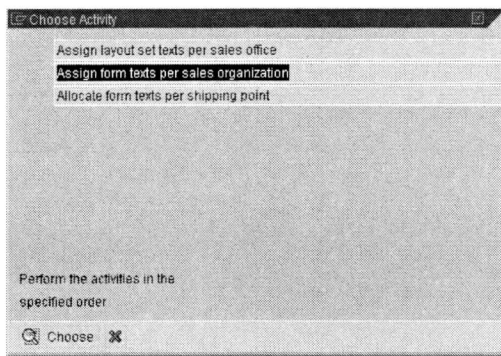

4. On the *Change View "Organizational Unit: Sales Organizations - Output": Overv* screen:

   a. Enter the standard text names for *Addr* (sending address), *Lett* (letter header), and *Foot* (footer text).

   Make sure the text names start with "Y" or "Z."

   b. Save the standard text names.

   If you use the CTS, specify a transport request after saving.

This screen displays the sales organizations that you have defined.

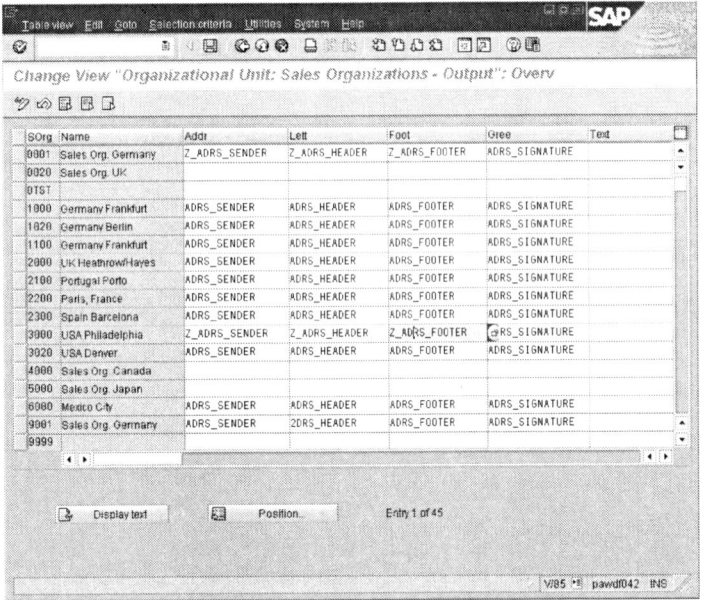

   c. Go *Back* to return to the *Choose activities* popup window.

5. On the *Choose Activity* screen, choose ✖ to return to the *Display IMG* screen.

   The system marks the activity with a check, indicating that you have already assigned form texts per sales organization.

To allocate form texts per shipping point, double-click on the desired activity and do **not** choose *Cancel*.

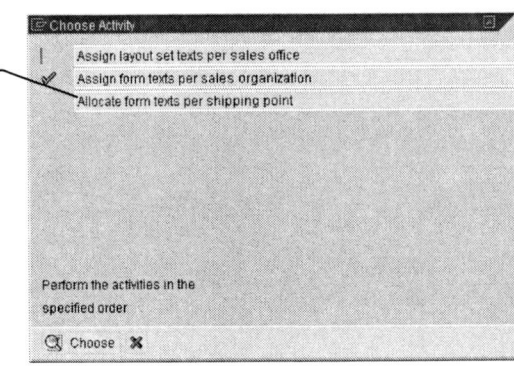

Allocating Standard Text per Shipping Point

Task

Allocate standard text for sender, header, and footer per shipping point.

1. Access the *SAP Reference IMG* (see "Accessing the IMG" on page 162).

2. Choose *Sales and Distribution → Basic Functions → Output Control → Output Determination → Process Output and Forms → Assign Form Texts.*

3. On the *Choose Activity* screen, to specify the standard texts for a picking list, double-click on *Allocate form texts per shipping point.*

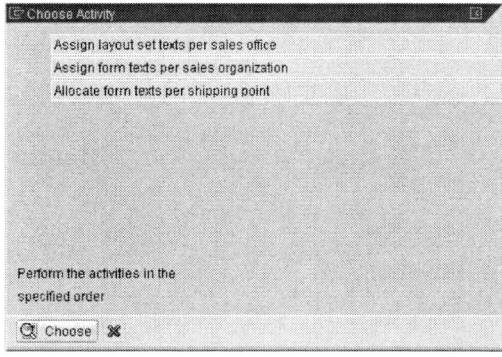

6

4. On the *Change View "Organizational Unit: Shipping Points - Output Determination* screen:

    a. Enter the standard text names for *Addr* (sending address), *Lett* (letter header), and *Foot* (footer text).

    Make sure the text names start with "Y" or "Z."

    b. Save the standard text names.

    c. Go *Back* to return to the *Choose activities* popup window.

This screen displays the shipping points that you defined.

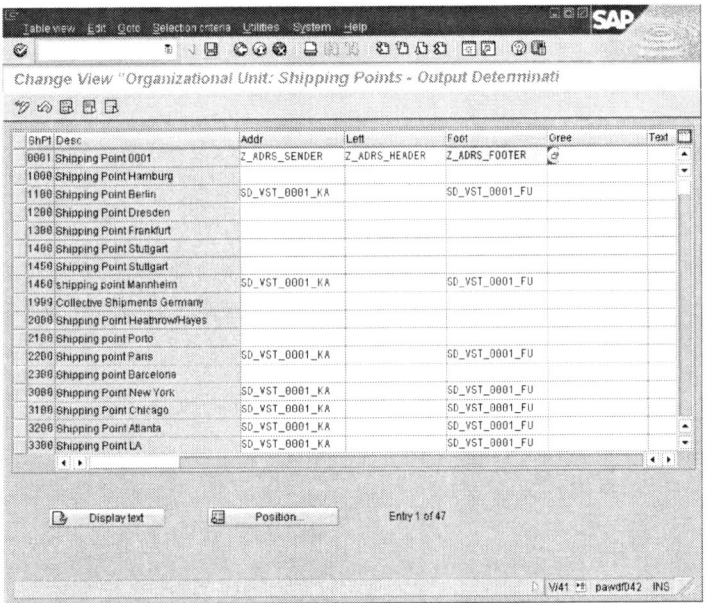

5. On the *Choose Activity* screen, choose ✖ to return to the *Display IMG* screen.

To assign form text per sales organization, double-click on the desired activity and do not choose *Cancel*.

The system marks the activity with a check, indicating that you have already allocated form texts per shipping point.

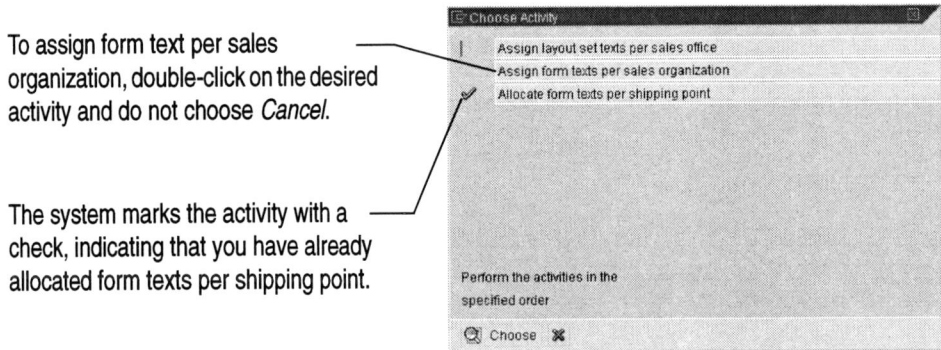

Maintaining Standard Text for Forms

Forms use standard text for recurring header, footer, sender, greetings, and other printed information. These standard texts are inserted in a form by the *INCLUDE* command.

If you create a new standard text, make sure that the form can refer to this new standard text. You have to create or change a *INCLUDE* command in the form.

The following task shows you how to create or change standard text using the PC Editor.

Task

Create or change standard text.

1. From the SAP standard menu, choose *Tools → SAPscript → SO10 - Standard text*.

2. On the *Standard Text: Request* screen:

   a. In the *Text name* field, enter **Z_ADRS_HEADER**.

   In this example, use the text name Z_ADRS_HEADER, specified for letter header in the section Specifying Standard Text for Sender, Header, and Footer.

   b. In the *Text ID* field, enter **ADRS**.

Tips & Tricks

> Since the forms use ADRS, it is easier to use this text ID here. If you use another text ID, you need to change the corresponding command line in the forms.

   c. If the standard text does not exist, choose 🗋 *Create*.

   If the standard text already exists, choose 🖉 *Change*.

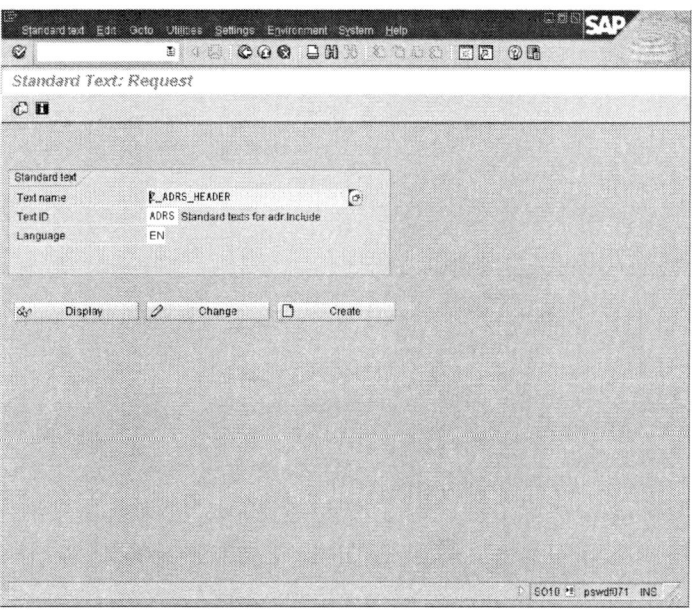

6

3. On the *Change Standard texts for adr.Include: Z_ADRS_Header Language EN* screen:

   a. Enter the desired text.

   b. Save the new or changed standard text.

This screenshot shows some examples of text formatting created with SAP-delivered paragraph and character formats.

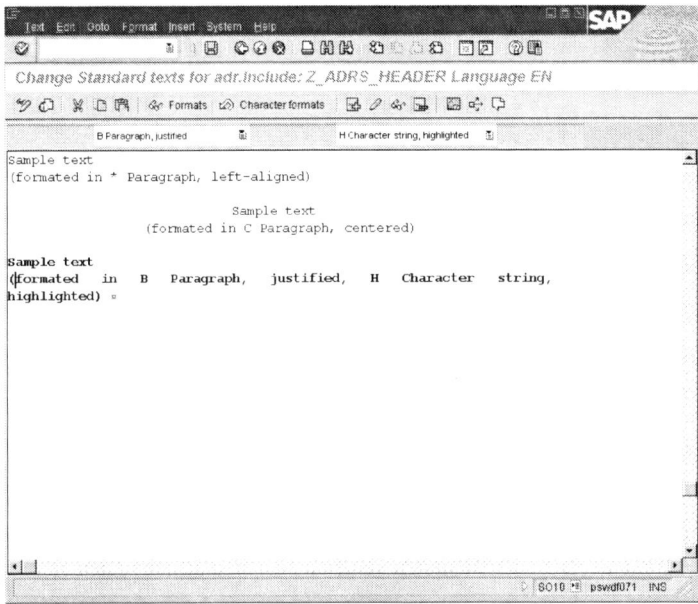

   c. Go *Back* to return to the *Standard Text: Request* screen.

   d. Go *Back* to return to the SAP standard menu.

4. If you create a new standard text, make sure that there is an INCLUDE command in the SAPscript form, which refers to the new standard text.

Tips & Tricks

If you replace an existing standard text, which is already referred by an INCLUDE command in a form, you do not have to create a new INCLUDE command, just replace the name of the standard text.

Maintaining Pricing Conditions to Appear in the Output

Pricing conditions can be marked to appear in the output, either at the item level or as a sum. During customizing, you can specify if the pricing conditions should appear:

- After each item

- As a sum at the end of all the items

Task

Maintain pricing procedures.

1. Access the *SAP Reference IMG* (see "Accessing the IMG" on page 162).

2. Choose *Sales and Distribution → Basic Functions → Pricing → Pricing Control → Define and Assign Pricing Procedures.*

3. On the *Choose Activity* screen, double-click on *Maintain pricing procedures.*

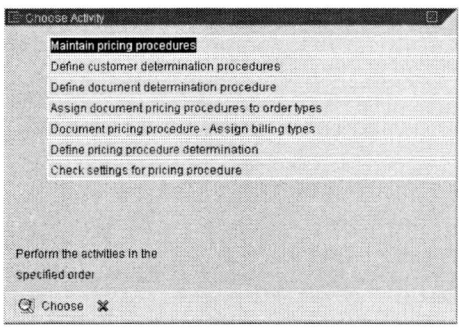

6

Note

Repeat steps 4 and 5 for relevant pricing procedures.

4. On the *Change View: "Procedures": Overview* screen:

   a. In the *Procedures* table, select the box in front of a pricing procedure.

   b. From the workplace menu, choose *Control*.

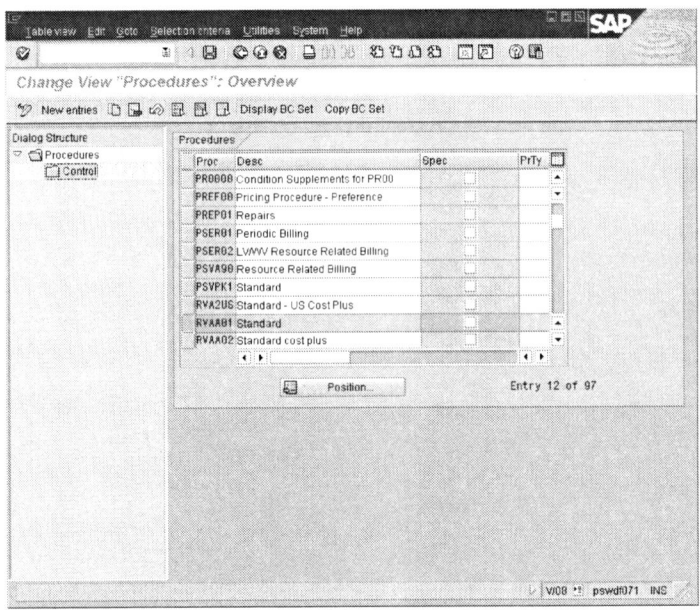

5. On the *Change View: "Control": Overview* screen:

    a. In the P column in the *Control* table, do one of the following subordinated steps:

- If the pricing condition should not appear on the output, delete X or S.

- If the pricing condition should appear for every item, enter X.

- If the pricing condition should appear as a sum, enter S.

    b. Save the controls.

    c. From the workplace menu, choose *Procedures*.

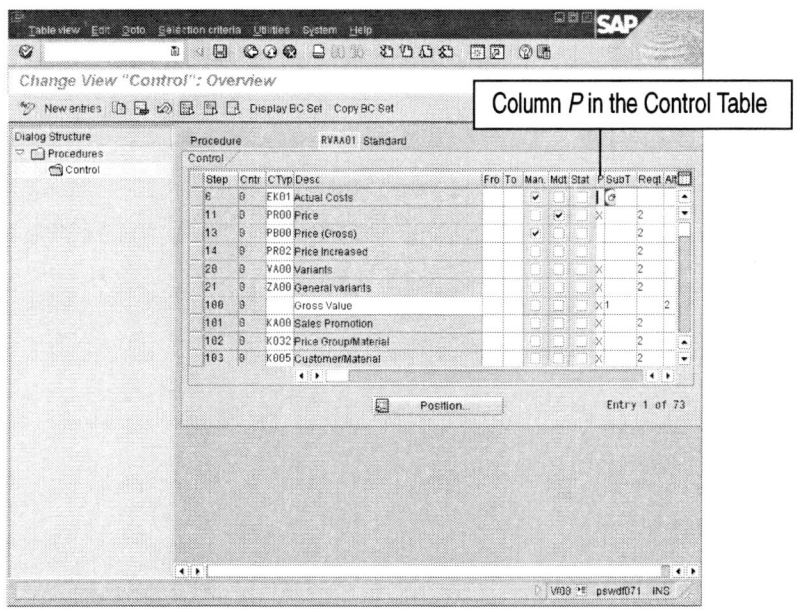

The *Change View: "Procedures": Overview* screen appears again.

Note

To maintain another pricing procedure, repeat steps 4 and 5.

6. Go *Back* to return to the *Choose Activity* screen.

7. On the *Choose Activity* screen, choose ✖ to return to the *SAP Reference IMG* screen.

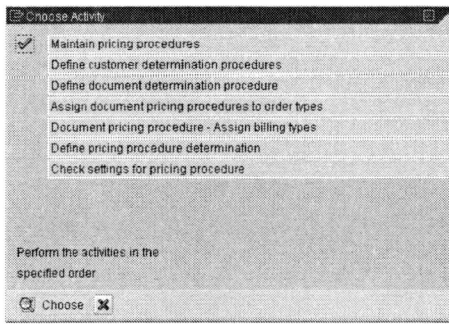

6

Customizing Materials Management for Print Forms

Overview

Before you can use print forms with your application, certain customizing steps may be needed.

This chapter covers the following two activities related to customizing Materials Management (MM) for print forms:

- How to use a modified form instead of a standard form

- How to get printing results that cannot be achieved by modifying the form

Assigning Print Programs and Forms to Documents

Before you can use your modified form for printing, you must assign it to the print program. If you do not assign your modified form, the system will use the standard form for printing.

A print program to collect and print data can also be specified. However, the print program does not need to be changed.

Task

Assign a new form for purchase orders.

1. Access the *SAP Reference IMG* (see "Accessing the IMG" on page 162).

2. Choose *Materials Management → Purchasing → Messages → Forms (Layout Sets) for Messages → Assign Form (Layout Set) and Print Program for Purchase Order.*

The *Change View: "Output Processing Programs": Overview* screen appears.

The *Med* column shows the different output media used for an output type ("1" for printer and "2" for fax).

NEU is the output type for the purchase order.

The *Form* column

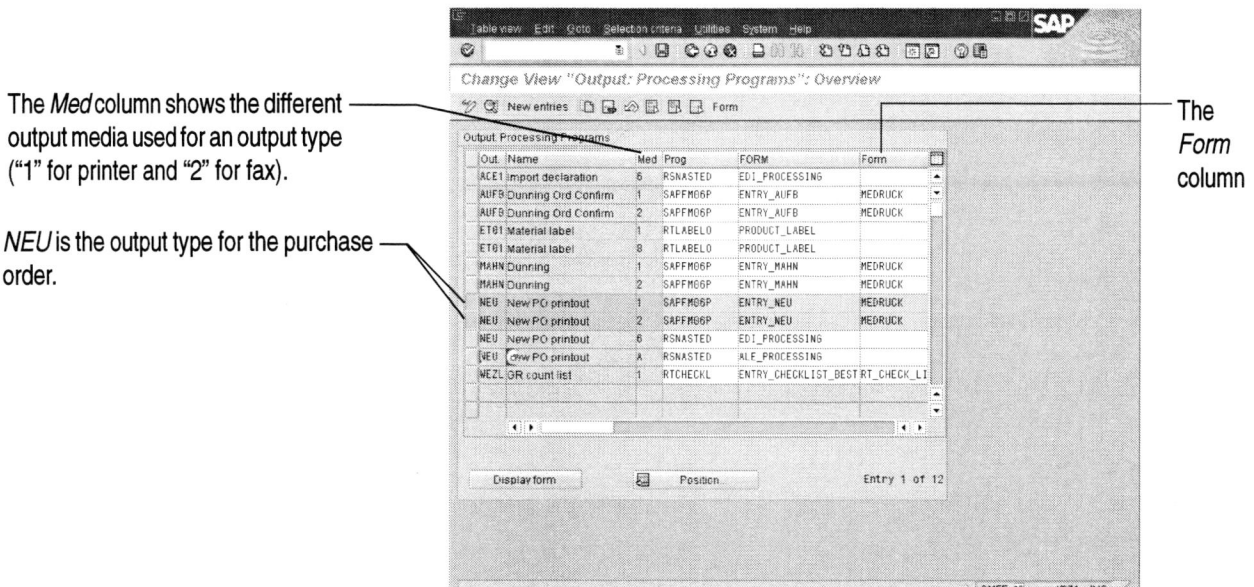

3. In the *Output Processing Programs* table, enter a form name in the *Form* field for each output type and medium you want to use.

For example, to send output to both printer and fax, use the preconfigured form *YPCC_PURCHORD_STD* instead of the standard form *MEDRUCK*.

4. Save the changes.

If you use the CTS, specify a transport request after saving.

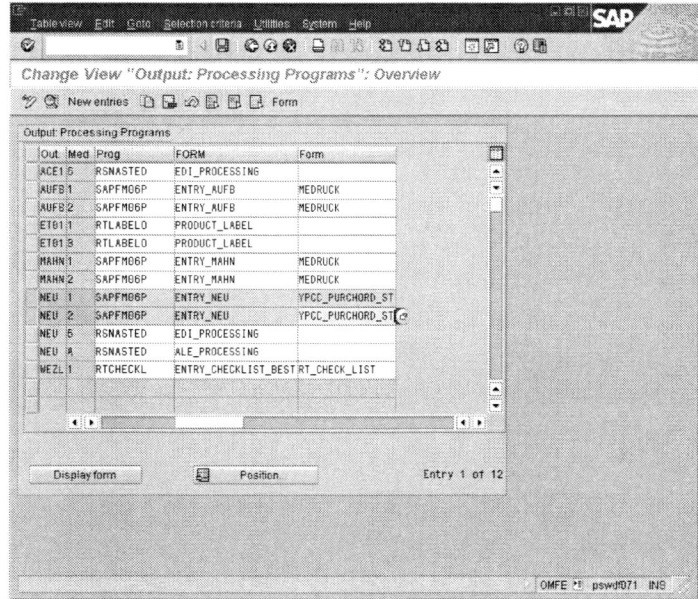

7

5. Go *Back* to return to the *Display IMG* screen.

Maintaining Document Text for Printing

The text from the purchase order, header, and item levels can appear in the output. Even if materials are included in the item, all material text can be selected to appear in the output at the item level of the purchase order.

You can maintain document text for:

- Document header

- Document item

- Document supplement

- Change text

- Headings

Figure 7–1 Purchase order (preconfigured SAPscript form)

Headings contain the document title, purchase order number, and date. The headings are printed in both first lines of the standard SAPscript form MEDRUCK for purchase order.

Document header text

Document item text

Document supplement text is usually printed at the end of all purchase order items.

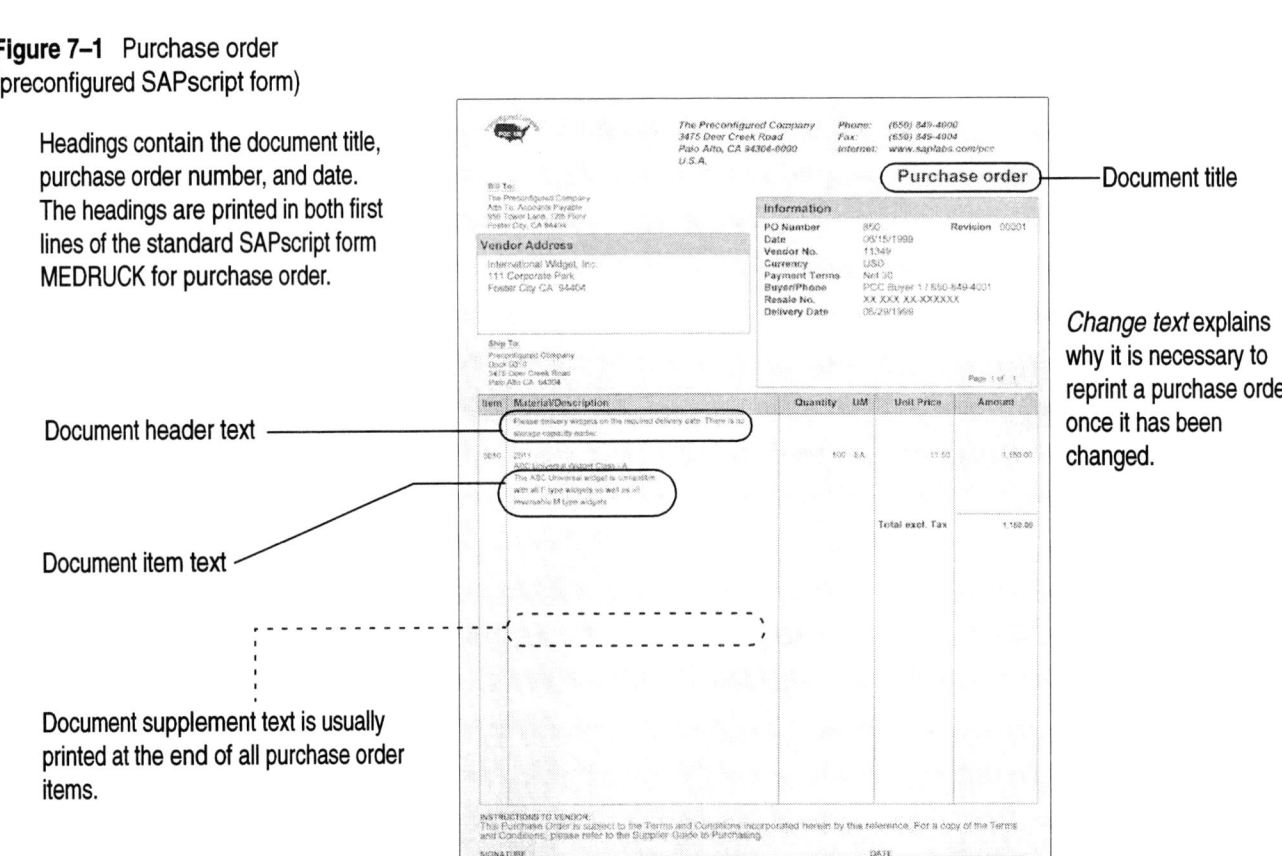

Document title

Change text explains why it is necessary to reprint a purchase order once it has been changed.

Where to Start Maintenance

The starting point for maintaining document text is the *Messages: Purchase Order* screen, where you can select the desired document text.

Task

Access the Messages: Purchase Order screen.

1. Access the *SAP Reference IMG* (see "Accessing the IMG" on page 162).

2. Choose *Materials Management → Purchasing → Messages → Texts for Messages → Define Texts for Purchase Order.*

3. On the *Choose Activity* screen, double-click on *Document Printout Purchase Order.*

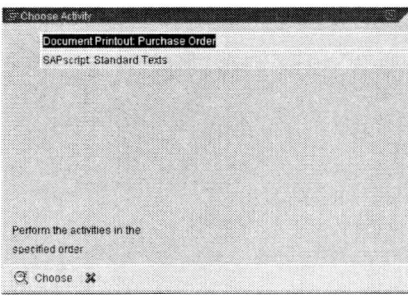

4. On the *Messages: Purchase Order* screen, choose the desired document text.

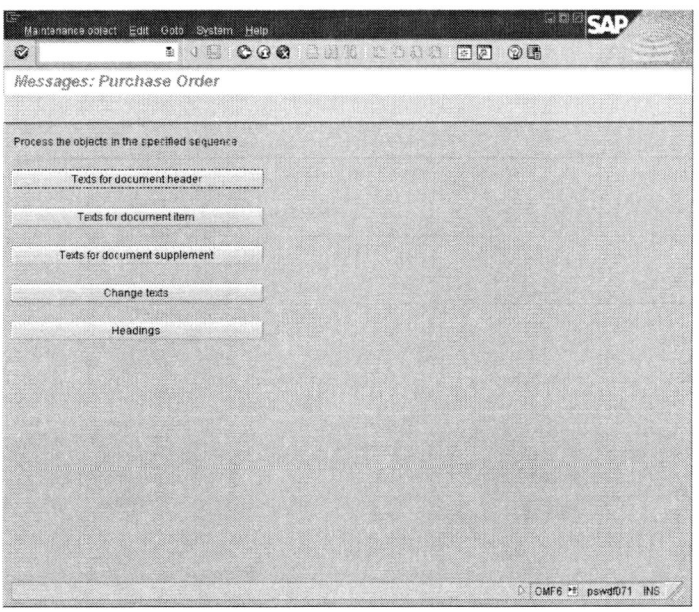

7

Table 7–1 provides an overview of the IMG activities related to maintaining document texts for purchase orders. To learn more about adding and deleting objects, or verifying print sequences, go to the appropriate page number.

Table 7–1   Overview of IMG activities related to document texts

Name of object	Adding an entry	Deleting an entry	Verifying a print sequence
Texts for document header	See page 187	See page 189	See page 189
Texts for document item	See page 191	See page 194	See page 194
Texts for document supplement	See page 196	See page 198	See page 198
Change texts	See page 200		
Headings	See page 201		

Maintaining Text for Document Header

Adding a New Entry for Document Header Text

1. Access the *SAP Reference IMG* (see "Accessing the IMG" on page 162).

2. Access the Messages: Purchase Order screen. For more information, see "Where to Start Maintenance" on page 185.

3. On the *Messages: Purchase Order* screen, choose *Texts for document header*.

4. On the *Change View: "Messages: Header Texts": Overview* screen:

   a. Review the text selected to appear in the output.

   This text is a subset of all text defined on the header level of the purchase order and comes either from the purchase order header or is individual text.

   b. Choose *New Entries*.

The most important lines are those with document type *NB* (*Standard PO*).

The important operations are:

- New purchase order: 1
- Changed purchase order: 2

EKKO is the Object and F01 (Header text) is the Text ID for text coming from the purchase order header.

TEXT is the Object and ST (Standard text) is the Text ID for individual text.

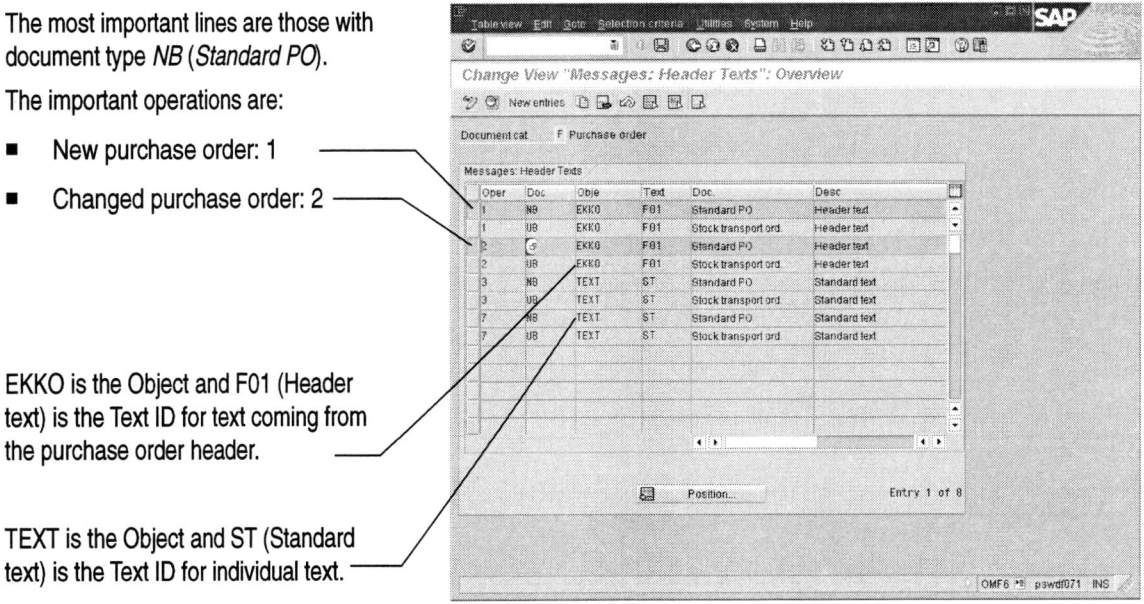

7

5. On the *New Entries: Details of Added Entries* screen:

   a. In the *Print operation* field, enter **1** (*New purchase order*) or **2** (*Changed purchase order*).

   b. In the *Purchasing doc. type* field, enter **NB** (*Standard purchase order*).

   c. In the *Text object* field, enter **EKKO** (*Purchasing document header texts*) or **TEXT** (*standard text*).

   d. In the *Text ID* field, enter **F02** (*Header note*) or **ST** (*standard text*).

   e. In the *Print sequence* field, enter a number that determines the text printing sequence for the text.

   f. If you use **TEXT** in the *Text object field*, enter a name for a standard text in the *Text name* field.

   g. Select *Print title* to print the text title.

   h. Save the new entry.

      If you use the CTS, specify a transport request after saving.

   i. Go *Back* to return to the *Change View: "Messages: Header Texts": Overview* screen.

The print sequence determines the sequence in which text will be printed.

The numbers you enter can be used only once, but you are not required to enter numbers in sequence.

For example, the following sequences are valid:

- 1, 3, 4, 6, and 8
- 1, 2, 3, 4, and 5
- 3, 5, 6, and 9

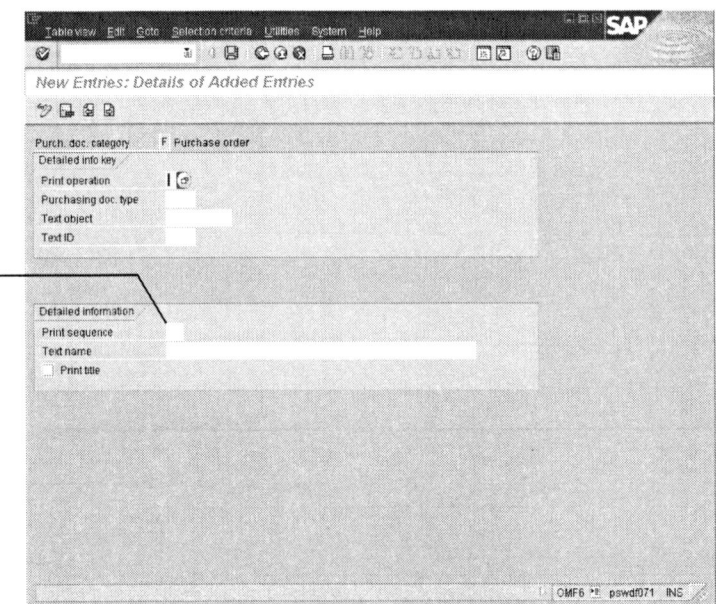

6. Go *Back* to return to the *Messages: Purchase Order* screen.

7. Choose ✖ twice to return to the *SAP Reference IMG* screen.

Deleting an Entry for Document Header Text

1. Access the *SAP Reference IMG* (see "Accessing the IMG" on page 162).

2. Access the *Messages: Purchase Order* screen (see "Where to Start Maintenance" on page 185).

3. On the *Messages: Purchase Order* screen, choose *Texts for document header*.

4. On the *Change View: "Messages: Header Texts": Overview* screen:

    a. Select the box at the beginning of the lines that you want to delete.

    b. Choose ⬜ .

    c. Save the changes.

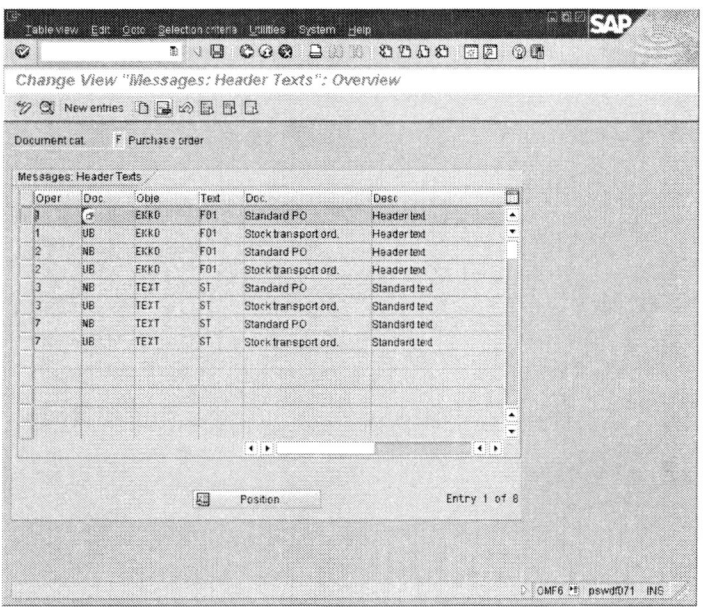

5. Go *Back* to return to the *Messages: Purchase Order* screen.

6. Choose ✖ twice to return to the *SAP Reference IMG* screen.

7

Verifying the Print Sequence for Document Header Text

1. Access the *SAP Reference IMG* (see "Accessing the IMG" on page 162).

2. Access the *Messages: Purchase Order screen* (see "Where to Start Maintenance" on page 185).

3. On the *Messages: Purchase Order* screen, choose *Texts for document header*.

4. On the *Change View: "Messages: Header Texts": Overview* screen:

   a. Select the box at the beginning of the line you want to verify.

   b. Choose ⌐ .

5. On the *Change View "Messages: Header Texts": Details* screen:

   a. In the *Print sequence* field, you can change the number that determines the text printing sequence.

   b. Save the changes.

   If you use the CTS, specify a transport request after saving.

   c. Go *Back* to return to the *Change View: "Messages: Header Texts": Overview* screen.

The print sequence determines the sequence in which text will be printed.

The numbers you enter can be used only once, but you are not required to enter numbers in sequence.

For example, the following sequences are valid:

- 1, 3, 4, 6, and 8

- 1, 2, 3, 4, and 5

- 3, 5, 6, and 9

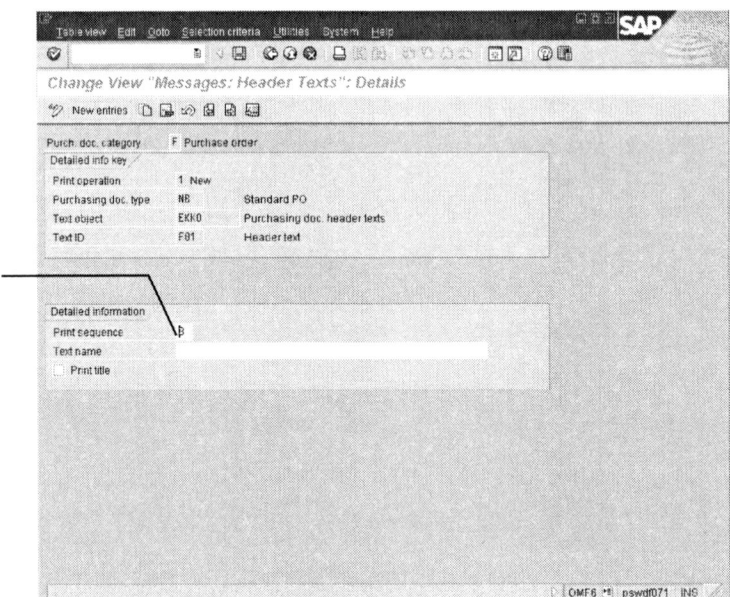

6. Go *Back* to return to the *Messages: Purchase Order* screen.

7. Choose ✖ twice to return to the *SAP Reference IMG* screen.

Maintaining Item Text

Text printed at the item level comes from various item categories. The most important item categories are:

Table 7–2 Item category indicators

Indicator	Description
(blank)	Standard item
B	Limit item
K	Consignment item
L	Subcontracting item
S	Third-party item
T	Text item
U	Stock transfer item
D	Service item

Text printed at the item level comes from various objects. The most important objects are:

Table 7–3 Objects at item level

Object	Description
EKPO	Purchase order items
MATERIAL	Materials
EINE	Purchasing info records
VBBP	Sales order items in case of a third-party item
ASMD	Service master records
ESLL	Services
TEXT	Standard texts

Adding a New Entry for Item Text

Task

Add a new entry for purchase order item text.

1. Access the *SAP Reference IMG* (see "Accessing the IMG" on page 162).

2. Access the *Messages: Purchase Order* screen (see "Where to Start Maintenance" on page 185).

7

3. On the *Messages: Purchase Order* screen, choose *Texts for document item*.

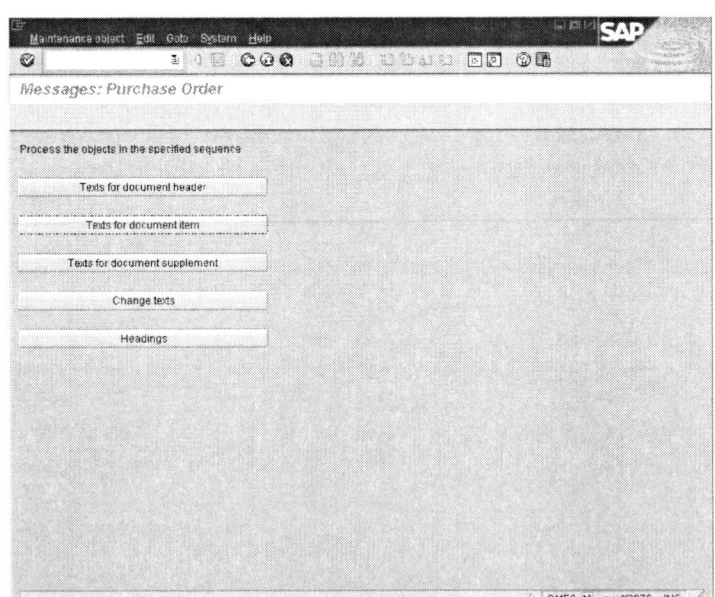

4. On the *Change View: "Messages: Item Texts": Overview* screen:

a. Review the text selected to appear in the output.

This text is a subset of all text defined on the item level of the purchase order.

b. Choose *New Entries*.

The output can be distinguished by item categories in the *I* column (see Table 7–2 on page 191).

The most important lines are those with document type *NB* (*Standard PO*).

The important operations are:

- New purchase order: 1
- Changed purchase order: 2

Text printed at the item level comes from various objects (see Table 7–3 on page 191).

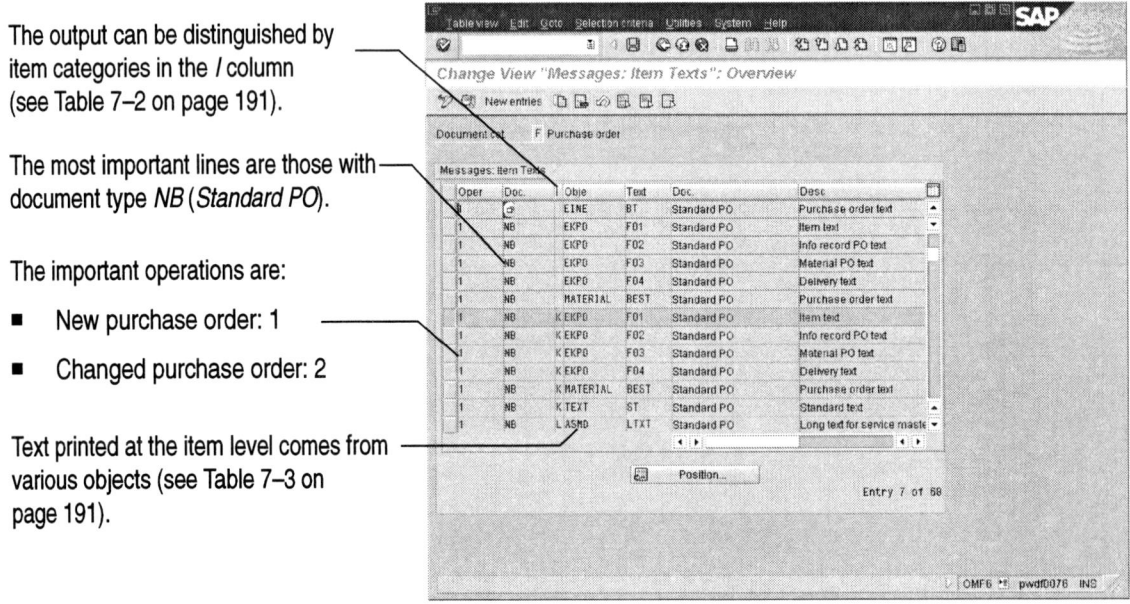

5. On the *New Entries: Details of Added Entries* screen:

a. In the *Print operation* field, enter **1** (*New purchase order*) or **2** (*Changed purchase order*).

b. In the *Purchasing document type* field, enter **NB** (*Standard purchase order*).

c. In the *Item category* field, enter the letter for the desired item category.

d. In the *Text object* field, enter **EKPO** (*Purchasing document item texts*) or **TEXT** (*Standard text*).

e. In the *Text ID* field, enter **F03** (*Material PO text*) or **ST** (*Standard text*).

f. If you use **TEXT** in the *Text object field*, enter a name for a standard text in the *Text name* field.

g. In the *Print Sequence* field, enter a number that determines the printing sequence for the text.

The *Printing priority* field can remain empty.

h. Select *Print title* to print the text title.

i. Save the new item text.

If you use the CTS, specify a transport request after saving.

j. Go *Back* to return to the *Change View: "Messages: Item Texts": Overview* screen.

Sequence and *Printing priority* determine the sequence in which text should be printed. It is a two-level sequence. Therefore, if the input for *Sequence* is equal for two text items, the *Printing priority* field determines the sequence. However, *Sequence* can accept up to 99 numbers, which is sufficient to determine a unique text sequence. Accordingly, we recommend that you leave *Printing priority* empty.

You must enter an increasing sequence in the *Sequence* and *Printing priority* fields. But within the sequence, you may skip numbers. For example, both "1, 2, 3, 4, and 5" and "3, 5, 6, and 9" are valid sequences.

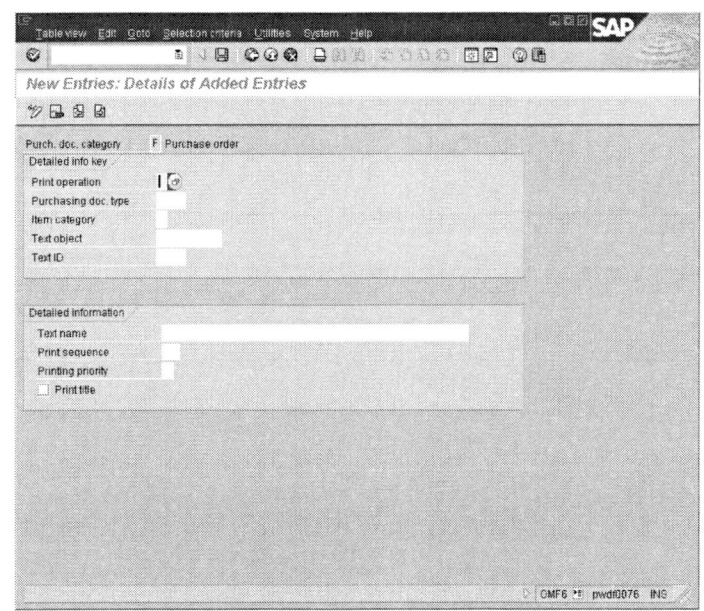

6. Go *Back* to return to the *Messages: Purchase Order* screen.

7. Choose ✖ twice to return to the *SAP Reference IMG* screen.

7

Deleting an Item Text

1. Access the *SAP Reference IMG* (see "Accessing the IMG" on page 162).

2. Access the *Messages: Purchase Order* screen (see "Where to Start Maintenance" on page 185).

3. On the *Messages: Purchase Order* screen, choose *Texts for document item*.

4. On the *Change View: "Messages: Item Texts": Overview* screen:

   a. Select the box at the beginning of the lines that you want to delete.

   b. Choose ▣ .

   c. Save the changes.

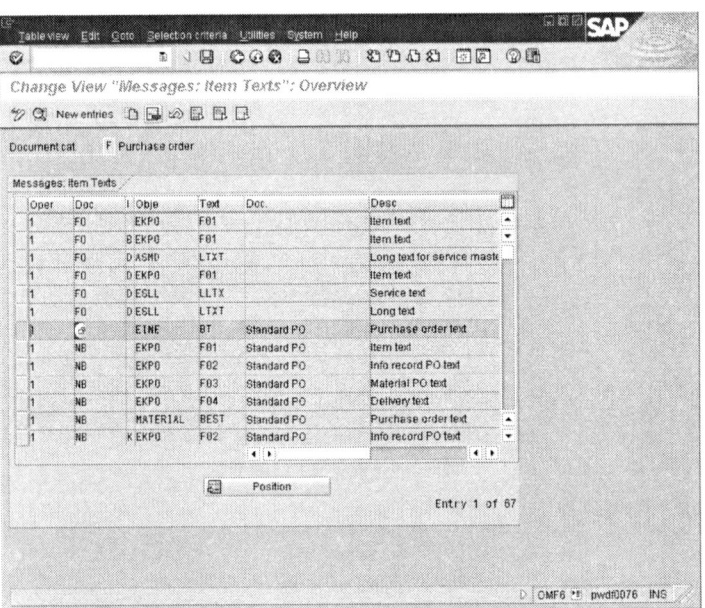

5. Go *Back* to return to the *Messages: Purchase Order* screen.

6. Choose ✖ twice to return to the *SAP Reference IMG* screen.

Verifying the Print Sequence for Item Text

1. Access the *SAP Reference IMG* (see "Accessing the IMG" on page 162).

2. Access the *Messages: Purchase Order* screen (see "Where to Start Maintenance" on page 185).

3. On the *Messages: Purchase Order* screen, choose *Texts for document item*.

4. On the *Change View: "Messages: Item Texts": Overview* screen:

    a. Select the box at the beginning of the line you want to verify.

    b. Choose 🔍 .

    The *Change View "Messages: Item Texts": Details* screen appears.

5. On the *Change View "Messages: Item Texts": Details* screen:

    a. In the *Print Sequence* field, you can change the number that determines the text printing sequence.

    b. In the *Printing priority* field, you can change the number that determines the text printing priority.

    This field can remain empty.

    c. Save the changes.

    If you use the CTS, specify a transport request after saving.

    d. Go *Back* to return to the *Change View: "Messages: Item Texts": Overview* screen.

You must enter an increasing sequence in the *Print Sequence* field, but, you may skip numbers.

For example, the following sequences are valid:

- 1, 2, 3, 4, and 5

- 3, 5, 6, and 9

You must enter an increasing sequence in the *Printing priority* field.

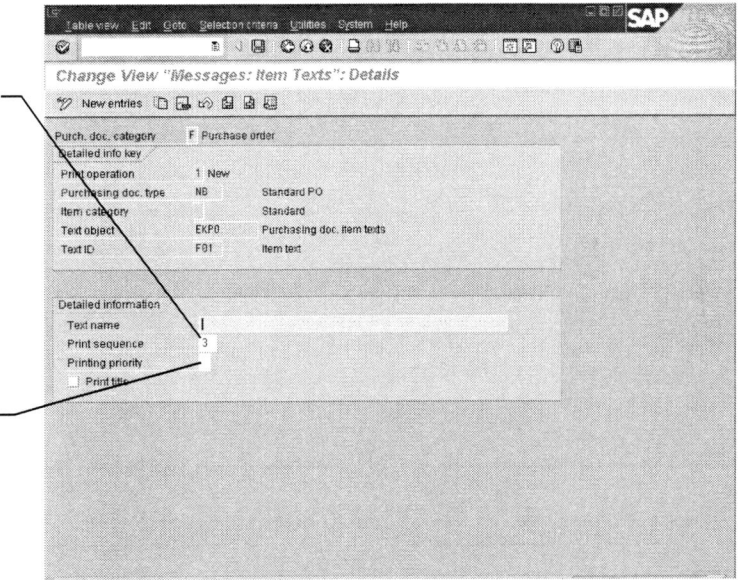

6. Go *Back* to return to the *Messages: Purchase Order* screen.

7. Choose ✖ twice to return to the *SAP Reference IMG* screen.

Maintaining Supplement Texts

Adding a New Entry for Supplement Text

1. Access the *SAP Reference IMG* (see "Accessing the IMG" on page 162).

2. Access the *Messages: Purchase Order* screen (see "Where to Start Maintenance" on page 185).

3. On the *Messages: Purchase Order* screen, choose *Texts for supplement text.*

4. On the *Change View: "Messages: Supplement Texts": Overview* screen:

   a. Review the text selected to appear in the output at the end of all purchase order items.

   b. Choose *New Entries.*

The most important lines are those with document type *NB* (*Standard PO*).

The important operations are:

- New purchase order: 1
- Changed purchase order: 2

Note

Text, printed as supplements, comes either from the purchase order header or is standard text.

For a purchase order header, *EKKO* is the *Object* and the supplement text *ID* varies (for example, *F06*).

For standard text, *TEXT* is the Object and *ST* is the *Text ID* (not shown).

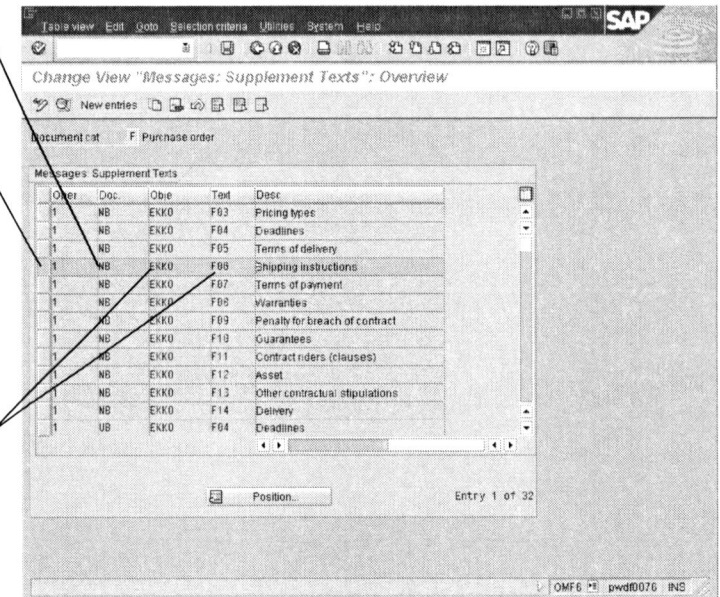

5. On the *New Entries: Details of Added Entries* screen:

a. In the *Print operation* field, enter **1** *(New purchase order)* or **2** *(Changed purchase order)*.

b. In the *Purchasing doc. type* field, enter **NB** *(Standard purchase order)*.

c. In the *Text object* field, enter **EKKO** *(Purchasing document header texts)* or **TEXT** *(standard text)*.

d. In the *Text ID* field, enter the desired text ID (for example *F06*).

e. In the *Print sequence* field, enter a number that determines the text printing sequence.

f. If you use **TEXT** in the *Text object* field, enter a standard text name in the *Text name* field.

g. Select *Print title* to print the text title.

h. Save the new entry.

If you use the CTS, specify a transport request after saving.

i. Go *Back* to return to the *Change View: "Messages: Supplement Texts": Overview* screen.

The print sequence determines the sequence in which text will be printed.

The numbers you enter in the *Print sequence* field can be used only once, but you are not required to enter numbers in sequence.

For example, the following sequences are valid:

- 1, 3, 4, 6, and 8
- 1, 2, 3, 4, and 5
- 3, 5, 6, and 9

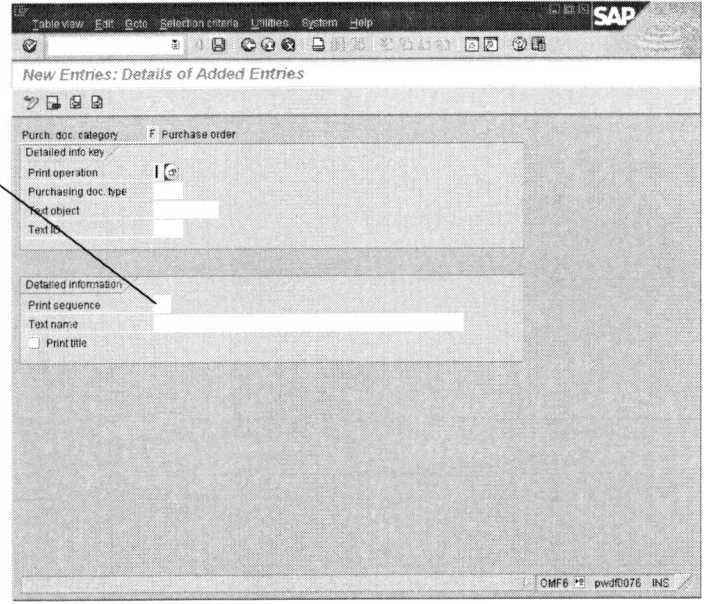

6. Go *Back* to return to the *Messages: Purchase Order* screen.

7. Choose ✖ twice to return to the *SAP Reference IMG* screen.

7

Deleting a Supplement Text

1. Access the *SAP Reference IMG* (see "Accessing the IMG" on page 162).

2. Access the *Messages: Purchase Order* screen (see "Where to Start Maintenance" on page 185).

3. On the *Messages: Purchase Order* screen, choose *Texts for supplement text*.

4. On the *Change View: "Messages: Supplement Texts": Overview* screen:

   a. Select the box at the beginning of the lines you want to delete.

   b. Choose 🔲 .

   c. Save the changes.

   If you use the CTS, specify a transport request after saving.

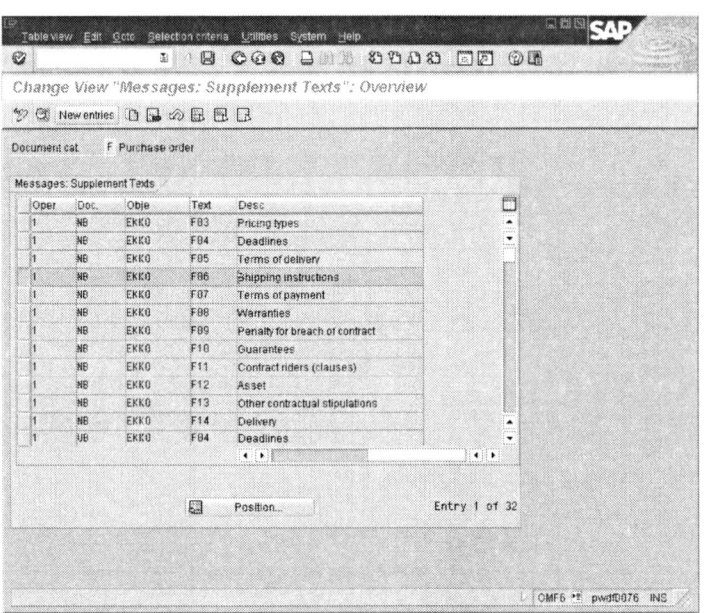

5. Go *Back* to return to the *Messages: Purchase Order* screen.

6. Choose ✖ twice to return to the *SAP Reference IMG* screen.

Verifying the Print Sequence for Supplement Text

1. Access the *SAP Reference IMG* (see "Accessing the IMG" on page 162).

2. Access the *Messages: Purchase Order* screen (see "Where to Start Maintenance" on page 185).

3. On the *Messages: Purchase Order* screen, choose *Texts for supplement text*.

4. On the *Change View: "Messages: Supplement Texts": Overview* screen:

   a. Select the box at the beginning of the line you want to verify.

   b. Choose 🔍 .

5. On the *Change View "Messages: Supplement Texts": Details* screen:

   a. In the *Print sequence* field, change the number that determines the text printing sequence.

   b. Save the changes.

      If you use the CTS, specify a transport request after saving.

   c. Go *Back* to return to the *Change View: "Messages: Supplement Texts": Overview* screen.

The print sequence determines the sequence in which text will be printed.

The numbers you enter in the *Print sequence* field can be used only once, but you are not required to enter numbers in sequence.

For example, the following sequences are valid:

- 1, 3, 4, 6, and 8

- 1, 2, 3, 4, and 5

- 3, 5, 6, and 9

6. Go *Back* to return to the *Messages: Purchase Order* screen.

7. Choose ✖ twice to return to the *SAP Reference IMG* screen.

Maintaining Change Texts

The *change text* explains why a change in a purchase order makes it necessary to reprint the purchase order. If it is applicable, this text appears in the output.

1. Access the *SAP Reference IMG* (see "Accessing the IMG" on page 162).

2. Access the *Messages: Purchase Order* screen (see "Where to Start Maintenance" on page 185).

3. On the *Messages: Purchase Order* screen, choose *Change texts*.

4. On the *Change View: "Messages: Change Texts": Overview* screen:

   a. Review the change texts.

   b. To change the text, overwrite it.

   c. Save the changes.

      If you use the CTS, specify a transport request after saving.

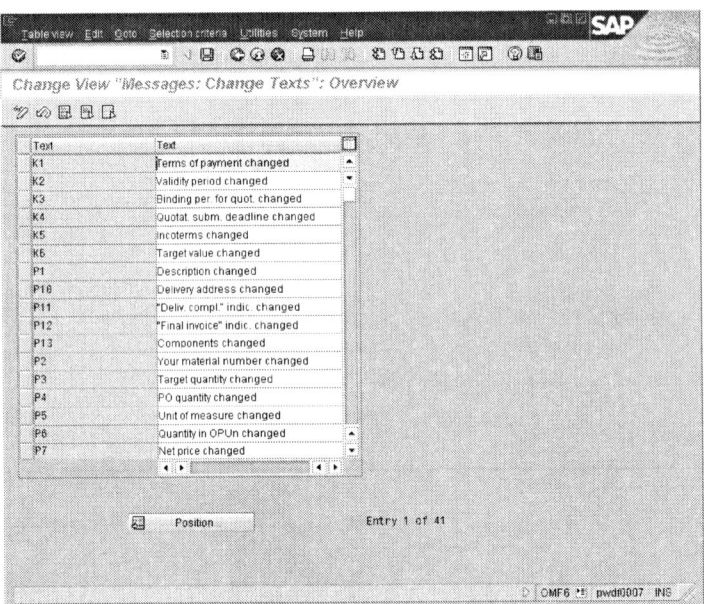

5. Go *Back* to return to the *Message: Purchase Order* screen.

6. Choose ✖ twice to return to the *SAP Reference IMG* screen.

Maintaining Headings

You can change the title of the output, the field headings for the purchase order number, and the purchase order date.

The content of the title and the document type are printed in the first two lines of purchasing documents outputted with the standard SAPscript form *MEDRUCK*.

The content of the heading document number is printed above the document number or document date.

1. Access the *SAP Reference IMG* (see "Accessing the IMG" on page 162).

2. Access the *Messages: Purchase Order* screen (see "Where to Start Maintenance" on page 185).

3. On the *Messages: Purchase Order* screen, choose *Headings*.

4. On the *Change View "Messages: Headings": Overview* screen:

    a. Select the box at the beginning of the lines that you want to change.

    b. Choose 🔍 .

The important operations are:

■ New purchase order: 1

■ Changed purchase order: 2

The most important lines are those with document type NB (Standard PO).

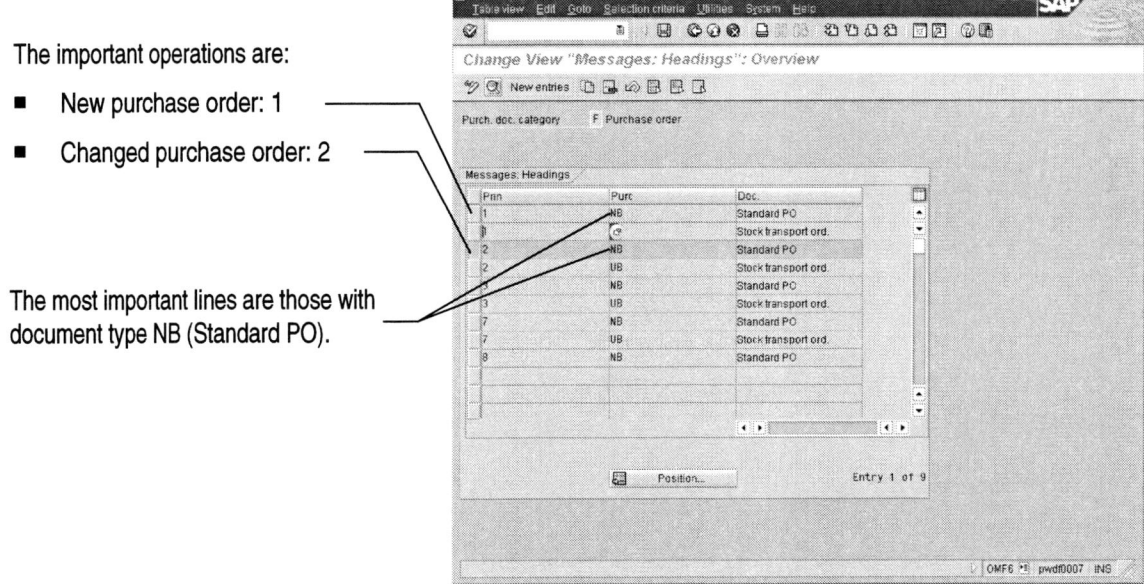

Changes in the heading for the document number and date can cause changes in the form. Before changing the headings, see where the variables for the document number and date are used in the form, and if the form needs to be changed.

5. On the *Change View "Messages: Headings": Details* screen:

    a. Overwrite the title and heading for the document number and date.

    b. Save the changes.

        If you use the CTS, specify a transport request after saving.

    c. Go *Back* to return to the *Change View "Messages: Headings": Overview* screen.

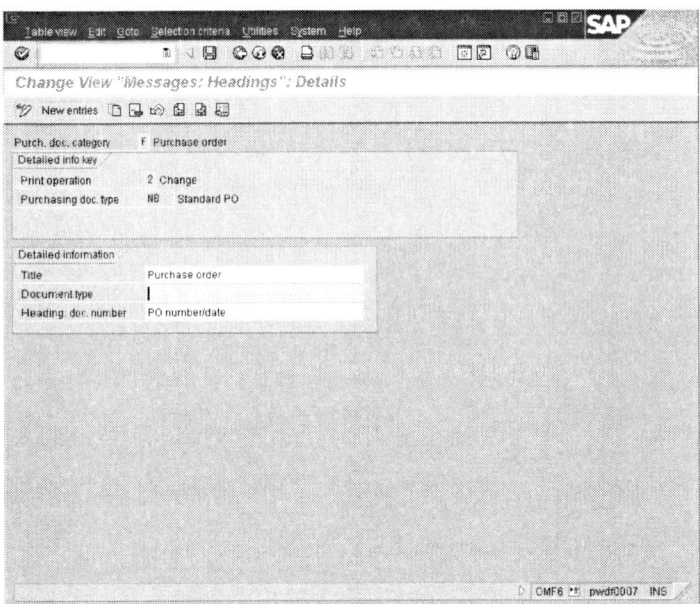

6. Go *Back* to return to the *Message: Purchase Order* screen.

7. Choose ✖ twice to return to the *SAP Reference IMG* screen.

Maintaining Standard Text for Forms

In the previous tasks, you might have created new entries using the text object *TEXT* and specified text names for standard texts. The following steps show how to create or change standard texts. In this example, use the text name *Z_PURCHORD_HEADER* and the text ID *ST*.

Task

Maintaining standard text.

1. From the SAP standard menu, choose *Tools → SAPscript → SO10 - Standard text*.

2. On the *Standard Text: Request* screen:

  a. In the *Text name* field, enter **Z_PURCHORD_HEADER**.

  b. In the *Text ID* field, enter **ST**.

  c. If the standard text does not exist, choose ☐ *Create*.

  If the standard text already exists, choose ⟋ *Change*.

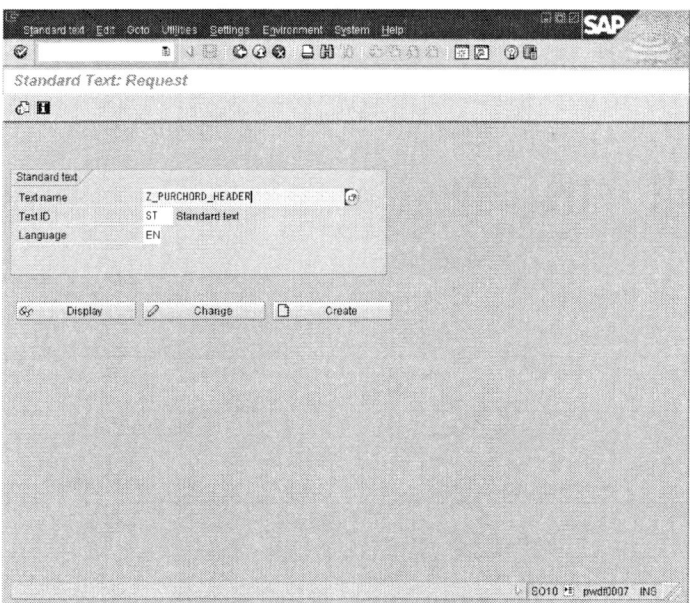

3. On the *Change Standard text: <...> Language <...>* screen:

   a. Enter the desired text.

   b. Save the new or changed standard text.

   c. Go *Back* to return to the *Standard Text: Request* screen.

This screen shows some examples of text formatting created with SAP-delivered paragraph and character formats.

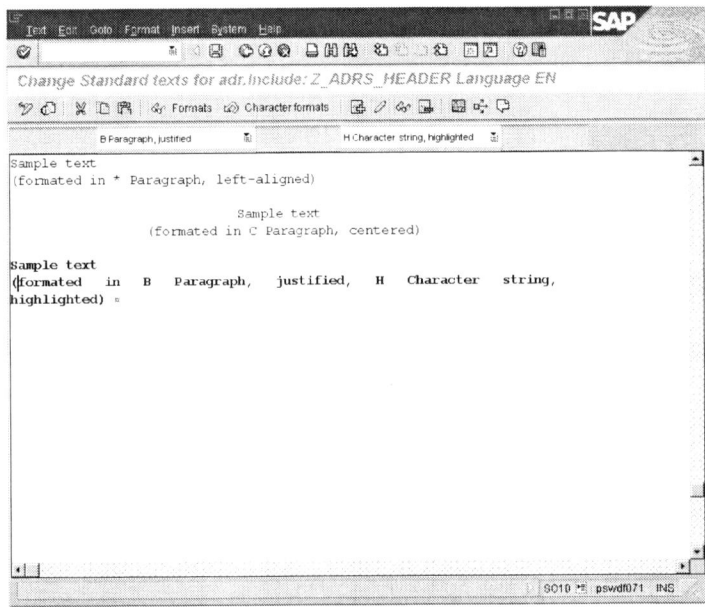

4. Go *Back* to return to the SAP standard menu.

5. If you create a new standard text, make sure that there is an INCLUDE command in the SAPscript form, which refers to the new standard text.

Tips & Tricks

If you replace an existing standard text, which is already referred to by an INCLUDE command in a form, you do not have to create a new INCLUDE command. Simply replace the name of the standard text.

7

CHAPTER

8

Customizing Financial Accounting
for Print Forms

Overview

Before you can use print forms with your application, certain customizing steps may be needed.

This chapter covers the following two activities related to customizing Financial Accounting (FI) for print forms:

- How to use a modified form instead of a standard form

- How to get printing results that cannot be achieved by modifying the form

Assigning a Print Program to Checks

If you copy and modify the standard print program for checks, you must inform the system that you want to use this new print program for printing checks. The following example shows how you can assign a print program to checks for a specific country.

Task

Assign a new print program to checks.

1. Access the *SAP Reference IMG* (see "Accessing the IMG" on page 162).

2. Choose *Financial Accounting → Accounts Receivable and Accounts Payable → Business Transactions → Outgoing Payments → Automatic Outgoing Payments → Payment Method/Bank Selection → Configure payment program.*

3. On the *Payment Program Configuration: Initial Screen*, choose *Payment methods/country.*

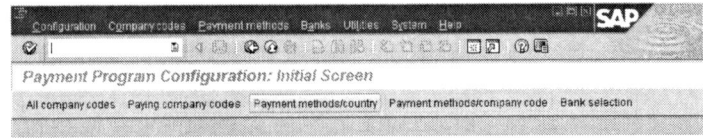

4. On the *Maintain Payment Program Configuration: Countries* screen, double-click on the appropriate country.

In this example double-click on U.S. (United States). If you cannot find the line US, scroll down the screen.

5. On the *Maintain Payment Program Configuration: Country Pmnt Methods – List* screen, choose the appropriate payment method for checks.

   In this example double-click on *C* (Checks). The *Maintain Payment Program Configuration: Country Pmnt Methods – Details* screen appears.

   a. In the *Name of the print program* field, enter the new print program name.

   b. Save the changes.

   If you use the CTS, specify a transport request after saving.

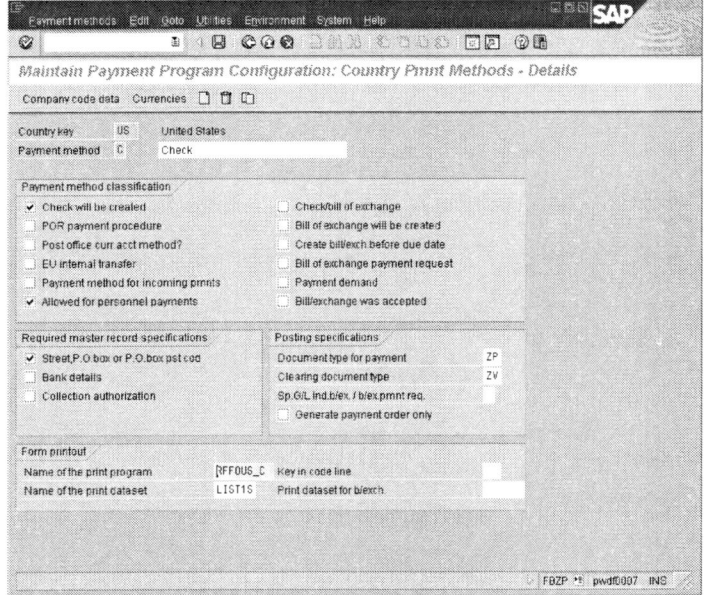

6. Choose *Exit* to return to the *Payment Program Configuration: Initial Screen*.

7. Choose *Back* to return to *Display IMG* screen.

Assigning Forms to Checks

If you copied and modified a form for checks, inform the system that you want to use the new form for check printing. The following example shows how to assign a new form to checks (per company code).

8

Task

Assign a new form to a print program for checks.

1. Access the *SAP Reference IMG* (see "Accessing the IMG" on page 162).

2. Choose *Financial Accounting → Accounts Receivable and Accounts Payable → Business Transactions → Outgoing Payments → Automatic Outgoing Payments → Payment Method/Bank Selection → Configure payment program.*

3. On the *Payment Program Configuration: Initial Screen*, choose *Payment methods/company code.*

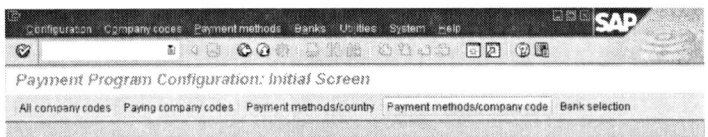

Note

Repeat steps 4 through 8 for each company code you want to assign a new form to.

4. On the *Maintain Payment Program Configuration: Company Codes* screen, double-click on a company code.

   In our example, we use *3000* (*IDES US INC New York*).

5. On the *Maintain Payment Program Configuration: Pmnt Methods in CC – List* screen, choose the appropriate payment methods for checks.

   In our example, we use *C* (Check).

6. On the *Maintain Payment Program Configuration: Pmnt Methods in CC – General Data* screen, choose *Form Data.*

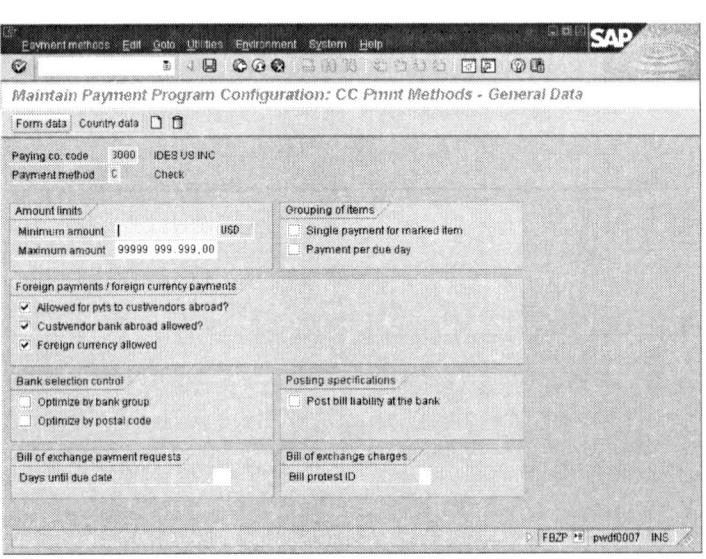

7. On the *Maintain Payment Program Configuration: Pmnt Methods in CC – Form Data* screen:

    a. Enter the new form name in the *Form for the payment transfer medium* field.

    b. Save the changes.

    If you use the CTS, specify a transport request after saving.

    c. Go *Back* to return to the *Maintain Payment Program Configuration: Pmnt Methods in CC – List* screen.

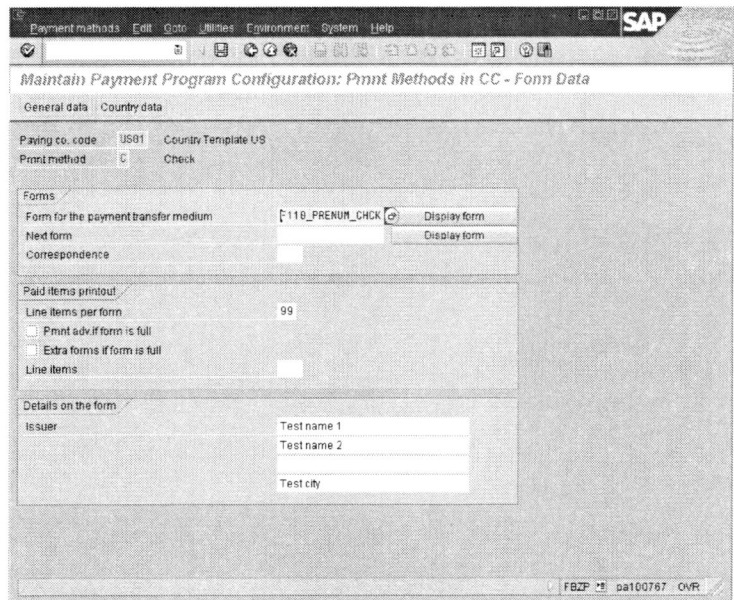

8. Go *Back* to return to the *Maintain Payment Program Configuration: Company Codes* screen.

9. Go *Back* to return to the *Payment Program Configuration: Initial Screen*.

10. Go *Back* to return to the *Display IMG* screen.

Specifying Standard Text for Header, Footer, Signature and Sender

Note

The form for the check normally prints only standard text such as letter header, but you can easily add the commands to print standard text for footer, signature, and sender.

You can specify standard text to appear in the output. The form for the check normally prints only standard text, such as letter header.

The header is printed at the top of the check. The *letter header* can use different standard text depending on the company code. If you do not specify standard text, or if the specified standard text does not exist, there is no resulting error.

8

Task

Assign text elements for header, footer, signature and sender per company code.

1. Access the *SAP Reference IMG* (see "Accessing the IMG" on page 162).

2. Choose *Financial Accounting → Accounts Receivable and Accounts Payable → Business Transactions → Outgoing Payments → Automatic Outgoing Payments → Payment Method/Bank Selection → Configure payment program.*

3. On the *Payment Program Configuration: Initial Screen*, choose *Paying company codes.*

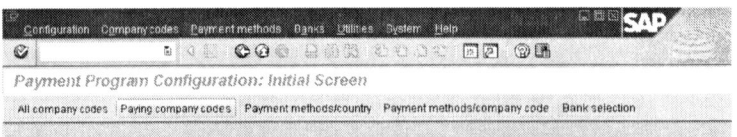

4. On the *Payment Program Configuration: Paying company codes* screen, double-click on the appropriate company code.
   In our example, we use *3000 (IDES US INC)*.

5. On the *Payment Program Configuration: Paying company codes data* screen, choose *Sender.*

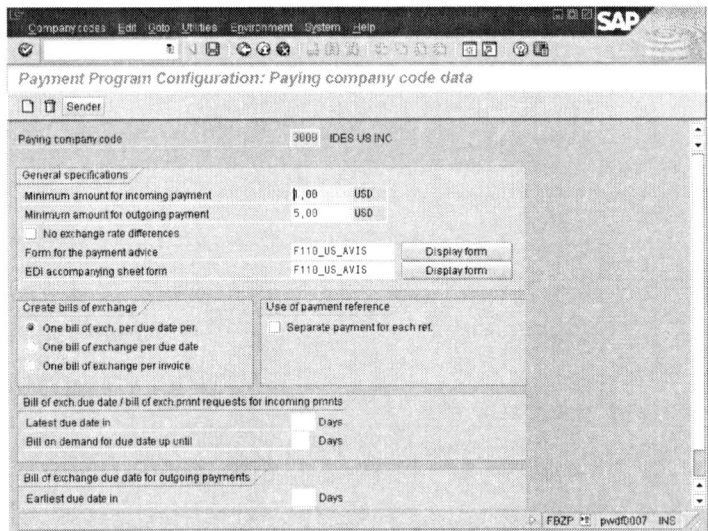

6. On the *Payment Program Configuration: Sender Details* screen:

a. Enter **ADRS** in the *Text ID* field.

b. To specify standard text enter names in the *Letter header, Footer text, Signature,* and *Sender* fields.

c. Save you changes.

If you use the CTS, specify a transport request after saving.

d. Choose *Exit* to return to the *Payment Program Configuration: Initial Screen*.

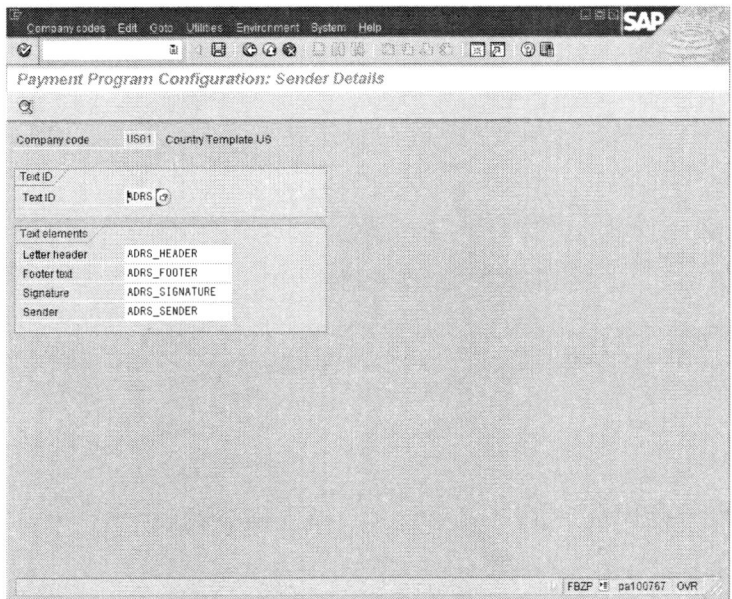

7. Go *Back* to return to *Display IMG* screen.

8. To print specified standard text for footer text, signature, and sender, make sure that the following control commands are used in the form:

TechTalk

To print the standard texts for footer text, signature, and sender, you must use the following control commands in the form:

Footer:
```
INCLUDE &REGUD-TXTFU& OBJECT TEXT ID ADRS
```

Signature:
```
INCLUDE &REGUD-TXTUN& OBJECT TEXT ID ADRS
```

Sender:
```
INCLUDE &REGUD-TXTAB& OBJECT TEXT ID ADRS
```

Make sure that you use the correct text ID in the control commands.

8

Maintaining Standard Text for Forms

In the previous task, you might have specified standard text names for letter header, footer text, signature, or sender. The following example shows how you can create or change standard texts. In this example, we use the text name Z_F_US01_HEADER and the text ID ST.

Task

Create or change standard text.

1. From the SAP standard menu, choose *Tools → SAPscript → SO10 - Standard text*.

2. On the *Standard Text: Request* screen:

   a. In the *Text name* field, enter a name of the standard text (for example, **Z_F_US01_HEADER**).

   b. In the *Text ID* field, enter a text ID (for example, **ST**).

   c. If the standard text does not exist, choose ☐ *Create*.

   d. If the standard text already exists, choose ✐ *Change*.

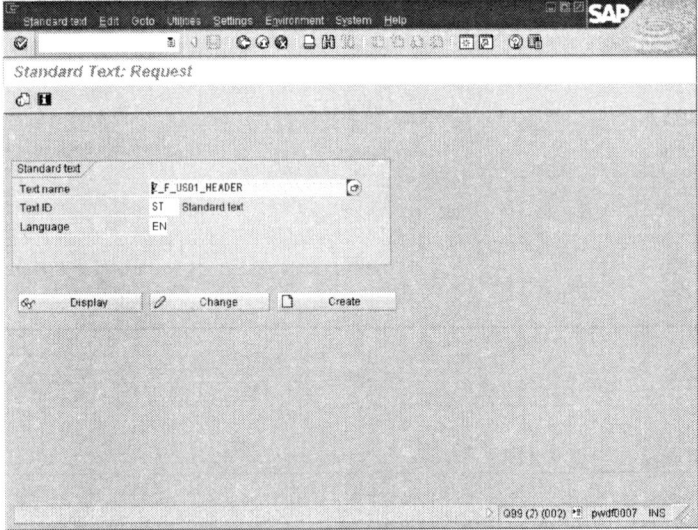

3. On the *Change Standard text: <...> Language <...> screen*:

   a. Enter the desired text.

   b. Save the new or changed standard text.

   c. Go *Back* to return to the *Standard Text: Request* screen.

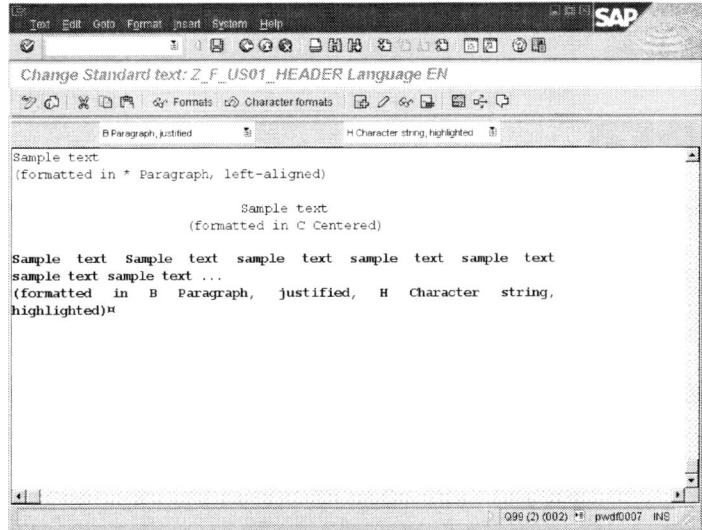

The illustration above shows you some examples of text formatting created with SAP-delivered paragraph and character formats.

4. Go *Back* to return to the SAP standard menu.

5. To print specified standard text for footer text, signature, and sender, make sure, that the following control commands are used in the form:

TechTalk

> To print the standard texts for footer text, signature, and sender, you must use the following control commands in the form:
>
> Footer:
> INCLUDE &REGUD-TXTFU& OBJECT TEXT ID ADRS
>
> Signature:
> INCLUDE &REGUD-TXTUN& OBJECT TEXT ID ADRS
>
> Sender:
> INCLUDE &REGUD-TXTAB& OBJECT TEXT ID ADRS
>
> Make sure that you use the correct text ID in the control commands.

8

Specifying Check Printing Options

In this section you will learn how to:

- Specify the number of test prints before a check run
- Specify multiple printers for:
  - printing checks
  - check run summary

To adjust your printer before a check run, specify the number of test prints you want. You specify the number of test prints in the variant of the print program (for example, program *RFFOUS_C*, variant *Z1*).

To adjust the variant of the print program to print the checks and a summary of checks run on different printers, specify multiple printers.

Task

Create a variant of the print program and specify the number of test prints. Specify multiple printers for printing checks and the check run summary.

1. Access the *SAP Reference IMG* (see "Accessing the IMG" on page 162).

2. Choose *Financial Accounting → Accounts Receivable and Accounts Payable → Business Transactions → Outgoing Payments → Automatic Outgoing Payments → Payment Method/Bank Selection → Configure payment program.*

3. On the *Payment Program Configuration: Initial Screen*, choose *Payment methods/country.*

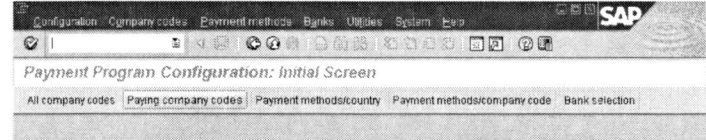

4. On the *Maintain Payment Program Configuration: Countries* screen, double-click on the appropriate country.

   In this example double-click on *U.S. (United States)*. If you can not find the line U.S., scroll down the screen.

5. On the *Maintain Payment Program Configuration: Country Pmnt Methods – List* screen, choose the appropriate payment method for checks.

   In this example double-click on *C (Checks)*.

6. On the *Maintain Payment Program Configuration: Country Pmnt Methods – Details* screen, choose *Environment → Print prog. variants*.

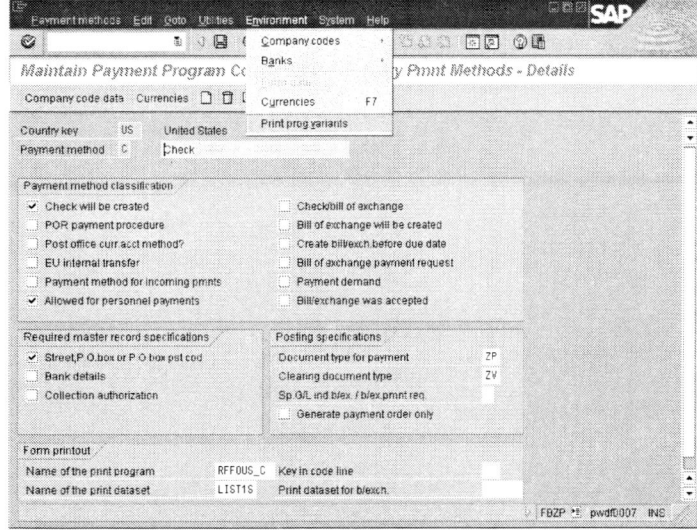

7. On the *ABAP: Variants – Initial Screen:*

a. Enter the name of your variant (for example, **Z1**) in the *Variant* field.

b. If the variant already exist choose 🖉 *Change*.

If the variant does not exist, choose 🗋 *Create*.

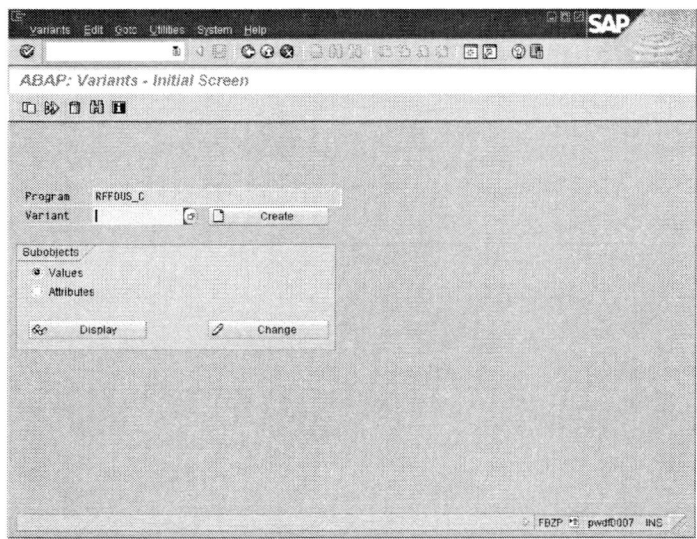

8

8. On the *Maintain Variants: Report RFFOUS_C, Variant Z1* screen:

    a. Scroll down until you see the *Print Control* section.

    b. In the *Print control* section, select the *Print checks* and *Print payment summary* fields and enter different printer names in the corresponding *Printer* fields.

    c. Scroll down until you see the *Output Control* section.

    d. In the *Output control* section, enter the number of desired test prints in the *Number of sample printouts* field.

    e. Save your changes.

       If you use the CTS, specify a transport request after saving.

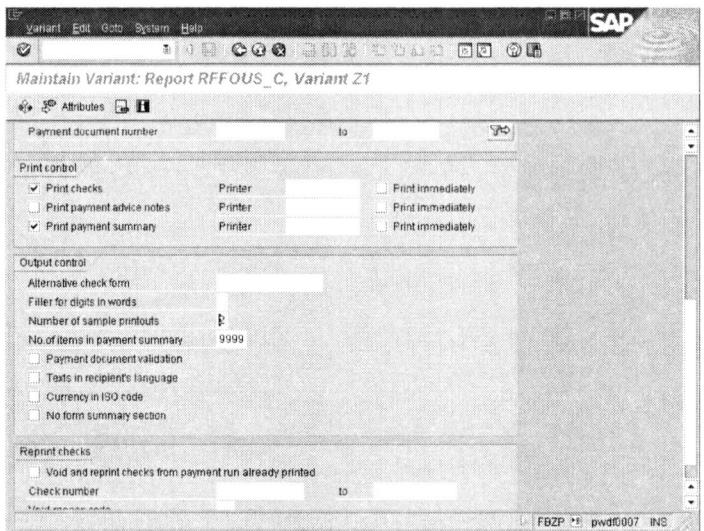

9. Choose *Exit* three times to return to the *Payment Program Configuration: Initial Screen*.

10. Go *Back* to return to the *Display IMG* screen.

PART FOUR

Appendixes

SAPscript Control Commands

Overview

The functionality of the SAPscript editor is determined by a number of commands, which you can either choose from the menu or call with function keys. These commands edit the text in the editor based on your requirements, and commands are immediately executed.

In contrast, SAPscript recognizes another type of commands, the control commands, which:

- Correspondingly influence the output formatting

- Are not interpreted by the SAPscript editor

- Only affect the SAPscript Composer

The Composer is a program that converts text from the editor display into the print display. This program formats the line and pages where symbols are replaced by their current values and text formatting is based on the paragraph and the character style formats.

Overview of SAPscript Control Commands

Table A–1 SAPscript control commands

SAPscript Commands	Description
ADDRESS	Formatting of addresses
BOTTOM, ENDBOTTOM	Define footer text in a window
BOX, POSITION, SIZE	Boxes, lines and shading
CASE, ENDCASE	Case distinction
DEFINE	Value assignment to text symbols
HEX, ENDHEX	Hexadecimal values
IF, ENDIF	Conditional text output
INCLUDE	Include other texts
NEW-PAGE	Explicit forms feed
NEW-WINDOW	Next window MAIN
PERFORM, ENDPERFORM	Calling ABAP Subroutines
PRINT-CONTROL	Insert print control character
PROTECT, ENDPROTECT	Protect from page break
RESET	Initialize outline paragraphs
SET COUNTRY	Country-specific formatting
SET DATE MASK	Formatting of date fields
SET SIGN	Position of +/- sign
SET TIME MASK	Formatting of time fields
STYLE	Change style
SUMMING	Summing variables
TOP	Set header text in window MAIN

Overview of Formatting Options

Formatting options format variables and override the format described in the *Dictionary*. Formatting options are always specified within &-& variable brackets.

Table A–2 SAPscript formatting options

Formatting Options	Description
Changing the value of a counter	Increasing or decreasing the value of a counter
Country dependent formatting	Specifying formats for country dependent values
Date mask	Formatting date fields
Exponent for floating point numbers	Specifying an exponent for floating point values
Fill characters	Replacing leading spaces with fill characters
Ignoring conversion rules	Ignoring conversion rules from Dictionary
Leading sign to the left	Leading sign of numeric values is on the left
Leading sign to the right	Leading sign of numeric values is on the right
Number of decimals	Specifying the number of decimal places
Offset	Specifying an offset of n characters
Omitting leading zeros	Omitting the leading zeros
Omitting the leading sign	Omitting the leading sign of numeric values
Omitting the separator for 'Thousands'	Omitting the separator for "Thousands" in numeric values

Syntax of Control Commands

SAPscript control commands differ from normal text lines in the following ways:

PC Editor

- Control commands are highlighted gray.

- Control commands are inserted, changed or deleted using a dialog window.

Text Editor

- Control commands are indicated with the paragraph format /: in the tag column.

- Control commands are entered, changed, or deleted in the SAPscript editor in the same way as other text lines.

PC Editor and Text Editor

- All key words and specifications, not defined in quotes as literal, are automatically converted to upper case.

- Enter the complete control command and the necessary parameters on one line.

- Enter only one control command per line.

- Editor formatting does not affect lines with control commands.

If the control command is unknown or syntactically incorrect, the command line is treated as a comment line, and is not interpreted or printed.

Tips & Tricks

If a parameter of a control command is written in square brackets ([ ]) on the following pages, then this parameter is optional for the command.

TechTalk

Some of the control commands are global settings, which are valid until they are explicitly switched off. Therefore, it is important to know that, on a page, the MAIN window is always processed first. For example, if you want to set the date format with the control command *SET DATE FORMAT* and this format must be valid for the entire form, then specify this command at the top of *MAIN*.

Note

All examples in appendix A show the syntax for the Text Editor. The syntax for the PC Editor is identically except the paragraph format /: in the tag column, because the PC Editor does not use a tag column anymore.

ADDRESS–ENDADDRESS: Formatting of Addresses

The command formats an address according to the postal standards of the destination country defined in the parameter *COUNTRY*. The reference fields are described in the structure *ADRS*. Both constants and symbols can be assigned to the parameters.

A

Syntax

```
/:  ADDRESS [DELIVERY] [PARAGRAPH a] [PRIORITY p] [LINES 1]
/:  TITLE title
/:  NAME name1[,name2[,name3[,name4]]]
/:  STREET street
/:  POBOX PO box [CODE zip code]
/:  POSTCODE zip code
/:  CITY town1[,town2]
/:  REGION region
/:  COUNTRY country
/:  FROMCOUNTRY from country
/:  ENDADDRESS
```

Both formatting data and address data are parameters. Address data is formatted for output based on the *COUNTRY, PRIORITY* and *LINES* parameters. As the default, the P.O. Box is used, if it is available, rather than the street address.

- **DELIVERY** defines the street address.

  If this parameter is selected, the system prints the street address on the layout output instead of the P.O. Box.

- **PARAGRAPH** defines in which paragraph format the address is output.

  If the parameter is not defined, the address is output in the default paragraph format.

- **PRIORITY** defines which address lines can be omitted if there is not enough space on the output.

  You can enter a combination of the following values:

Table A–3 PRIORITY parameter values

Value	Description
A	form of address
P	mandatory blank line 1
Q	mandatory blank line 2
2	name 2
3	name 3
4	name 4
L	country name
S	line for the street
O	line for the city

- *LINES* define how many lines are available to format the address. If the address data cannot be completely formatted due to an insufficient number of lines, the data entered in the parameter PRIORITY is omitted. If the LINES specification is missing and this command is in a form window whose type is not MAIN, the lines available for the address layout are automatically calculated with the current output line item and window size.

- *TITLE* is a required form of address.

- *NAME* means that up to four separate names, separated by commas, can be defined.

- *STREET* means the street specification, including address number.

- *POBOX* is the Post Office box number.

- *CODE* is the P.O. box, postal, or zip code, if this code is different from the postal code of the city.

- *POSTCODE* is city's postal, or zip, code.

- *CITY* means that up to two place names can be defined.

- *REGION* determines the administrative area.

- *COUNTRY* specifies the country based on specific postal standards and the address format.

- *FROMCOUNTRY* defines in which language the destination country's name is formatted. In EEC countries, only the international country identification letter is placed, with a hyphen, before the postal code.

Example

```
/: ADDRESS
/: TITLE 'Company'
/: NAME 'Widget Technology, Inc.', 'All Kinds of Widgets'
/: STREET '1005 Lido Lane'
/: POBOX '2935' CODE '94400'
/: POSTCODE '94404'
/: CITY 'Foster City'
/: REGION 'CA'
/: COUNTRY 'USA'
/: FROMCOUNTRY 'USA'
/: ENDADDRESS
```

This list generates the following address:

Company
Widget Technology, Inc.
All Kinds of Widgets
PO box 2935
Foster City, CA 94400

If the DELIVERY supplement is specified for the ADDRESS command, then the street, not the P.O. Box, is entered.

Company
Widget Technology, Inc.
All Kinds of Widgets
1005 Lido Lane
Foster City, CA 94404

TechTalk

> SAPscript calls the ADDRESS_INTO_PRINTFORM function module to format the address. If the display is not in the required form, check the settings that are valid for this function module (see the documentation on the function module).

BOTTOM: Define Footer Text in a Window

For *MAIN*, determine the lines, also known as footer texts, which are always automatically output at the bottom of that window.

Syntax

```
/:  BOTTOM
      :
      :
/:  ENDBOTTOM
```

The text lines between the two commands are output at the bottom of *MAIN*.

Example

To switch a footer text off, enter the command pair BOTTOM.. ENDBOTTOM with no text lines in between:

```
/:  BOTTOM
/:  ENDBOTTOM
```

Footer text no longer appears at the bottom of the page from and including this page.

TechTalk

> If there is sufficient space in the window, a footer text is output on the current page.
>
> Only use footer texts in texts that are not printed with application programs, such as dunning texts, ordering texts. These application programs also work with footer texts with the form interface, which can lead to unwanted results.

BOX, POSITION, SIZE: Boxes, Lines, Shading

The *BOX, POSITION* and *SIZE* commands draw boxes, lines, and shadows. Within any particular form, these commands specify window or passage of window text can be output in a frame or with shadowing. The SAP printer drivers based on page-oriented printers (the HP LaserJet PCL-5 driver HPLJ4, the Postscript driver POST, the Kyocera Prescribe driver PRES) use these commands when creating output. Line printers and nonsupported page-oriented printers ignore these commands. The resulting output may be viewed in the SAPscript print previewer.

BOX

Syntax

```
/: BOX [XPOS] [YPOS] [WIDTH] [HEIGHT] [FRAME] [INTENSITY]
```

This command draws a box of the specified size at the specified position. For each parameter (*XPOS, YPOS, WIDTH, HEIGHT,* and *FRAME*), both a measurement and a unit of measure must be specified. The *INTENSITY* parameter should be entered as a percentage between 0 and 100.

- **XPOS, YPOS** specify the upper left corner of the box, relative to *POSITION* command values.
  Default is the values specified in the *POSITION* command.
  The following calculation is performed internally to determine the absolute output position of a box on the page:
  $X(abs) = XORIGIN + XPOS$
  $Y(abs) = YORIGIN + YPOS$

- **WIDTH** determines the width of the box.
  Default: *WIDTH* value of the *SIZE* command

- **HEIGHT** determines height of the box.
  Default: *HEIGHT* value of the *SIZE* command

- **FRAME** determines the thickness of frame.
  Default: 0 (no frame)

- **INTENSITY** determines the box contents as a grayscale percentage.
  Default: 100 (full black)

When determining the measurements, use decimal numbers to specify literal values (like ABAP numeric constants) and enclose these values in inverted commas. Use a period for the decimal point character. See also the examples listed below.

Use the following units of measure:

- TW (twip)

- PT (point)

- IN (inch)

- MM (millimeter)

- CM (centimeter)

- LN (line)

- CH (character)

The following conversion factors apply:

- 1 TW = 1/20 PT

- 1 PT = 1/72 IN

- 1 IN = 2.54 CM

- 1 CM = 10 MM

- 1 CH = height of a character relative to the CPI specification in the form header

- 1 LN = height of a line relative to the LPI specification in the form header

Example

```
/: BOX FRAME 10 TW
```

The above command draws a frame around the current window with a thickness of 10 TW (= 0.5 PT).

```
/: BOX INTENSITY 10
```

The above command fills the window background with shadowing having a gray scale of 10 %.

```
/: BOX HEIGHT 0 TW FRAME 10 TW
```

The above command draws a horizontal line across the complete top edge of the window.

```
/: BOX WIDTH 0 TW FRAME 10 TW
```

The above command draws a vertical line along the complete height of the left hand edge of the window.

```
/: BOX WIDTH '17.5' CM HEIGHT 1 CM FRAME 10 TW INTENSITY 15
/: BOX WIDTH '17.5' CM HEIGHT '13.5' CM FRAME 10 TW
/: BOX XPOS '10.0' CM WIDTH 0 TW HEIGHT '13.5' CM FRAME 10 TW
/: BOX XPOS '13.5' CM WIDTH 0 TW HEIGHT '13.5' CM FRAME 10 TW
```

The above commands draw two rectangles and two lines to construct a table of three columns with a highlighted heading.

POSITION

Syntax

```
/: POSITION [XORIGIN] [YORIGIN] [WINDOW] [PAGE]
```

This command sets the origin for the coordinate system used by the *XPOS* and *YPOS* parameters of the *BOX* command. When a window is first started, the *POSITION* value is set to refer to the upper left corner of the window (default setting). If a parameter value does not have a leading sign, then its value is interpreted as an absolute value, which is a value that specifies an offset from the upper-left corner of the output page. If a parameter value is specified with a leading sign, then the new value of the parameter is calculated relative to the old value. If a parameter specification is missing, then this parameter is unchanged.

- *XORIGIN, YORIGIN* is the origin of the coordinate system.

- *WINDOW* sets the values for the left and upper edges to be the same of those of the current window (default setting).

- *PAGE* sets the values for the left and upper edges to be the same as the current output page (*XORIGIN* = 0 cm, *YORIGIN* = 0 cm).

Example

```
/: POSITION WINDOW
```
The above command sets the origin for the coordinate system to the upper-left corner of the window.

```
/: POSITION XORIGIN 2 CM YORIGIN '2.5 CM'
```
The above command sets the origin for the coordinate system to a point 2 cm from the left edge and 2.5 cm from the upper edge of the output page.

```
/: POSITION XORIGIN '-1.5' CM YORIGIN -1 CM
```
The above command shifts the origin for the coordinates 1.5 cm to the left and 1 cm up.

SIZE

Syntax

```
/: SIZE [WIDTH] [HEIGHT] [WINDOW] [PAGE]
```

This command sets the values of the *WIDTH* and *HEIGHT* parameters used in the *BOX* command. When a window is first started, the *SIZE* value is set to the same values as the window (default setting). If one of the parameter specifications is missing, then no change is made to its current value. If a parameter value does not have a leading sign,

A

then its value is interpreted as an absolute value. If a parameter value is specified with a leading sign, then the new value of the parameter is calculated relative to the old value.

- *WIDTH, HEIGHT* sets the dimensions of the rectangle or line.

- *WINDOW* sets the values for the width and height relative to the values of the current window (default setting).

- *PAGE* sets the values for the width and height to the values of the current output page.

Example

```
/: SIZE WINDOW
```

The above command sets WIDTH and HEIGHT to the current window dimensions.

```
/: SIZE WIDTH '3.5' CM HEIGHT '7.6' CM
```

The above command sets WIDTH to 3.5 cm and HEIGHT to 7.6 cm.

```
/: POSITION WINDOW
/: POSITION XORIGIN -20 TW YORIGIN -20 TW
/: SIZE WIDTH +40 TW HEIGHT +40 TW
/: BOX FRAME 10 TW
```

With the above commands, a frame is added to the current window. The frame edges extend beyond the window itself, to avoid obscuring the leading and trailing text characters.

CASE: Case Distinction

The *CASE* command is a special case of multi-level case distinction with IF commands. As a condition for the different cases, only one symbol can be queried for equality with different values.

Syntax

```
/: CASE symbol
/: WHEN value1
     :
/: WHEN value2
     :
/: WHEN value n
     :
/: WHEN OTHERS
     :
/: ENDCASE
```

The symbol entered in the *CASE* line is formatted. If it has a value specified in the individual *WHEN* lines, the text following the valid *WHEN* line is output. If none of the listed values apply, the lines between the *WHEN OTHERS* line and *ENDCASE* are output. The *WHEN OTHERS* case is optional. Comparison is always carried out as a literal comparison as for the IF command.

TechTalk

> *ENDCASE* must end a *CASE* command, but the *WHEN OTHERS* command is optional.

DEFINE: Value Assignment to Text Symbols

Text symbols receive their value through an explicit assignment. This assignment can be made interactively in the editor by choosing *Include → Symbols → Text*. This step lists all the text symbols of a text module and those of the allocated form. If the transaction is exited, the contents defined in this way are lost. To continue printing the text module, you would have to enter the symbol values again.

The *DEFINE* command allows you to anchor this value assignment in the text and to have it available when you next call up the text. Furthermore, you can allocate another value to a text symbol in the course of the text.

Syntax

```
/: DEFINE &symbolname& = 'value'
```

Example

```
/: DEFINE &re& = 'Your correspondence of 3/17/94'
/: DEFINE &symbol1& = 'xxxxxxx'
/: DEFINE &symbol2& = 'yyy&symbol1&'
/: DEFINE &symbol1& = 'zzzzzzz'
```

Result:

&symbol2& → yyyzzzzzzz

The assigned value may have a maximum of 60 characters, but it can also contain more symbols. When a symbol is defined using *DEFINE*, symbols which occur in the value are not immediately replaced by their value. They are replaced only when the target symbol is output.

If operator *:=* is used in *DEFINE*, the symbols that occur in the value to be assigned are immediately replaced by their current values. The resulting character string is only then assigned to the target symbol when all occurring symbols have been replaced. The length of the value is limited to 80 characters, and the target symbol must be a text symbol.

Syntax

```
/: DEFINE &symbolname& := 'value'
```

HEX: Hexadecimal Data

This command sends printer commands in a printer language directly to a printer that supports that language. SAPscript does not interpret the data enclosed by the *HEX* and *ENDHEX* command pair, but inserts unchanged data into the output stream. This technique allows objects with a pixel-oriented format to be printed as part of a SAPscript text. The *HEX* and *ENDHEX* command pair enclose the printer commands and data as hexadecimal text, so that the printer formatting routines interpret each successive pair of characters as a single hexadecimal value in the 0..255 range.

The characters 0..9 and A..F to represent the values 10..15 are valid hexadecimal characters. The text may also include comment lines (these begin with /* in the format column), which will not be interpreted as hexadecimal data but are simply passed over by the formatting routines.

Syntax

```
/: HEX [TYPE printer_language]
      :
      :
/: ENDHEX
```

HEX denotes the start of the hexadecimal data. Subsequent text lines are interpreted as described above. If the *TYPE* parameter is present, the data will be sent to the printer only if the printer understands the specified printer language. The following printer languages are currently supported:

- *POST* (Postscript)

- *PRES* (Kyocera Prescribe)

- *PCL* (HP Printer Control Language)

```
/: HEX [TYPE printer_language] [XPOS x_position] [YPOS
y_position]
```

Before the hexadecimal data is output, the output cursor is set to the absolute position indicated by the specified X and Y position parameters. If either the X or the Y position is not specified, then 0 will be assumed for this parameter.

```
/: HEX [TYPE printer_language] [HEIGHT height] [LEFT
left_indentation]
```

The *HEIGHT* parameter determines the amount of space to be reserved on the page for the output of the hexadecimal data. Any text after *ENDHEX* will be output below this point. If the *LEFT* parameter is also specified, then the output of the hexadecimal data will be indented from the left margin by the specified amount.

Example

```
/* Creator: report ZQVNTE30 date 19940705 time 125129 user
SAPSCRIPT
/=
1B2A7230461B2A743735521B2A7231411B2A62304D1B2A62343057FFFFFF
FFFFFF
/=
FF1B2A62343057FFFFFFFFFFFFC0007D00DFC0F7D0000000000000000000
000017
/: ENDHEX
```

This data will be printed only by an HP PCL printer (7.5 cm of space will allocated on the page for the output of the data and the output cursor will be indented 2.25 cm to the right of the form window edge).

TechTalk

The *RSTXLDMC* program uploads correctly formatted pixel data to the R/3 System and prepares it as a *HEX-ENDHEX* control command. This data can be saved then as normal SAPscript text.

IF: Conditional Text Output

With the *IF* control command, define those lines that are output under certain conditions. If the logical expression entered for the *IF* command is fulfilled, the lines parenthesized by *IF ... ENDIF* are output. If this expression is not enclosed in parentheses, the commands are ignored.

Syntax

```
/: IF Condition
      :
      :
/: ENDIF
```

In the condition, the following relational operators are possible:

Table A–4 Relational operators overview

Relational Operator	Description
= or *EQ*	equals
< or *LT*	less than
> or *GT*	greater than
<= or *LE*	less than or equal to
>= or *GE*	greater than or equal to

As logical link operators use *OR, NOT,* or *AND.*

The sequence of processing the logical operations and the sequence of processing the conditions is always from left to right. There is no order of binding, and bracketing is not allowed.

Comparison is always carried out as a literal comparison, that is, symbols are compared in their formatted form as a character string and not with their internal representation. This comparison must be taken into account for program symbols whose format depends on different parameters. Examples include currency fields that are output with different number of places after the decimal point depending on the currency key, or that use a comma or a period as the decimal separator depending on the setting.

The *IF* command can be extended to make a two-sided case distinction with the *ELSE* command. If the specified *IF* condition is true, then the lines listed between *IF* and *ELSE* are formatted, otherwise the lines between *ELSE* and *ENDIF* are formatted.

Syntax

```
/: IF Condition
      :
/: ELSE
      :
/: ENDIF
```

A multilevel case distinction is possible using the *ELSEIF* command.

Syntax

```
/: IF Condition
      :
/: ELSEIF Condition
      :
/: ELSE
      :
/: ENDIF
```

You can use as many *ELSEIF* commands as required. The specification of an *ELSE* command is optional in this case.

TechTalk

The condition must not extend over several lines, and must be contained in one line with the IF or ELSEIF command.

IF commands can also be nested.

An IF command must always end with ENDIF. If this command is forgotten, and if the condition is not true, nothing more is output after the IF command.

If a syntax error is found when interpreting these commands, the corresponding command is not executed. This can have various effects on the following text output. If, for example, the IF statement is incorrectly structured, since IF is missing, the following ELSEIF or ELSE commands are ignored. All lines are output.

INCLUDE: Include Other Texts

Use *INCLUDE* to include the contents of another text into your text. The text to be included exists separately from yours and is only copied at the time of the output formatting. With *INCLUDE*, since the text is only read and inserted during the output formatting, the most current version of the required text is always available.

Syntax

```
/: INCLUDE name [OBJECT o] [ID i] [LANGUAGE l] [PARAGRAPH p]
[NEW-PARAGRAPH np]
```

The name of the text to be inserted must be specified and can have up to 70 characters. If the text name contains blanks, put it in quotes as a literal. It can also be specified with a symbol. All further parameters of *INCLUDE* are optional. If these parameters are missing, SAPscript uses default values based on the respective call environment for them.

Example

```
/: INCLUDE MYTEXT
```
The text MYTEXT is included in the language of the calling text.

```
/: INCLUDE MYTEXT LANGUAGE 'E' PARAGRAPH 'A1'
```
The text with the name MYTEXT and the language E is included, regardless of the language in which the calling text is created. The paragraph format A1 is valid as the standard paragraph for this call.

Optional Specifications

- *LANGUAGE*

  A

  If a language is unspecified, the calling text's language or the form is set for the text to be included. If a language is specified, the text is always loaded in this language, regardless of the language of the calling text.

- *PARAGRAPH*

  The text to be included is formatted with its style allocation. With this parameter, the standard paragraph of this style can be redefined for the current call. All * paragraphs of the inserted text are formatted with the paragraph specified here.

- *NEW-PARAGRAPH*

  The first line of the included text has this format flag, provided it is not a command or comment line. If the optional entry PARAGRAPH (see above) is empty, all * paragraphs of the included text are formatted with the paragraph np specified with NEW-PARAGRAPH.

- *OBJECT*

  To completely specify a text, create additional specifications about the text object. There are different rules and restrictions for this specification that depends on the calling text's object type. All texts can be included in a form. If no object is entered here, *TEXT* is used (standard texts). With a documentation text (object *DOKU*), you can only include documentation texts. This object is assumed even if no object is specified in this environment.

  Only hypertext or documentation text can be included into a hypertext (object *DSYS*). If the *OBJECT* specification is missing, *DSYS* is set as a default value.

  Only standard text (object *TEXT*), documentation text or hypertext can be included in any other type of text. The default object is *TEXT* if nothing is entered.

- *ID*

  The text ID allows further text types within an object, is a further part of the text key. If the ID is not entered, the default *Include ID* from table *TTXID* is used to call text. If the specification is not in this table, the text ID of the calling text is used.

The ID and the object are now the basis of a further consistency check:

- All text IDs are allowed for a form.

- Only documentation texts with the text IDs *TX* (general texts), *UO* (authorization objects), and documentation texts (with the same text ID as the calling documentation text) may be included in documentation texts.

- All *DSYS* texts may be included in *DSYS* texts, regardless of their ID. Documentation texts that will be inserted may only have IDs *TX* and *UO*.

- Standard texts with the allowed text IDs, *DSYS* texts with IDs, and documentation texts with IDs *TX* and *UO* may be included in the text types.

NEW-PAGE: Explicit Form Feed

SAPscript automatically inserts a page break if MAIN of one page is filled. Using *NEW-PAGE*, a page break can be forced at any point. The text after this command is written on a new page. The form feed is independent of any conditions. The command now outputs the current page.

If you have entered *NEW-PAGE* without additional parameters, the page defined in the form as the next page is accessed. If, however, there are various pages in your form, you can jump to any particular next page by specifying the page name.

Syntax

```
/: NEW-PAGE [page name]
```

Example

```
/: NEW-PAGE
```

The current page is completed and the text in the following lines is written on the next page as determined in the form.

```
/: NEW-PAGE S1
```

Same as before, but S1 is accessed as the next page.

Caution

If an explicitly specified page for *NEW-PAGE* is not in the form, this page specification is ignored. Make sure that there are no blank lines immediately before a *NEW-PAGE* command. If an implicit form feed was carried out within these blank lines, this step could lead to an unwanted empty page being printed.

A

NEW-WINDOW: Next Window MAIN

You can have up to 99 *MAIN* windows on one page. These windows are distinguished by a serial number (0..98) and assigned in this order. So, with SAPscript, it is possible to print labels or to output text in multiple columns. If one *MAIN* window is filled, then the next *MAIN* window on the page is automatically accessed. A page break is inserted at the end of the final *MAIN* window.

Using *NEW-WINDOW*, even if the current window is not completely filled, you can explicitly call the next window *MAIN*. If you are currently in the last *MAIN* window of the page, the command works as a *NEW-PAGE*.

Syntax

```
/: NEW-WINDOW
```

PERFORM: Calling ABAP Subroutines

You can use the *PERFORM* command to call an ABAP subroutine (form) from any program, subject to the normal ABAP runtime authorization checking. You can use such calls to subroutines for carrying out calculations, for obtaining data from the database that is needed at display or print time, for formatting data, and so on.

PERFORM commands, like all control commands, are executed when a document is formatted for display or printing. Communication between a subroutine that you call and the document is by way of symbols whose values are set in the subroutine.

Syntax

```
In a form window:
/: PERFORM <form> IN PROGRAM <prog>
/: USING &INVAR1&
/: USING &INVAR2&
        :
/: CHANGING &OUTVAR1&
/: CHANGING &OUTVAR2&
        :
/: ENDPERFORM
```

INVAR1 and **INVAR2** are variable symbols and may be any of the four SAPscript symbol types.

OUTVAR1 and **OUTVAR2** are local text symbols and must therefore be character strings.

The ABAP subroutine called via the command line stated above must be defined in the ABAP report **prog** as follows:

```
FORM <form> TABLES IN_TAB STRUCTURE ITCSY
OUT_TAB STRUCTURE ITCSY.
:
ENDFORM.
```

The values of the SAPscript symbols passed with / : USING... are now stored in the internal table *IN_TAB* . Note that the system passes the values as character string to the subroutine, since the field *Feld VALUE* in structure *ITCSY* has the domain *TDSYMVALUE (CHAR 80)*. See the example below on how to access the variables.

The internal table **OUT_TAB** contains names and values of the *CHANGING* parameters in the *PERFORM* statement. These parameters are local text symbols, that is, character fields. See the example below on how to return the variables within the subroutine.

Example

From within a SAPscript form, a subroutine *GET_BARCODE* in the ABAP program *QCJPERFO* is called. Then the simple barcode contained there ('First page', 'Next page', 'Last page') is printed as local variable symbol.

Definition in the SAPscript form:

```
/: PERFORM GET_BARCODE IN PROGRAM QCJPERFO
/: USING &PAGE&
/: USING &NEXTPAGE&
/: CHANGING &BARCODE&
/: ENDPERFORM
/
/ &BARCODE&
```

Coding of the calling ABAP program:

```
REPORT QCJPERFO.

FORM GET_BARCODE TABLES IN_PAR STUCTURE ITCSY
OUT_PAR STRUCTURE ITCSY.
```

PRINT-CONTROL: Insert Print Control Character

This command allows you call certain printer functions from SAPscript text. The control characters for the printer cannot be directly entered into your text. First, with the spool transaction *SPAD*, define a print control that contains the required printer commands. This print control can now be called with the SAPscript command *PRINT-CONTROL*.

Syntax

```
/: PRINT-CONTROL name
```

The name of the required print control can be entered with or without quotes.

Caution

SAPscript has no idea of what is contained in the print control. It cannot check whether the printer commands hidden behind it are functional. If problems result when printing such a text, first print the text without the print controls, and then activate each *PRINT-CONTROL* command to help you locate the error more easily.

On completion, make sure that the defined print control sequences restore the printer to a defined status. When printing subsequent texts, SAPscript assumes that certain settings are still valid (type font, current page). If these settings are changed by the called printer commands, this change can have unwanted effects.

After performing *PRINT-CONTROL*, SAPscript inserts a blank at the start of the following line. If this is not required, this line must have the paragraph format "=."

PROTECT: Protect from Page Break

You can determine whether a paragraph should or should not be separated by a page break in the style or form. If the attribute page protection is set, then all the lines of this paragraph are always output together on one page. This attribute is linked to the respective paragraph.

It is not beneficial to provide all paragraphs with a page protection attribute to neutralize unwanted page breaks. This event is too dynamic and only results from the current text. Furthermore, you may also want to protect only parts of a paragraph from a page break.

In principle, this problem could be solved with *NEW-PAGE* by explicitly starting a new page before the affected parts of the text. However, it is complicated to change this procedure. Using NEW-PAGE, if your text is formatted to have no unwanted page breaks, and new lines are inserted and existing ones are deleted, the *NEW-PAGE* commands inserted after this point will have to be checked and can result in the movement of page breaks.

With the command pair *PROTECT .. ENDPROTECT*, SAPscript offers the option to individually define protection from a page break. If you parenthesize text with these commands, SAPscript automatically guarantees that all of its lines are printed on one page. If the lines fit on the current output page, they are output there, as if *PROTECT* was not used. If, however, the space is not sufficient, *PROTECT* works like a NEW-PAGE and generates a form feed.

So, you can view *PROTECT/ENDPROTECT* are conditional *NEW-PAGE* commands, that determine whether the included lines fit into the current window *MAIN* or not.

Syntax

```
/: PROTECT
       :
       :
/: ENDPROTECT
```

The lines to be protected lie between the two commands.

TechTalk

An *ENDPROTECT* command without a preceding *PROTECT* command is ineffective.

If the last *ENDPROTECT* is missing, it is implicitly assumed at the end of the text.

PROTECT .. ENDPROTECT commands cannot be nested. If a second *PROTECT* command is recognized while another is active, the second is ignored.

If the text between *PROTECT* and *ENDPROTECT* is so extensive that it would not fit on an empty page, then only one form feed is generated and the text is normally output. Thus, in this case, the section to be protected is separated by a page break.

RESET: Initialize Outline Paragraphs

The *RESET* command resets the numbering of an outline paragraph to its initial value. If the user does not use *RESET*, all the outline paragraphs of a text are sequentially numbered. If the name of an outline paragraph is entered in *RESET*, the numbering of this paragraph, is initialized with subordinate outline levels.

Syntax

```
/: RESET paragraph format
```

The paragraph format specifies the outline paragraph to be initialized.

Example

Assume that paragraph N1 is defined in the style you are using. This paragraph should be used for listings and each time it generates an output of a list number. This is the SAPscript editor:

```
AS If you want to work with the SAP R/3 System, proceed as
follows:
N1 Make sure that you have a PC
N1 Switch on the PC
```

```
N1 Click on the SAP icon.
AS The SAP logon screen appears. To log on, you must carry
out the following steps:
/: RESET N1
N1 Enter your user ID
N1 Enter your password
N1 Choose the application you require
```

Result:

If you want to work with the SAP R/3 System, proceed as follows:

1. Make sure that you have a PC

2. Switch on the PC

3. Click on the SAP icon.

The SAP logon screen appears. To log on, you must carry out the following steps:

1. Enter your user ID

2. Enter your password

3. Choose the application you require.

If the *RESET* command between the two lines in the previous example is missing, then both of the listings would be sequentially numbered:

Result:

If you want to work with the SAP R/3 System, proceed as follows:

1. Make sure that you have a PC

2. Switch on the PC

3. Click on the SAP icon.

The SAP logon screen appears. To log on, you must carry out the following steps:

4. Enter your user ID

5. Enter your password

6. Choose the application you require.

SET COUNTRY: Country-Specific Formatting

Some field types are formatted to be country-specific. This includes the display of a date, the decimal point, or the thousands separator. Normally, the display types defined in the user master record are used here. With the control command *SET COUNTRY*, a format alternative to that in the user master record can be chosen, which is stored country-specifically in table *T005X*.

Syntax

```
/: SET COUNTRY Country key
```

This country key can be entered either directly in quotes or with a symbol.

Example

```
/: SET COUNTRY 'CAN'
/: SET COUNTRY &Country key&
```

By entering an empty country name, you can return to the values set in the user master record.

```
/: SET COUNTRY ' '
```

The corresponding ABAP command is called internally by SAPscript.

Tips & Tricks

If the required formats are incorrect, check the settings in table *T005X*.

SET DATE MASK: Formatting of Date Fields

Formatting date fields can be defined with the SAPscript command *SET DATE MASK*. After executing this command, all the date fields are output with this display.

Syntax

```
/: SET DATE MASK = 'date mask'
```

In the date mask, the following edit formats can be used:

Table A–5 Date mask: Edit formats

Edit format	Description
DD	Day (two-digit)
DDD	Day name abbreviated
DDDD	Day name in full
MM	Month (two-digit)
MMM	Month name abbreviated
MMMM	Month name in full
YY	Year (two-digit)
YYYY	Year (four-digit)

All other characters in the mask are interpreted as text and copied correspondingly.

Example

Assume that the current system date is March 1, 2000.

```
/: SET DATE MASK = 'Walldorf, DD.MM.YY'
&DATE&
```

Result:

Walldorf, 01.03.00

```
/: SET DATE MASK = 'DD, MMMM, YYYY'
&DATE&
```

Result:

01 March 2000

Example

By specifying an empty string as the date mask, you can switch back to the default display:

```
/: SET DATE MASK = ' '
```

Note

The texts for the month and day names, shortened or in full, are stored language-dependently in table *TTDTG* under the following arguments:

Table A–6 Table TTDTG: Date mask arguments

Argument	Description
%%SAPSCRIPT_DDD_dd	abbreviated day name
	dd = day number (01 = Monday ... 07 = Sunday)
%%SAPSCRIPT_DDDD_dd	full day name
%%SAPSCRIPT_MMM_mm	abbreviated month name
	mm = month number (01 = January ... 12 = December)
%%SAPSCRIPT_MMMM_mm	full month name

SET SIGN: The Position of +/-

For commercial applications, it is common for the "+/-" signs to be displayed to the right of the number value. In certain cases, however, it is necessary for these signs to be displayed to the left of the number value. This position can be determined with the control command *SET SIGN*. All program symbols formatted using this command and that have a "+/-" sign are displayed in the required fashion.

Syntax

```
/: SET SIGN LEFT
```

The +/- sign is displayed to the left of the number.

```
/: SET SIGN RIGHT
```

The +/- sign is displayed to the right of the number.

SET TIME MASK: Formatting of Time Fields

With the SAPscript command *SET TIME MASK* time fields can be alternatively formatted to the standard display.

Syntax

```
/: SET TIME MASK = 'time mask'
```

The following edit formats can be used in the time mask:

- HH = hours (two-digit)

- MM = minutes (two-digit)

- SS = seconds (two-digit)

All other characters in the mask are interpreted as text and printed correspondingly.

Example

Assume that the current time is 10:08:12.

```
/: SET TIME MASK = 'HH:MM'
&TIME&
```

Result:

10:08

```
/: SET TIME MASK = 'HH hours MM minutes'
&TIME&
```

Result:

10 hours 08 minutes

By specifying an empty string as a time mask, you can switch back to the default display:

```
/: SET TIME MASK = ' '
```

STYLE: Change Style

The control command *STYLE* changes style within a text. This other style is used until a new *STYLE* command is entered. If * is entered as a style name, switch back to the original style.

Syntax

```
/: STYLE style
/: STYLE *
```

If another text module is inserted by choosing *Include → Text* and immediately deleted, *STYLE* is automatically set in the editor. The same occurs if the text contents included in *INCLUDE* are copied into the text by choosing *Edit → Selected area → Delete INCLUDE*.

SUMMING

Program symbols can be added with the *SUMMING* command. The command needs to be defined only once. Each time that the specified symbol is edited, its current value is added to the sum field. Several program symbols can also be added in a sum field.

```
/:SUMMING program symbol INTO sum symbol
```

Since SAPscript can not dynamically define sum fields, the sum symbol must be in a calling program structure that was declared with *TABLES*.

TOP: Set Header Text in MAIN

In *MAIN*, lines that are always automatically output at the top of the window, called header texts, can be determined. Header texts can automatically repeat the table heading at the top of every page for an extensive tabular list.

Syntax

```
/: TOP
     :
     :
/: ENDTOP
```

Those text lines between the two commands will be output at the top of *MAIN*.

To switch a header text off, enter the command pair *TOP .. ENDTOP*, with no lines in between:

```
/: TOP
/: ENDTOP
```

Header text will not appear on subsequent pages.

Tips & Tricks

If the document window contains text, then the header text is effective from the next page.

The same applies to deleting a header text. That is, a header text that has already been output can no longer be canceled on the current page.

Only use header texts in texts that are not printed with application programs, such as dunning texts and ordering texts. These application programs can also work with header texts in the form interface, which can lead to unwanted results.

Syntax of Formatting Options

A

Changing the Value of a Counter

You can increase or decrease the value of *SAPSCRIPT-COUNTER_x* *(x=0.. 9)* counter variable by 1, before the current counter value is printed.

Syntax

```
&SAPSCRIPT-COUNTER_x(+)& Increases by 1 the contents
of the counter variable x
(x=0.. 9)
&SAPSCRIPT-COUNTER_x(-)& Decreases by 1 the contents
of the counter variable x
(x=0.. 9)
```

If you want to change the value of a counter variable without actually printing the new value, use this formatting option together with an additional option to set the output length to 0 (see above). If you want to set a counter variable to some specific value, use the *DEFINE* control command.

Example

Assume that *&SAPSCRIPT-COUNTER_1&* initially has the value *2*.

```
&SAPSCRIPT-COUNTER_1&   > 2
&SAPSCRIPT-COUNTER_1(+)&  > 3
&SAPSCRIPT-COUNTER_1(-)&  > 2
&SAPSCRIPT-COUNTER_1(-)&  > 1
&SAPSCRIPT-COUNTER_1(+0)& >
&SAPSCRIPT-COUNTER_1(+)&  > 3
```

Country Dependent Formatting

Certain fields are formatted specific to a particular country. These include fields for displaying a date and numeric fields containing either a decimal point or a 'thousands' separator character. The formatting applied is usually determined by the definitions contained in the user master record. You can use the *SET COUNTRY* control command to choose a different formatting operation. The various country-dependent formatting options are stored in table *T005X*.

Syntax

```
/: SET COUNTRY country_key
```

You can specify this country key either by quoting it directly enclosed in inverted commas or by using a symbol.

```
/: SET COUNTRY 'CAN'
/: SET COUNTRY &KNA1-LAND1&
```

You can revert to the settings of the user master record by using the *SET COUNTRY* control command again with an empty country name.

```
/: SET COUNTRY ' '
```

When SAPscript encounters this command it calls the corresponding ABAP command internally. The effect of the SAPscript command is thus identical with that of the ABAP command.

If the formatting turns out other than expected, check the settings in table *T005X*.

Date Mask

To format date fields, use the SAPscript *SET DATE MASK* command. Executing this command causes all subsequent date fields to be printed with the specified formatting.

Syntax

```
/: SET DATE MASK = 'date_mask'
```

In the date mask, the following edit formats can be used:

Table A–7 Date mask: Edit formats

Template	Description
DD	day (two digits)
DDD	name of day (abbreviated)
DDDD	name of day (written out in full)
MM	month (two digits)
MMM	name of month (abbreviated)
MMMM	name of month (written out in full)
YY	year (two digits)
YYYY	year (four digits)
LD	day (formatted as for the L option)
LM	month (formatted as for the L option)
LY	year (formatted as for the L option)

Any other characters occurring in the mask are interpreted as simple text and are copied directly to the output.

Example

Assuming a current system date of March 1, 2000.

```
/: SET DATE MASK = 'Foster City, MM.DD.YY'
&DATE&
```

Result:

Foster City, 03.01.00

```
/: SET DATE MASK = 'MMMM DD, YYYY'
&DATE&
```

Result:

March 01, 2000

You can revert to the standard setting by using the *SET DATE MASK* command again with an empty string in place of the date mask:

```
/: SET DATE MASK = ' '
```

Exponent for Floating Point Numbers

How a floating point number is formatted depends on whether an exponent is specified. The mantissa is adjusted by shifting the decimal point and, if necessary, introducing leading zeros, based on the chosen exponent. An exponent value of 0 means that the exponent representation will not be used to display the symbol.

Syntax

&symbol(En)&

Example

In this example the *PLMK-SOLLWERT* field is assumed to have the value 123456.78 and to be of data type *FLTP*.

Table A–8 Examples for floating point numbers

Symbol	Result
&PLMK-SOLLWERT&	+1.23456780000000E+05
&PLMK-SOLLWERT(E3)&	+123.456780000000E+03
&PLMK-SOLLWERT(E6)&	+0.12345678000000E+06
&PLMK-SOLLWERT(E0)&	+123456.780000000
&PLMK-SOLLWERT(E)&	+123456.780000000

Fill Characters

Leading spaces in a value can be replaced with a fill character. The character immediately following the *F* in the specification is used as the fill character.

Syntax

&symbol(F**f**)&

Example

The figure for customer sales in the *KNA1-UMSAT* field is *$700*. The *Dictionary* description of the field specifies an output length of eight.

Table A–9 Examples for fill characters

Symbol	Result
&KNA1-UMSAT&	700.00
&KNA1-UMSAT(F*)&	**700.00
&KNA1-UMSAT(F0)&	00700.00

Ignoring Conversion Rules

SAPscript conversion routines specified in the *Dictionary* are automatically recognized and used when program symbols are formatted. These conversions can be prevented with the *K* option.

Syntax

&symbol(K)&

Leading Sign to the Left

The leading sign is normally displayed to the right of a numeric value, except when using a floating point number. This option allows you to specify that the leading sign is placed to the left of the number.

Syntax

&symbol(<)&

Table A–10 Examples for leading sign

Symbol	Result
&ITCDP-TDULPOS&	100.00-
&ITCDP-TDULPOS(<)&	-100.00

Tips & Tricks

The *SET SIGN LEFT* control command specifies that all subsequent symbols with a numeric value should have a left-justified leading sign. Using this control command means that there is then no need to repeat the < option for each individual symbol.

A

Leading Sign to the Right

The default setting outputs the leading sign to the right of a numeric value. If you used the *SET SIGN LEFT* to specify that the leading sign should be output before the value, this specification can be overridden for individual symbols to enable these values to be output with the leading sign to the right.

Syntax

```
&symbol(>)&
```

Tips & Tricks

Use the *SET SIGN RIGHT* control command to switch back to the default setting to output the leading sign.

Number of Decimals

A program symbol of one of the data types *DEC*, *QUAN* and *FLTP* can contain decimal place data. This option overrides the *Dictionary* definition for the number of decimal places to format this symbol value.

Syntax

```
&symbol(.n)&
```

Example

The *EKPO-MENGE* field contains the value *1234.56.* The *Dictionary* definition specifies three decimal places and an output length of 17.

Table A–11 Examples for number of decimals

Symbol	Result
&EKPO-MENGE&	1,234.560
&EKPO-MENGE(.1)&	1,234.6
&EKPO-MENGE(.4)&	1,234.5600
&EKPO-MENGE(.0)&	1,235

Offset

Specifying an offset of "*n*" causes the "*n*" left-most characters of the symbol value will not be displayed. If the offset specified is greater than the length of the value, nothing is output.

Syntax

&symbol+n&

Example

If symbol has the value *123456789*, the following will be displayed:

Table A–12 Examples for offsets

Symbol	Result
&symbol&	123456789
&symbol+3&	456789
&symbol+7&	89
&symbol+12&	Blank
&symbol+0&	123456789

Omitting Leading Zeros

Certain symbol values are output with leading zeros. To suppress these values use the Z option.

Syntax

&symbol(Z)&

Example

Assuming the current date is January 1, 2000

Table A–13 Examples omitting leading zeros

Symbol	Result
&DAY&	01
&DAY(Z)&	1

Omitting the Leading Sign

A

Program symbols with numeric values can have a leading sign, which usually appears at the right of the numeric value as a space for positive numbers, or as a minus sign for negative numbers. The *S* option ensures that the value is formatted without the sign.

Syntax

&symbol(S)&

Example

The *ITCDP-TDULPOS* field contains the value -100.00. The *Dictionary* definition for this field includes a leading sign.

Table A–14 Examples of omitting leading sign

Symbol	Result
&ITCDP-TDULPOS&	100.00-
&ITCDP-TDULPOS(S)&	100.00

Omitting the Separator for "Thousands"

Symbols of the *DEC, CURR, INT* and *QUAN* data types are normally formatted with the "thousands" separator character. The *T* option allows you to specify that this separator character should be omitted.

Syntax

&symbol(T)&

Example

The *EKPO-MENGE* field contains the value *1234.56*. The *Data Dictionary* definition specifies three decimal places and the output length is set to 17.

Table A–15 Examples of omitting separator for thousands

Symbol	Result
&EKPO-MENGE&	1,234.560
&EKPO-MENGE(T)&	1234.560

Output Length

If you need only a part of the symbol value, or if the output has to fit in an on-screen box or field without overlapping the edges of this area, use an output length specification to define how many character positions should be copied from the value.

If a length is specified that is greater than the current value length, then spaces are appended to the symbol value.

The character * specifies the program symbol length. This specification causes the symbol value to be output based on the output length defined in the *Dictionary*.

Syntax

&symbol(l)&

Example

If symbol has the value 123456789.

Table A–16 Examples for output length

Symbol	Result
&symbol(3)&	123
&symbol(7)&	1234567

An output length specification can be combined with an offset specification. The specified length is then counted from the specified offset position.

&symbol+4(3)& → 567

Example

The *SYST-UNAME* field contains the logon name of a user called Einstein. The *Dictionary* entry for this field contains an output length of 12.

&SYST-UNAME&...Einstein...
&SYST-UNAME(9)&...Einstein ...
&SYST-UNAME(*)&...Einstein   ...

Preceding and Subsequent Text

In addition to using initial symbol values, additional texts that are output only when the symbol value is no longer the initial value can be specified. You can specify a text to be output immediately before the symbol value (the pretext), and text to be output immediately after it (the posttext). If the symbol has its initial value, these texts are suppressed.

Syntax

&'pre-text'symbol'post-text'&

Tips & Tricks

Ensure that the symbol, the pretext and the posttext, all appear on a single line of the editor. This may mean that you have to use a long line (paragraph attribute = or /=) in the editor.

The apostrophe character delimits these texts. If this character also appears as part of one of these texts, then it must be written twice at this point to avoid misinterpretation. A pretext or posttext may contain symbols in addition to normal text. These symbols are subject to the restriction that these symbols may not have a pretext or a posttext.

Example

The *KNA1-PFACH* field contains a customer PO Box number. Since "PO Box" is not stored in the field with the value, you would normally write the following for the PO Box line of an address:

```
PO Box &KNA1-PFACH&
```

However, if no "P.O. Box" has been specified then "PO Box" would still appear on its own in the address. Prevent this step by using pretext and/or posttext (in this case pretext).

```
PO Box &KNA1-PFACH&  → PO Box
&'PO Box 'KNA1-PFACH&
```

If "P.O. Box" is specified, then this information will be displayed with the appropriate text in the usual way.

```
&'PO Box 'KNA1-PFACH&  → PO Box 123456
```

Right-Justified Output

Symbol values other than numeric values are normally formatted to be left-justified. Right-justified formatting can be specified with the *R* option. This option has to be used with an output length specification.

Syntax

```
&symbol(R)&
```

Example

If symbol has the value *1234*.

Table A–17 Examples for right-justified output

Symbol	Result
&symbol&	1234
&symbol(8R)&	1234

Space Compression

The symbol value is viewed as a sequence of "words," each separated from the next by either one or a string of space characters. The C option replaces each string of space characters with a single space and shifting "words" to the left to close gaps. Leading spaces are completely removed. The results are the same as if the ABAP command *CONDENSE* was used.

Syntax

&symbol(C)&

Example

Assuming ' Albert   Einstein   ' is the symbol value.

Table A–18   Examples for space compression

Symbol	Result
&symbol&	Albert Einstein
&symbol(C)&	Albert Einstein

Suppressing Initial Values

The *I* option suppresses the output of symbols that still contain their initial value.

Syntax

&symbol(I)&

Example

Assuming *KNA1-UMSAT* contains the value *0* and the currency is USD.

Table A–19   Examples for suppressing initial values

Symbol	Result
&KNA1-UMSAT&	0.00
&KNA1-UMSAT(I)&	

If the field contains an amount other than *0*, this value will be output in the usual way.

Time Mask

You can use the SAPscript *SET TIME MASK* command to format time fields in a way that differs from the standard setting. Executing this command causes all subsequent time fields to be printed with the specified formatting.

A

```
/: SET TIME MASK = 'time_mask'
```

In the time mask, the following edit formats can be used:

Table A–20 Time mask: Edit formats

Template	Description
HH	hours (two digits)
MM	minutes (two digits)
SS	seconds (two digits)

Any other characters occurring in the mask are interpreted as simple text and are copied directly to the output.

Assuming the current time is 10:08:12.

```
&TIME&  →  10:08:12
/: SET TIME MASK = 'HH:MM'
&TIME&
```

Result:

10:08

```
/: SET TIME MASK = 'HH hours MM minutes'
&TIME&
```

Result:

10 hours 08 minutes

```
/: SET TIME MASK = 'HH hours MM minutes'
&TIME(Z)&
```

Result.

10 hours 8 minutes

You can revert to the standard setting by using the SET TIME MASK command again with an empty string in place of the time mask:

```
/: SET TIME MASK = ' '
```

System Variables

&SAPSCRIPT-COUNTER_x& (x = 0.. 9):

These fields represent ten counter variables that you can use in your text and forms for any counting purposes. You can use the '+' and '-' formatting options to increment or decrement a counter before its value is printed. You can use the *DEFINE* control command to assign any specific value to a counter.

&SAPSCRIPT-DRIVER&:

SAPscript formats a text for a specific output device. The initial formatting is independent of the specific language of this device. SAPscript then calls a driver to convert the device-independent format to device-specific control commands. This field contains the name of the driver.

POST Postscript driver

HPL2 HP Laserjet driver for the PCL4/PCL5 languages

PRES Driver for output devices using the PRESCRIBE language

The available drivers are stored in table *TSP09*.

&SAPSCRIPT-SUBRC&

After executing an *INCLUDE* statement, this contains a value that indicates whether the *INCLUDE* was found or not. This value can be queried with IF....

INCLUDE found = 0 and *INCLUDE* not found = 4

&SAPSCRIPT-FORMPAGES&

This contains the total number of pages output in a SAPscript form (all output between the functions *START_FORM* and *END_FORM*). The state of the page counter on the individual form pages (*START,HOLD,INC*) is not taken into account.

Tips & Tricks

Using this symbol impairs performance, since all output data for every form must be retained internally to fill the symbol.

A

TechTalk

The *CONDENSE* option cannot be used on the program icon *SAPSCRIPT-FORMPAGES (C)* without an explicit length specification. This symbol is replaced with a value only after the form has been completely edited, since the total number of pages of a form is first known in the program function *END_FORM* or *CLOSE_FORM*.

However, the symbol size (number of characters) is reserved correctly when the symbol first occurs, with the current page number. Therefore, only one character is reserved for option *C (CONDENSE)* on pages 1-9, two characters on pages 10-99, and so on.

&SAPSCRIPT-JOBPAGES&

This contains the total number of pages output in a SAPscript print run (all output between the functions *OPEN_FORM* and *CLOSE_FORM*). The state of the page counter on the individual form pages (*START,HOLD,INC*) is not taken into account.

Tips & Tricks

Using this symbol impairs performance, since all output data for every print job must be retained internally to fill the symbol.

&SAPSCRIPT-TELELAND&

This contains the country identifier for the fax destination with fax output with SAPscript (field *ITCPO-TDTELELAND* for the parameter *OPTIONS* of function *OPEN_FORM*).

&SAPSCRIPT-TELENUM&

This contains the local fax number for the fax destination with fax output with SAPscript (field *ITCPO-TDTELENUM* for the parameter *OPTIONS* of function *OPEN_FORM*).

&SAPSCRIPT-TELENUME&

This contains the complete fax number for the fax destination with fax output with SAPscript (field *ITCPO-TDTELENUME* for the parameter *OPTIONS* of function *OPEN_FORM*).

Variables of Structure SYST

All variables of structure *SYST,* called system variables, can be used in the form. Of particular interest are the variables for the system date and time. These variables indicate the date and time that the output was created. For the system date, use *SYST-DATUM* variable, for the system time, use *SYST-UZEIT*. Note that you have the formatting options for date and time variables.

Sample Forms

Overview

This appendix presents samples of some of the preconfigured forms used by R/3 customers in the U.S. and Canada. To help you visualize the layout and components of printed forms, the following forms are shown:

- Account statement
- Credit memo
- Debit memo
- Delivery note
- Invoice
- Prenumbered check
- Unnumbered check
- Remittance advice
- Sales order confirmation

To find current versions of preconfigured SAPscript forms, visit http://www.saplabs.com/forms.

Account Statement Form

SAP Labs, Inc.	Phone: (650) 849-4000	**Account**
3475 Deer Creek Road	Fax: (650) 849-4004	**Statement**
Palo Alto, CA 94304-0000	Internet: www.saplabs.com/simple	
U.S.A.		

Acme Widgets Inc.
customer -jc-CA0000000-tx-0
123 Deer Creek Road
Palo Alto CA 94304

Customer No.: **1003238**
Statement Date: **04/27/1999**
Our accounting clerk:
Our account with you:
Page: **1 of 1**
Account statement from **01/01/1999** to **04/27/1999**

Document Number Text/Reference	Doc Type	Document Date	Arrears On 04/27/1999	Amount	Clearing
Balance carried forward 01/01/1999.........				0.00	
0018001006	01	01/22/1999	65	100.00	
0018001007	01	02/21/1999	35	200.00	
0018001008	01	03/23/1999	5	300.00	
0018001009	01	04/17/1999	20-	400.00	
0018001010	01	04/27/1999	30-	500.00	
Closing balance 04/27/1999.........				1,500.00	
Items due on 04/27/1999.........				600.00	

Document Type: 01=Invoice; 06=Charge Back; 11=Credit Memo; 15=Payment; 16=Payment Difference

CURRENT	OVERDUE 1-30	OVERDUE 31-60	OVERDUE 61-90	OVERDUE 91+	ACCT BALANCE
900.00	300.00	200.00	100.00	0.00	$1,500.00

Credit Memo Form

SAP Labs, Inc.
3475 Deer Creek Road
Palo Alto, CA 94304-0000
U.S.A.

Phone: **(650) 849-4000**
Fax: **(650) 849-4004**
Internet: **www.saplabs.com/simple**

Credit Memo

B

Billing Address

SuperStore-MegaMart Stores Incorpor
Office - Home - Corporate - Interna
PO Box MBOX123456
Palo Alto CA 94304-1213

Information

Document Number	90000462
Document Date	04/27/1999
Invoice Number	90000461
Payment Terms	Net 30
Currency	USD

Shipping Address

Acme Widgets Inc. 99999999999999999
customer -jc--tx-0BBBBBBBBBBBBBBBBBB
123 Deer Creek Road
Palo Alto CA 94304

1 of 1

Credit Memo Details

Item	Material Description	Quantity	Unit Price	Amount
	This is the header very long text for testing purpose. It is supposed to print before the details line items.			
0020	2396 Hi-Grade Widget Composite Kit 45-rtr-093 Cust. Material No.: CUST 2396	1EA	1,300.21 /1EA	1,300.21
			Items total............	1,251.20
			Tax amount..........	75.07
			Total amount........	$ 1,326.27

Debit Memo Form

SAP Labs, Inc. *3475 Deer Creek Road* *Palo Alto, CA 94304-0000* *U.S.A.*	*Phone:* **(650) 849-4000** *Fax:* **(650) 849-4004** *Internet:* **www.saplabs.com/simple**	**Debit Memo**

Billing Address

SuperStore-MegaMart Stores Incorpor
Office - Home - Corporate - Interna
PO Box MBOX123456
Palo Alto CA 94304-1213

Information

Document Number	90000463
Document Date	04/27/1999
Invoice Number	90000461
Payment Terms	Net 30
Billing Date	04/27/1999
Currency	USD

1 of 1

Debit Memo Details

Item	Material Description	Quantity	Unit Price	Amount
	This is the header very long text for testing purpose. It is supposed to print before the details line items.			
0010	2395 Super Performance Widget Class A-234-56G	10EA	1,300.00 /1 EA	13,000.00
0020	2396 Hi-Grade Widget Composite Kit 45-rtr-093 Cust. Material No.: CUST 2396	15EA	1,300.21 /1 EA	19,503.15
			Items total............	31,378.06
			Tax amount..........	1,882.68
			Total amount........	$ 33,260.74

Delivery Note Form

SAP Labs, Inc.
3475 Deer Creek Road
Palo Alto, CA 94304-0000
U.S.A.

Phone: (650) 849-4000
Fax: (650) 849-4004
Internet: www.saplabs.com/simple

Delivery Note

Shipping Address

SuperStore-MegaMart Stores Incorpor
Office - Home - Corporate - Interna
23457 Industrial Park - Square Rout
Palo Alto CA 94304

Information

Document Number	80000358
Document Date	04/27/1999

Purchase Order No.	Ref. # 45-GGJ-09	**Purchase Order Date**	04/27/1999	
Sales Order Number	515	**Customer Number**	1000755	
Shipping Conditions	Standard	**Incoterms**	CIF San Francisco	
Gross Weight	1,350 LB	**Net Weight**	1,350 LB	

1 of 1

Shipping Details

Item	Material Description	Quantity	Weight
0010	2395 Super Performance Widget Class A-234-56G *This super performance widget class A-234-56g is the most superior widget in its class.* *This is text from the Material Master Record.*	50 BOX	1,200 LB
0020	2396 Hi-Grade Widget Composite Kit 45-rtr-093 Customer material number CUST 2396 *This hi-grade widget composite kit isa special kit made up of our finestproducts. It has many components whichare compatible with other Widget products.* *This is text from the material master record.*	150 EA	150 LB

Invoice Form

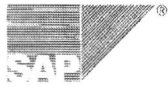

SAP Labs, Inc.
3475 Deer Creek Road
Palo Alto, CA 94304-0000
U.S.A.

Phone: **(650) 849-4000**
Fax: **(650) 849-4004**
Internet: **www.saplabs.com/simple**

Invoice

Billing Address

SuperStore-MegaMart Stores Incorpor
Office - Home - Corporate - Interna
PO Box MBOX123456
Palo Alto CA 94304-1213

Information

Document Number	90000461
Document Date	04/27/1999
Purchase Order No.	Ref. # 45-GGJ-09
Purchase Order Date	04/27/1999
Packing List Number	80000358
Sales Order Number	515
Payment Terms	Net 30
Billing Date	**04/27/1999**
Currency	USD

1 of 1

Invoice Details

Item	Material Description	Quantity	Unit Price	Amount
	This is the header very long text for testing purpose. It is supposed to print before the details line items.			
0010	2395 Super Performance Widget Class A-234-56G *This super performance widget class A- 234-56g is the most superior widget in its class.* *This is text from the Material Master Record.*	50BOX	1,300.00 /1 EA	1,560,000.00
0020	2396 Hi-Grade Widget Composite Kit 45-rtr-093 Cust. Material No.: CUST 2396 *This hi-grade widget composite kit is a special kit made up of our finest products. It has many components which are compatible with other Widget products.* *This is text from the material master record.*	150EA	1,300.21 /1 EA	195,031.50
			Items total...........	1,700,880.55
			Tax amount.........	102,052.83
			Total amount........	$ 1,802,933.38

B

Prenumbered Check Form

SAP Labs, Inc.	Phone: (650) 849-4000
3475 Deer Creek Road	Fax: (650) 849-4004
Palo Alto, CA 94304-0000	Internet: www.saplabs.com/simple
U.S.A.	

005359

Acme Supplies
3475 Deer Creek Road,
Palo Alto CA   94304

Payment No.: 20000337
Check No.: 05359
Payment Date: 04/26/1999
Vendor No.: 13587
Page: 1 of   1

Invoice Number	Invoice Date	Document Number Text	Gross Amount	Discount	Net Amount
56173446	04/26/1999	19004018	162.35	3.25	159.10
		text to be printed on correspondence			
56173447	04/26/1999	19004019	224.70	4.49	220.21
		text to be printed on correspondence			
56173448	04/26/1999	19004020	287.05	5.74	281.31
		text to be printed on correspondence			
56173449	04/26/1999	19004021	349.40	6.99	342.41
		text to be printed on correspondence			
56173450	04/26/1999	19004022	411.75	8.24	403.51
		text to be printed on correspondence			
56173451	04/26/1999	19004023	474.10	9.48	464.62
		text to be printed on correspondence			
56173452	04/26/1999	19004024	536.45	10.73	525.72
		text to be printed on correspondence			
56173453	04/26/1999	19004025	598.80	11.98	586.82
		text to be printed on correspondence			
56173454	04/26/1999	19004026	661.15	13.22	647.93
		text to be printed on correspondence			
56173455	04/26/1999	19004027	723.50	14.47	709.03
		text to be printed on correspondence			
		Check Total............................			$ **4,340.66**

DETACH FROM CHECK AND KEEP FOR YOUR RECORDS

SAP TECHNOLOGY, INC.
900 TOWER LANE   16TH FLOOR
FOSTER CITY, CA 94404

PNC BANK, N.A.   71
LESTER, PA 19113-1523
3-5/310-676

005359

04/26/1999

PAY TO THE
ORDER OF   Acme Supplies   4,340.66

*** FOUR THOUSAND THREE HUNDRED FORTY and 66/100 ***   DOLLARS

VOID

Acme Supplies
3475 Deer Creek Road,
Palo Alto CA   94304

MEMO

⑆005359⑆ ⑈031000053⑈ 8611743221⑆

Unnumbered Check Form

| | SAP Labs, Inc.
3475 Deer Creek Road
Palo Alto, CA 94304-0000
U.S.A. | Phone:
Fax:
Internet: | (650) 849-4000
(650) 849-4004
www.saplabs.com/simple | 10513 |

Acme Supplies
3475 Deer Creek Road,
Palo Alto CA 94304

Payment No.: **20000336**
Payment Date: **04/26/1999**
Vendor No.: **13586**

Page: **1** of **1**

Invoice Number	Invoice Date	Document Number Text	Gross Amount	Discount	Net Amount
56173435	04/26/1999	19004008 *text to be printed on correspondence*	162.35	3.25	159.10
56173436	04/26/1999	19004009 *text to be printed on correspondence*	224.70	4.49	220.21
56173437	04/26/1999	19004010 *text to be printed on correspondence*	287.05	5.74	281.31
56173438	04/26/1999	19004011 *text to be printed on correspondence*	349.40	6.99	342.41
56173439	04/26/1999	19004012 *text to be printed on correspondence*	411.75	8.24	403.51
56173440	04/26/1999	19004013 *text to be printed on correspondence*	474.10	9.48	464.62
56173441	04/26/1999	19004014 *text to be printed on correspondence*	536.45	10.73	525.72
56173442	04/26/1999	19004015 *text to be printed on correspondence*	598.80	11.98	586.82
56173443	04/26/1999	19004016 *text to be printed on correspondence*	661.15	13.22	647.93
56173444	04/26/1999	19004017 *text to be printed on correspondence*	723.50	14.47	709.03
		Check Total.............................			$ **4,340.66**

DETACH FROM CHECK AND KEEP FOR YOUR RECORDS

	SAP Labs, Inc. 3475 Deer Creek Road Palo Alto, CA 94304	PNC BANK, N.A. 71 LESTER, PA 19113-1522 3-5/310-76	10513
			04/26/1999

PAY TO THE
ORDER OF   Acme Supplies $ 4,340.66

*** FOUR THOUSAND THREE HUNDRED FORTY and 66/100 ***   DOLLARS

Acme Supplies
3475 Deer Creek Road,
Palo Alto CA 94304

MEMO

⑈ 1 0 5 1 3 ⑈ ⑆ 0 1 1 0 0 0 3 9 0 ⑆   1 2 3 4 ⑈ 5 6 7 8 ⑈

Remittance Advice Form

SAP Labs, Inc.
3475 Deer Creek Road
Palo Alto, CA 94304-0000
U.S.A.

Phone: **(650) 849-4000**
Fax: **(650) 849-4004**
Internet: **www.saplabs.com/simple**

Remittance Advice

Vendor Address

Acme Supplies
3475 Deer Creek Road.
Palo Alto CA 94304

Remittance Address

SAP Labs, Inc.
Attn To: Accounts Payable
PO BOX 1234
Palo Alto, CA 94304-0000

Vendor No.:   13590
Payment Date: 04/27/1999
Notification: Please use Check No. **10517** (Our payment document **20000340**) to clear the items listed below

1 of 1

Invoice Number	Inv Date	Document Number/Text	Gross Amount	Discount	Net Amount
56173489	04/27/1999	19004058	113.10	2.26	110.84
		vendor invoice line item text			
56173490	04/27/1999	19004059	175.45	3.51	171.94
		vendor invoice line item text			
56173491	04/27/1999	19004060	237.80	4.76	233.04
		vendor invoice line item text			
56173492	04/27/1999	19004061	300.15	6.00	294.15
		vendor invoice line item text			
56173493	04/27/1999	19004062	362.50	7.25	355.25
		vendor invoice line item text			
56173494	04/27/1999	19004063	424.85	8.50	416.35
		vendor invoice line item text			
56173495	04/27/1999	19004064	487.20	9.74	477.46
		vendor invoice line item text			
56173496	04/27/1999	19004065	549.55	10.99	538.56
		vendor invoice line item text			
56173497	04/27/1999	19004066	611.90	12.24	599.66
		vendor invoice line item text			
56173498	04/27/1999	19004067	674.25	13.49	660.76
		vendor invoice line item text			
56173499	04/27/1999	19004068	736.60	14.73	721.87
		vendor invoice line item text			
56173500	04/27/1999	19004069	798.95	15.98	782.97
		vendor invoice line item text			
56173501	04/27/1999	19004070	861.30	17.23	844.07
		vendor invoice line item text			
56173502	04/27/1999	19004071	923.65	18.47	905.18
		vendor invoice line item text			
		Check Total			**$ 7,112.10**

B

Sales Order Confirmation Form

SAP Labs, Inc.
3475 Deer Creek Road
Palo Alto, CA 94304-0000
U.S.A.

Phone: (650) 849-4000
Fax: (650) 849-4004
Internet: www.saplabs.com/simple

Order
Confirmation

Sold-to Party Address

SuperStore-MegaMart Stores Incorpor
Office - Home - Corporate - Interna
PO Box MBOX123456
Palo Alto CA 94304-1213

Information

Order Number	515
Document Date	04/27/1999
Customer No.	1000755

Purchase Order No.	Ref. # 45-GGJ-09	Purchase Order Date	04/27/1999
Delivery Terms	CIF San Francisco	Delivery Date	04/27/1999
Gross weight	1,350 LB	Payment Terms	NT30
Net weight	1,350 LB	Currency	USD

1 of   1

Sales Order Details

Item	Material Description	Quantity	Unit Price	Amount
	This is a test header.			
	This Sales note is specifically for our customers. This text comes from			
	the sales data section of the customer master record.			
	This customer requires special attention!!!			
0010	2395	50 BOX	1,300.00	1,560,000.00
	Super Performance Widget Class A-234-56G		per 1 EA	
	Customer Discount			46,800.00-
	Net Value for Item			1,513,200.00
	This super performance widget class A- 234-56g is the most superior			
	widget in its class.			
	This is text from the Material Master Record.			
0020	2396	150 EA	1,300.21	195,031.50
	Hi-Grade Widget Composite Kit 45-rtr-093		per 1 EA	
	Cust. Material No.: CUST 2396			
	Customer Discount			5,850.95-
	Material			1,500.00-
	Net Value for Item			187,680.55
	This hi-grade widget composite kit isa special kit made up of our			
	finestproducts. It has many components whichare compatible with			
	other Widget products.			
	This is text from the material master record.			
			Items Total......	1,700,880.55
			Tax Amount.....	102,052.83
			Total Amount...	$ 1,802,933.38

Third-Party Solutions

SAPscript should be used whenever possible because it is the only integrated solution. However, many vendors offer output solutions for the R/3 System. This appendix presents an overview of some of the solutions provided by third-parties:

- Formscape (AFP Technology)

- Professional printing solutions for SAP R/3 environments (Hewlett Packard)

- JetCAPS BarSIMM (Hewlett Packard)

- Flash SIMM (Hewlett Packard)

- JetForm Output Pak for R/3 (JetForm)

- StreamServe Connectivity Pack for R/3 (StreamServe)

Note

The companies featured in this appendix do not represent a complete list of vendors with output solutions for the R/3 customers.

Caution

- SAP does not endorse any particular third-party solution.

- Product information covered here has been supplied by company representatives and has not been reviewed for accuracy.

- For the most current product information, visit the company web sites.

AFP: FormScape®

FormScape is an enterprise wide, text management solution that dramatically reduces the time associated with the creation and management of modern documents. Essentially, the program takes the burden of formatting output off the host and places it onto Network servers within the organization. This approach helps reduce network load because users are able to print improved documents without sending the entire formatted print job across the network wire.

FormScape Components

The FormScape suite of products consists of four core modules:

- FormScape Server™

- FormScape Developer™

- FormScape Inquisitor™

- FormScape Administrator™

The modules are also complemented by a suite of other advanced "add-ons" that work together to provide organizations with a scalable text management solution.

FormScape Server

FormScape Server receives the data users want to improve and recomposes it into a modern dynamic document for example:

- Changing the font styles and sizes

- Changing the layout or

- Adding and removing logos—on the fly

One FormScape Server can handle multiple document types and will process each one uniquely. Once the Server has finished processing the data, it can route the final output to any printer, fax, email or other archive device. This component runs without user intervention as a background service on the Windows NT4 machine.

FormScape Developer

FormScape Developer is used to configure how the FormScape Server component captures and processes print jobs. FormScape Developer refers to each unique set of instructions of a project. When a project for FormScape Server is defined, users specify:

- What input is used

- What process on the data is to be performed

- How it will design and redirect output

C

The Developer module provides powerful "drag and drop" programming that removes the need to "script," together with a "What-You-See-Is-What-You-Get" (WYSIWYG) interface for form layout. The Developer also allows for remote testing and debugging of projects, further reducing implementation times.

FormScape Inquisitor

The third module, FormScape Inquisitor, is a management system providing centralized control of the FormScape environment.

Using Inquisitor, an administrator can install, move or remove any FormScape core or add-on module remotely across the WAN. In-built functionality also allows for the off-line backup of Server services for mission critical applications.

FormScape Administrator

FormScape Administrator allows central control of multiple FormScape projects across multiple servers within the environment, over the WAN. Its functionality includes timed project replication and server activity logging.

FormScape Enabler

For the SAP R/3 Release 4.x user, AFP has an advanced "add-on" module called FormScape Enabler. This module interacts with the SAP system via the certified Raw Data Interface (RDI).

RDI is an SAP proprietary specification that allows developers to define document structure and content, but leave the layout and other formatting attributes to FormScape. In-addition to RDI, Enabler comes with new Wizbar™ technology that further reduces development time.

Via RDI, Enabler allows the SAP R/3 System to produce high quality documents, both in batch and single output modes, across a wide range of output methods.

Cross-Platform Features

FormScape ideally sits within a TCP/IP network environment hosted by the NT4 operating system. You can therefore, access FormScape services from any PC, UNIX, mainframe, or midrange system as either an LPR printer queue or by using FTP to put data files into a file queue.

If an alternative protocol is required, this can be provided through third-party inter-connectivity products, or by using FormScape's POP3/SMTP compliant e-mail input queue.

For example, a user on a SCO UNIX machine running SCO's Advanced File and Print Server can direct output data for an invoice, via LPR to an NT print queue. FormScape intercepts the data, reformats it, and prints the invoice, complete with graphical formatting.

The open nature of the FormScape architecture allows seamless integration with a wide range of third-party solutions such as volume print systems, global archives, fax systems, workflow systems, and "end-to-end" delivery systems.

The Concept

The FormScape Server is driven by a project built with the Developer module. SAP R/3 outputs RDI to a printer that is actually a FormScape print queue. FormScape then massages the raw data based upon the rules in the project and routes the data to its final destination(s).

The FormScape Server module works in three distinct phases:

1. *Collection*—Collection is the point where the FormScape Server receives the data by either a printer queue, e-mail queue, or via file queues.

2. *Identification*—this stage determines which set of defined rules should act upon this particular job.

3. *Reporting*—after identification, the specific rules and routing

procedures are applied to the data and then sent to the destination.

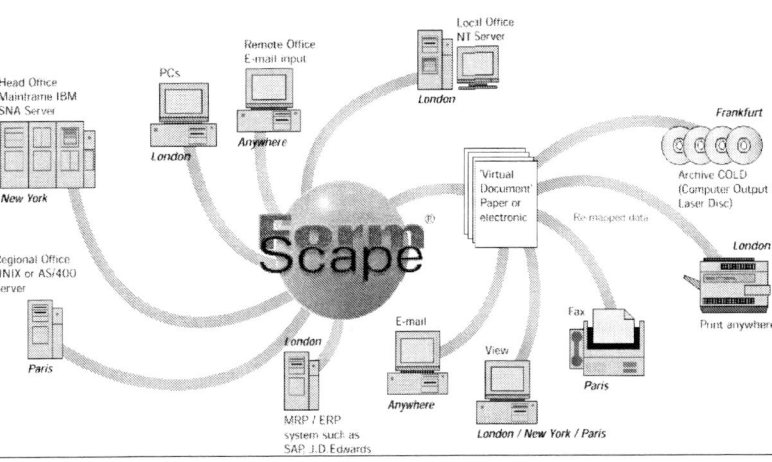

Contact Information

AFP Technology
Internet: http://www.formscape.com
E-mail: info@formscape.com

HP: Professional Printing Solutions for SAP R/3 Environments

The HP corporate printer family is synonymous with office printing. Many companies use them, but most have not made full use of the benefits offered by state-of-the-art printing. By consolidating various business printing tasks on your HP corporate printers, especially in SAP R/3 environments, HP's printing solutions for SAP R/3 environments lead the way to massive savings.

Even better, HP brings you the complete printing solution—including consulting and services—therefore addressing all your SAP R/3 printing needs:

- Electronic forms with corporate logos, typefaces and signatures

- Bar-codes including scaling and automatic checksum calculations

- MICR check printing for highest quality checks

- Implementation services and support

Professional Electronic Forms Printing

Electronic forms with corporate logos, boxes, grey-shading, and special typefaces offer you a simple way to enhance the output quality of your SAP R/3 System. Even double-sided or color printing are available. Greater flexibility, together with cost savings, will be easily achieved. Thanks to HP's corporate printer family you can now revolutionize the way you print forms. In the past, preprinted forms and stationery were the best way to produce quality results. Now, an HP LaserJet 5 printer with its definition of 600 dpi and HP's Resolution Enhancement Technology (RET) almost matches the printing press. Instead of preprinting you can now print forms on demand on plain paper.

Simultaneous Printing of Form and Data

The powerful HP LaserJet printers allow simple insertion of downloaded variable data such as names, addresses or other information into fields along with the fixed data that makes up the form layout. Completed forms can then be printed in any order on plain paper. The need for multiple paper trays is eliminated, as is the manual feeding of various types of preprinted paper.

Printing Features

- Two-sided printing with duplex option

- Multiple copies printed automatically (duplicates, triplicates)

- Automatic labeling of carbon copies

- Duplication of signature with special carbon paper (up to two copies)

- High quality gray-scale printing or color printing for logos or highlighting (Color LaserJet 5 or DeskJet 1600C)

- Just-in-time simultaneous printing of form and data (on demand)

- Printing in any order without paper changes

Contact Information

Hewlett Packard

http://www.hp.com/go/sap_hp

HP: JetCAPS Intelligent Bar Code SIMM

JetCAPS BarSIMM is an exclusive bar coding solution for HP LaserJet printers, available in PCL mode only.

Solution

A unique feature of HP bar code SIMM is the full EAN 128 set A, and the EAN 128 autoswitch, able to analyze incoming data to perform data compression and to switch dynamically between sets A, B, and C within the same bar code. This feature makes the HP LaserJet printers one of the only standard laser printers that are fully compatible with the new international shipping labels standard UCC/EAN-128 defined by ANSI/MH 10.8 and the ENC/MITL (European Normalization Committee/Multi-Industry Transport Label).

C

Features

- Data integrity check
- Checksum calculations
- Text value automatically printable
- Automatic font selection and scaling

Supported Bar Codes

- UPC-A, UPC-A +2, UPC-A +5
- UPC-E, UPC-E +2, UPC-E +5
- EAN/JAN-8, EAN/JAN-8 +2, EAN/JAN-8 +5
- EAN/JAN-13, EAN-JAN-13 +2, EAN/JAN-13 +5
- 2 of 5 interleaved (+CHK), 2 of 5 Matrix (+CHK)
- 2 of 5 Industrial (+CHK)
- 3 of 9 (+CHK), 3 of 9 extended (+CHK)
- 93 (+CHK), 93 extended (+CHK)
- 128 autoswitch
- 128 A/B/C
- UCC-128
- Codabar-Monarch (+CHK Mod 16)

- MSI Plessey (+CHK 10), MSI Plessey (+CHK 11 & CHK 10)
- Danish, French and German postal bar-codes
- ZIP+4 Postnet 5 and 9 digits, contents of HP's Barcode & More cartridge

Supported HP Printer Models

- HP LaserJet 4/ 4M
- HP LaserJet 4 Plus/4M Plus
- HP LaserJet 4P/ 4MP
- HP LaserJet 4 Si/ 4SI MX
- HP LaserJet 4V/ 4MV
- HP LaserJet 5P/ 5MP
- HP LaserJet 5/ 5N/ 5M
- HP LaserJet 5Si/ 5Si MX
- HP LaserJet 6P/ 6MP

SAP R/3-Specific Information

Fully compatible with SAP R/3, HP bar code SIMM supports the printing of bar codes through the SAP R/3 device type HPLJ4, designed for HP PCL5 printers. HPLJ4 contains the PCL5 commands necessary to drive the bar code SIMM and is delivered with SAP R/3 Release 3.0. Customers using SAP R/3 Releases 2.1/2.2 may install this device type into their systems following R/3 note #8928.

Contact Information

http://www.hp.com/go/sap_hp).

HP: Flash SIMM for HP LaserJet Printers

Solution

HP's new Flash SIMM stores your document formats on a non-volatile chip within your printer—so you can use ordinary plain paper to produce high quality forms and stationery on demand.

Features

- Integration of graphics, company logos, signatures, etc.
- Update formats instantly
- Boost network efficiency
- Ensure high security
- Produce consistent documents
- Guaranteed quality
- Effective management control

C

Supported Printers

- HP LaserJet 4/ 4M
- HP LaserJet 4 Plus/4M Plus
- HP LaserJet 4P/ 4MP
- HP LaserJet 4 Si/ 4SI MX
- HP LaserJet 4V/ 4MV
- HP LaserJet 5P/ 5MP
- HP LaserJet 5/ 5N/ 5M
- HP LaserJet 5Si/ 5Si MX
- HP LaserJet 6P/ 6MP

Management Software Systems Requirements

PC running Windows 3.1 or later, Windows NT, Windows 95, or OS/2.

Contact Information

http://www.hp.com/go/sap_hp

JetForm: JetForm Output Pak for SAP R/3

JetForm Output Pak for SAP R/3 allows SAP customers to merge R/3 data with a JetForm electronic form and print or fax it using existing devices. JetForm Output Pak for SAP R/3 consists of the following products and services.

JetForm Design

JetForm Design for Microsoft® Windows® is a comprehensive WYSIWYG graphical design tool for creating electronic replicas of paper forms. Design forms that contain company logos, graphics, and bar codes as well as customizing the format of data. Easy to use tools such as user-defined grids allow for precise placement of graphics and text. JetForm Design provides full font support, as well as shaded or rotated text. JetForm Central merges forms developed with JetForm Design with data from R/3 applications. The Form Builder is a utility that ships with JetForm Output Pak for SAP R/3 and works with JetForm Design.

When a R/3 SAPscript form is imported into JetForm Design, the Form Builder creates a form containing the specifics of the SAPscript form. This provides for fast easy creation and integration of new forms beyond those included in the JetForm Output Pak for SAP R/3.

JetForm Central

JetForm Central is a server-based application, with which customers can deliver presentation-quality forms output from information stored in the R/3 databases. JetForm Central's data merge functions replace preprinted forms and unformatted reports. The custom print drivers of JetForm Central guarantee print speed three to five times faster than standard operating system print drivers. JetForm Central is a multi-platform product that runs under a variety of operating systems.

JetForm Output Pak for SAP R/3 enhances the basic functionality of JetForm Central by providing two additional Agents: the Sort Agent and the RDI Agent. The Sort Agent allows you to sort forms on specified data before printing or faxing the form. The RDI Agent converts RDI output from SAP R/3 Release 4.x to a JetForm field nominated data stream for further processing by JetForm Central.

JetForm SAPscript forms for R/3

JetForm Output Pak contains a number of simplified versions of the standard R/3 SAPscript forms. These SAPscript forms generate SAP data in a format that a JetForm Central can process. Table C-1 lists the SAPscript forms included with JetForm Output Pak for SAP R/3. These SAPscript forms are available for both Release 3.x and Release 4.x (RDI interface) users.

C

JetForm Forms for R/3

JetForm Output Pak also contains a number of production ready forms to work with the JetForm forms. These forms are the best business practice examples, and can be modified to meet customer-specific needs such as the addition of company logos. Table C-1 lists the forms available with JetForm Output Pak for SAP R/3.

How It Works

Table C–1 The JetForm Output Pak forms and SAPscript forms

SAP Module	SAPscript form	Form
SD	RVORDER01	Order Confirmation
SD	RVDELNOTE	Delivery Note
SD	RVINVOICE01	Invoice
SD	SD_PACKING_LIST	Packing List
SD	RVPICKSIN	Picking List
SD	SD_LOADING_LIST	Loading List
SD	SD_CASH_SALE	Cash Sale
FI	F110_IN_CHECK	International Check
FI	F140_PAY_CONF_01	Payment Notice
FI	F150_DUNN_01	Dunning Letter
FI	F110_PRENUM_CHCK	Prenumbered Check
MM	MEDRUCK	Purchase Order
MM	MEDRUCK	Request for Quote
A&D	ZJ_SF1034	SF 1034 Public Voucher for Purchases and Services other than personal
A&D	ZJ_SF1035	SF1035 Public Voucher for Purchases and Services other than personal — Continuation
A&D	ZJ_SF1443	SF1443 Contractor's Request for Progress Payment
A&D	ZJ_DD250	DD250 Material Inspection and Receiving Report

With JetForm Output Pak for SAP R/3, the formatting attributes now reside in the form instead of in the SAPscript form. Use JetForm Design to move, change, add, or delete the formatting attributes on the form. Page sizes, font types, line spacing, justification, shading, logos, and field sizes are all specified within the form itself and is independent of the SAPscript form.

The Print Process

When a user initiates a print request, R/3 executes an ABAP print program, which calls the SAPscript subsystem and opens the appropriate SAPscript form. The print program then passes the application data, extracted from the R/3 database, to SAPscript by calling the elements defined in the SAPscript form. SAPscript is responsible for formatting the data output stream according to instructions defined in the SAPscript form, as well as specific commands issued by the print program.

The forms that ship with JetForm Output Pak, allow the R/3 application to generate the data stream in a format that JetForm Central can process. The SAPscript subsystem sends the application data stream to the R/3 spool subsystem. The R/3 spooler output device type is specified as a plain ASCII printer, which results in a JetForm data stream being passed to the host spool system. The corresponding operating system print queue is configured to send the data stream unmodified to JetForm Central. JetForm Central then merges the data and places it on the form created using JetForm Design. When forms and graphic files, such as company logos are stored on the server, there is no need to download them for each print job. JetForm Central contains its own print drivers and converts the merged form to the appropriate printer language and sends it to the specified printer, which outputs the document as a printed form.

C

Figure C–1 R/3 print processing steps using JetForm

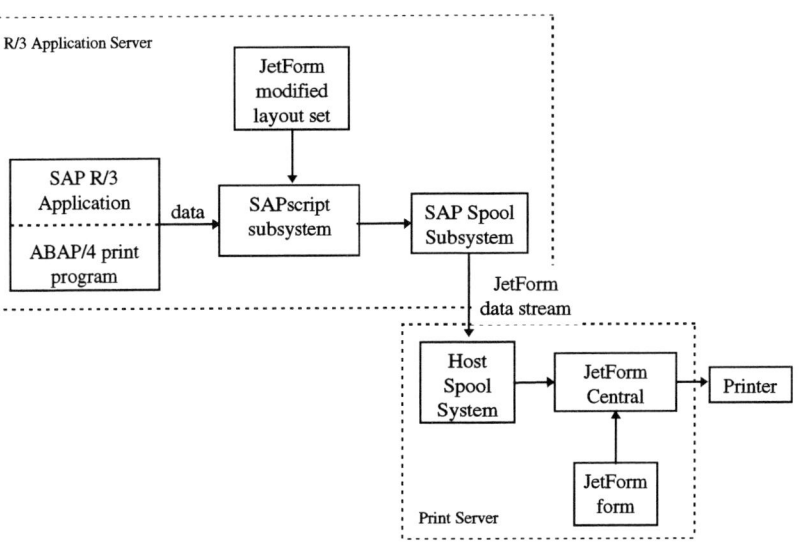

Features

Forms are language independent, so only one version needs to be maintained. (Language-dependent "boilerplate" is stored within the JetForm form file.) Since the form is simpler, the SAPscript composer requires less processing time. Downloading the forms only once and storing them on the print server reduces the amount of data transferred across the network. Network traffic is also reduced since the spool system data stream sent across the network is significantly smaller than a standard SAP data stream with embedded formatting information—as small as one tenth of the typical size.

JetForm Output Pak Features

- Easy to use WYSIWYG forms drawing tool. No programming is required to create the forms.

- Extensive forms processing capabilities (graphics, bar codes, logos, watermarks, rotated text, multi-part forms). High quality professional forms output, comparable to preprinted forms.

- The Form Builder utility converts layout sets to forms. Eliminates the need to create new forms from scratch, automatically creates and positions fields on the form.

- Bar codes done in software. Print bar codes on any supported printer with no additional hardware required.

- Print data values anywhere on a form, for example, print "amount due" total at the top, as well as at the bottom of the page. Create flexible forms that support customers' business requirements.

- Intelligent dynamic forms. Create market-focused, personalized messages on customer documents.

- The look and feel of each document can be dynamically controlled by the data. For example, processing automatically allocates space on an invoice to accommodate the number of line items. This saves paper and improves the appearance of printed documents as well as makes documents easy for customers to read and process.

- Nonprogrammers can make the necessary changes to the forms. Easy and inexpensive to maintain using existing staff.

- Layout sets generate plain ASCII data that can simultaneously output several types of documents in multiple formats. For example, you can print or fax an invoice, packing list, and credit memo from a single data stream.

- Create one output stream from the R/3 application for all users. Customize and print documents locally at remote subsidiaries using different languages, logos, or terms and conditions without impacting application development or deployment.

- JetForm data streams sent across the network contain only data, no formatting. This greatly reduces the network traffic, as small as one tenth of the typical size.

- Supports most common languages. This supports global business requirements to deliver documents worldwide in languages that require double-byte characters.

- Forms and logos are stored on the server. Reduces the amount of data transferred across the network.

- Implement JetForm forms and layout sets without changing the standard R/3 print program.

- Installation routines automatically install all components. Get up and running quickly.

- JetForm Central print drivers are three to five times faster than operating system print drivers.

- Can sort documents prior to printing. Allows documents to be printed in any order, for instance, by postal code to support external mail handling systems.

- Perform calculations on a data stream including +, - , *, /, **, log, ln, abs, exp, floor, frac, int, round, sqrt and trunc. Create new fields such as running totals without changing the R/3 application.

- SAP BAPI-certified. Assures interface with R/3 has been tested and certified by SAP.

Contact Information

JetForm Corporation

`http://www.jetform.com.`

StreamServe: StreamServe Connectivity Pack for R/3

The StreamServe Connectivity Pack for R/3 is certified for the SAPscript Raw Data Interface (BC-RDI). It includes tools and runtime software components that allow customers to meet their output processing requirements in all situations.

Design principles applied to the creation of the Connectivity Pack are:

- Universally applicable - all versions and release levels of SAP R/3 are supported

- Based on standards - SAP tools and interfaces are used wherever possible

- Flexible and adaptable - customer modifications to standard SAP forms are taken into consideration

- Easy to use - graphical tools ensure quick and easy creation and maintenance of documents

- Maximum functionality - all processing, formatting, and distribution requirements are supported

- High performance - any output device driven at any speed

The following graphic gives an overview of the StreamServe Connectivity Pack architecture:

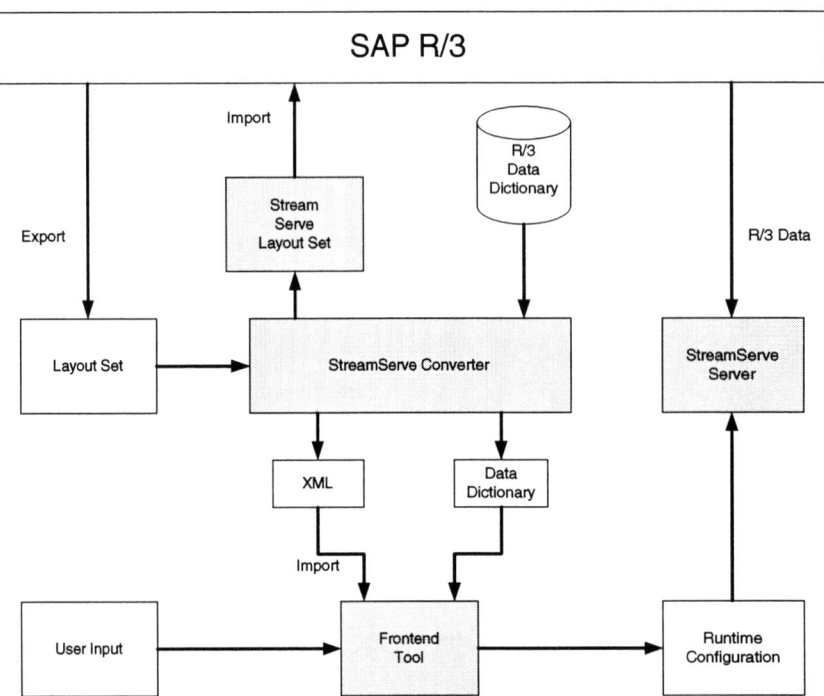

StreamServe Output Format Converter for R/3

The StreamServe Output Format Converter for R/3 can read existing R/3 SAPscript forms and translate them into StreamServe format. Alternatively, it is possible to use RDI data streams as input to the Converter, as is necessary for the Customer Care and Services module in the R/3 Industry Solution Utilities (IS-U/CCS), where SAPscript forms don't contain all the information required for conversion.

The Converter is a graphical tool running on 32-bit Microsoft Windows platforms. It allows users to recreate their existing R/3 forms for enhancement by StreamServe Tool, the graphical StreamServe application used for defining the formatting, processing, and distribution of documents; all changes and modifications to the standard SAPscript forms provided by SAP are reflected accurately.

Data items are added to a StreamServe Data Dictionary, allowing for flexible use of all data variables anywhere in a document, such as the highlighted display of the total of a multi-page invoice on top of the first page.

Layout information, such as the positioning of text elements, can be transferred to StreamServe Tool using an Extensible Markup Language (XML) file.

RDI Support for SAP R/3 Release 4

RDI Certification means that StreamServe Server can directly interpret data from SAP R/3 Release 4.

The formatting and processing capabilities of StreamServe ensure that all customer requirements can be met:

- Documents complying with legal and Corporate Image requirements

- Use of all printer features (fonts, tray selection, ...)

- Support for high speed/high volume printing

- Post-processing of output data for envelope and postal machines

- Distribution to the correct output channels, depending on data content

StreamServe Layout Sets

If a customer's R/3 system is still at Release 3, or if RDI is not be used in Release 4, the Converter allows the transformation of any SAPscript form to StreamServe format.

When such a transformed form is re-imported into the R/3 system, it causes SAPscript to generate data in a format nearly identical to RDI. In this way, StreamServe Server can handle all data streams in the same manner, regardless of whether they originate from SAP R/3 Release 3 or 4. In other words, the benefits of RDI support for Release 4 equally apply to Release 3 of SAP R/3.

StreamServe Server

StreamServe Server is the real-time output processing, formatting and distribution engine. It is available on Microsoft Windows NT and most UNIX platforms, including IBM AIX, HP-UX, Sun OS, Digital UNIX and DG-UX. By adding optional modules, a wide variety of output formats and distribution channels, such as IBM AFPDS, Xerox VIPP, Fax, Email, HTML and XML can be used.

StreamServe Tool

StreamServe Tool is a Windows-based end-user tool for output design and formatting, entering distribution rules, and system configuration and maintenance. Built-in graphical functions are supplemented by a powerful scripting language that provides full control over all aspects of output processing.

Features and Benefits

SAP customers and System Integrators derive a whole range of benefits through using StreamServe:

- Powerful, Easy-to-use Design Tools

  Formatting and layout changes no longer require modifications to R/3 SAPscript forms, thereby reducing implementation time. Device independent document design facilitates Spool Administration in R/3.

- Conformance to Corporate Image Requirements

  StreamServe supports graphics, barcodes and all printer features. This allows for very precise document design, resulting in consistent and professional looking documents. This is difficult, if not impossible, to achieve using standard R/3 tools.

- External Processing of Output Data

  StreamServe supports post-processing of output data, for example to add marks for enveloping or postal machines, along with many other functions, including database lookups via ODBC.

- Intelligent Routing to Multiple Channels

  One of the core functions of StreamServe is its ability to select the appropriate output medium and channel, according to the content of the output data stream. This includes generating multiple documents from one data stream, for example faxing an invoice to a customer, generating a confirmation for the sales representative, and producing a PDF file for archiving.

- Application Independence

  Output Processing is treated as a separate module. A clearly defined interface ensures most changes in output requirements do not require changes in the application, and vice versa. As the output module processes raw application data, new data fields are easily accommodated, keeping programming changes to an absolute minimum.

- Release Independence

  The StreamServe solution uses R/3 standards, such as RDI. As a result, you can install new releases of R/3 without having to worry about the impact on output processing.

Contact Information

StreamServe Corporation

`http://www.streamserve.com/`

INDEX